A PROCESS MODEL

Northwestern University
Studies in Phenomenology
and
Existential Philosophy

Founding Editor †James M. Edie

General Editor Anthony J. Steinbock

Associate Editor John McCumber

A PROCESS MODEL

Eugene T. Gendlin

Foreword by Robert A. Parker

Northwestern University Press
Evanston, Illinois

Northwestern University Press
www.nupress.northwestern.edu

Printed in the United States of America

10 9 8 7 6 5 4 3 2 1

Library of Congress Cataloging-in-Publication Data

Names: Gendlin, Eugene T., 1926–2017, author.
Title: A process model / Eugene T. Gendlin ; foreword by Robert A. Parker.
Other titles: Northwestern University studies in phenomenology & existential
    philosophy.
Description: Evanston, Illinois : Northwestern University Press, 2018. |
    Series: Northwestern University studies in phenomenology and existential
    philosophy | Originally published 1997 by the Focusing Institute. | Includes
    bibliographical references and index.
Identifiers: LCCN 2017028695 | ISBN 9780810136205 (cloth : alk. paper) |
    ISBN 9780810136199 (pbk. : alk. paper) | ISBN 9780810136212 (e-book)
Subjects: LCSH: Knowledge, Theory of. | Human body (Philosophy) |
    Perception (Philosophy) | Experience. | Meaning (Philosophy) | Meaning
    (Psychology)
Classification: LCC BD214.5 .G46 2018 | DDC 121.34—dc23
LC record available at https://lccn.loc.gov/2017028695

Contents

Foreword

Robert A. Parker

In their recent book *Retrieving Realism*, Hubert Dreyfus and Charles Taylor identify two powerful but deeply mistaken ways of construing our relation to the surrounding world: "mediational" and "contact" theories (Dreyfus and Taylor 2014). According to the first, we have no meaningful relationship to the outside world except through intermediate terms (for example, sense data, images, representations); for the second, we are directly contiguous with the world at all times, and this basic contact sanctions knowledge about its contents. Eugene Gendlin takes up a third approach whereby the body ingresses into its environment. Body and the environment *are* always already an interaction. In bold and innovative ways, he spells out just how this happens in *A Process Model*, a text that draws together his many contributions in ongoing debates over the past several decades. This book is an important and original contribution in contemporary debates that span fields as diverse as cognitive psychology, neuroscience, epistemology, and theory of meaning.

A New Way of Thinking

A cornerstone of Gendlin's thinking is the role of the body in the generation of meaning. It is increasingly recognized that humans must be understood as embodied: a theme first argued by Edmund Husserl and deepened by Maurice Merleau-Ponty. Gendlin goes further, showing that such understanding must already itself be interaction between the body and the environment rather than the result of the bare perception of the environmental particulars. This requires not only a rethinking of body, behavior, perception (sentience), language, and explicit and implicit thought; but also a rethinking of the very process of thinking, and of how we use concepts. Gendlin demonstrates that we need new concepts about the body, and these concepts must come from direct reference to body-environment interaction.

The book before you brings the body into a discourse that has until now concentrated mainly on the perceptual intakes of the five senses, rather than concerning itself with the things we encounter and the events of which we form part. Gendlin gives the name en#1 to a model of an ostensibly external perceptual world of colors and sounds that are the contents of separate acts of sensing. This is a world of sheer sensory inputs mistakenly taken as real objects (seeing is believing), as if they were out there, fully formed, waiting to be discovered.[1] He contrasts this world with the world generated by body-environment interactions, which he designates as en#2. On this very different model, neither body nor environment figures as a separate term: each is what it is only in its identity with the other. Taking en#1 as ultimate has been a mistake in the Western tradition. Gendlin outlines an alternative paradigm, a process model in which the environment is reciprocally identical with our own bodies in the multiple modes of our interaction with it.

En#2 is not separate from us, it *is* us, it is already both the environment and the body. Your chest expands as the air goes in, and contracts as the air goes out. But it's not as if the chest expands first and then the air goes in; chest expanding and air going in are the same event (same going on, same happening, same occurring).

Perception develops from this basic interaction, not the other way around as in most mediational models. There is a lot to account for before actual perception develops. Seeing the couch across the room is more than just seeing colors and shapes. One sees something to sit on, one sees the texture of the fabric and the softness of the cushions. When I hear a horn honking as I cross the street, I don't just hear a frequency of sound, I hear the possibility of getting run over.

When a baby finds its mother's breast for the first time, the mother is a continuation of the baby's own bodily process. The body *is* interaction with its environment; the baby's body and the baby's environment are the same event.

It is a mistake to take mere percepts (colors, sounds, etc.) as reality, as if the reality we live with were mere colors and sounds. Such a merely perceptual reality would exclude the body's interaction with its environment. In this scenario, perception, actual consciousness, and even life would become impossible (see section VI-A).

Moreover, the en#1 model makes it seem as if the world were first of all a vacuous space and time, like an empty theater within which the events of the world play out. But the perceptual world is a development, not a beginning; everything develops from the interaction of body and environment. Space and time are *generated* by living, by doing something: getting out of the way of a moving car, or walking from here to there.

Empty space and time are later abstractions from body-environment interaction, not prior to it.

Bodily Knowing

This new model opens a new way to think about the body. As ongoing interaction with the world, our bodies are also a bodily knowing of the world. It is what Merleau-Ponty calls "the knowing body" (*le corps connaissant*). Such knowing consists in much more than external observation; it is the body always already interacting directly with the situation it finds itself in. We know situations in a bodily way, even when we can't say verbally what they are. The body *implies* what to do in *situations* because the body is living through the situation; the situation is the body's process.

Bodily knowing consists in a "feel" for a situation or problem, such as the tip of the tongue phenomenon as described by William James in his *Principles of Psychology*:

> Suppose we try to recall a forgotten name. The state of our consciousness is peculiar. There is a gap therein; but no mere gap. It is a gap that is intensely active. A sort of wraith of the name is in it, beckoning us in a given direction. . . . If wrong names are proposed to us, this singularly definite gap acts immediately so as to negate them. . . . And the gap of one word does not feel like the gap of another, all empty of content as both might seem necessarily to be when described as gaps. When I vainly try to recall the name of Spalding, my consciousness is far removed from what it is when I vainly try to recall the name of Bowles. (James 1890, 251)

As James noted, this bodily felt, more-than-conceptual knowing is very precise, yet it is not anything like a fixed verbal or conceptual pattern. Words can come if one's attention on the bodily feeling is maintained. What James showed in 1890 is the still largely unknown fact that we can feel something with our bodies that is very precise even though it doesn't have a single pattern.

This bodily knowing that is more than a pattern is of crucial importance in modern psychotherapy. When we directly refer to the bodily feeling without first knowing what the trouble is—calling it "this" without trying for an exact description in words—then after some time we experience a *felt shift*; we feel the situation differently, even though we might not be able to say what the difference is in words and concepts.

Suddenly one knows and can say something significant about the trouble that one didn't know before, and this brings a deep sense of relief. This bodily felt, more-than-verbal knowing allows new words to come from direct reference to the body-feeling: honoring it in its pre-articulate state as it were.

In the method called focusing (Gendlin 1996), developed by Gendlin in the 1970s, an openness to the bodily sense of a situation—a sense that, despite being nonverbal, is distinctly felt—is encouraged and cultivated. This practice has been of major import in psychotherapy and in many other fields, including environmental management and interdisciplinary studies. Gendlin's concern with this practice, however, is first and foremost philosophical. He sets out how the bodily based knowing that is at stake in focusing and in a later practice he calls *thinking at the edge* (Gendlin 2004a) can be directly referred to and *thought from*. For it is in this way that genuinely new ideas can emerge from a process of attending to the bodily felt dimension of human experience.

Coming Full Cycle

Gendlin says that "body and environment are one." This may not seem to make much sense on a first reading; in their usual meanings, "body" and "environment" are clearly two things, not one thing. Gendlin thinks otherwise: "En#2 . . . is identical with the organism's living process. Body and en are one event, one process. For example, it is air-coming-into-lungs-and-blood cells. We can view this event as air (coming in), or as (a coming into) lungs and body cells. Either way it is one event, viewed as en or as body" (4). The same event is the bodily expansion and the environmental coming in: both at once and as one. In saying this, we have changed the meaning of the words *body* and *environment*, as well as *process* and *imply*. Moreover, all four terms now imply each other.

The reason Gendlin was able to expand and develop so much in *A Process Model* is that so much was skipped by a large segment of the philosophical tradition.[2] Too many previous philosophers went directly to a mediational model of perceptual intakes, or else to a naive notion of direct contact. This ignored radically different ways of conceiving the world and our relationship with it. Just these ways are what Gendlin sets forth in this remarkable book.

Chapters I through III each show a specific difference between en#1 and en#2. Chapter I establishes body-environment interaction as the same single event, as in breathing. Chapter II shows that a body interacting with its environment *implies* both that environment and further action with regard to it. This implying means that events have their own internal continuity, not only the continuity imposed by an observer. En#2 is the body's *own* process, which generates its own space and time. On this basis, chapter III shows that "objects," far from being original givens, are derivative from body-environment interaction.

Chapters IV through VIII develop new concepts for body-environment interaction in plants, animals, and humans. And these concepts themselves involve and are implied by our own ongoing bodily experiencing. Moving in this direction, we lose none of the power of older conceptual models; but by acknowledging a bodily mode of knowing we gain a different ground to stand on. We gain powerful insights into the nature of life, sentience, and much more.

In the last three chapters of this book, Gendlin derives the actuality of perceiving (chapter VI), showing how it too is derivative. From there—in chapter VII—he goes on to treat language in the light of the Process Model. In chapter VIII he offers an account of a kind of thinking that refers continuously to bodily knowing, enabling new insight and creativity by doing so.

The furthest edge at which a logical conceptual chain of thought leaves us can be a bodily knowing that has as yet no words, but is altogether more precise than words could be. From this bodily knowing, new conceptual steps can come—steps we may never before have taken or thought to take. Yet these same steps can lead to a revolution in our thinking philosophically as well as in our concrete lives.[3]

White Plains, New York

Acknowledgments

Many people were indispensable in the making of this book.

I am grateful to the teachers—Richard McKeon and others—who taught me philosophy.

Thanks are also due to Zack Boukydis, the listener to whom much of the thinking in this volume was first articulated over the course of ten years.

I am grateful to Ed Casey and Donata Schoeller, who initiated the project of getting it published. Kye Nelson, Rob Parker, David Young, and Christina Honde also made crucial contributions.

Most especially, I am grateful to my wife, Marion Hendricks.

Eugene T. Gendlin
October 2016

Introduction

Eugene T. Gendlin and David Young

Even though we humans do perceive, we are also an interacting living that is more primal and immediate. We share this living with everything else that lives. Like plants, our bodies interact *as bodies*, and not as what comes only with the five senses. Our bodies *are* interactings.

However, if we discuss how human beings interact with their environment, including each other, without bringing in perception before we have systematically derived it from what is prior, this provides a vast expansion. This expansion is needed because there is a lot to account for in our nonperceiving bodily interacting. That is what chapters I, II, III, IV, and V of this book do, and they do it before we move to perceptual intakes (colors, sounds, smells). So when we get to chapter VI, we are bringing all this implicit complexity of "not yet actually perceiving" body and environment interaction ("body-en") into play. And in the course of this later chapter, we do get to perceiving.

Central to the not yet actually perceiving body-en interaction is "implying." Whatever happens occurs into implying. Occurring-into-implying is ongoingly fundamental to all living bodies in their environmental interacting.

Occurring-into-implying does not assume preexisting fixed units which just get rearranged. Rather, each chapter brings further ways of articulating what is at first only the bodily feeling (the bodily implying) from which new words and actions can come.

Chapter I starts by saying that "body and environment are one"—a statement progressively developed throughout the book. This chapter shows how certain body-en interactings are the same event, that is, body and en are one process and imply each other. For example, air-coming-in (environment) and lungs-expanding (body) are the same happening, one "-ing," one activity. We need not split between lungs-expanding (body) and air-coming-in (environment). .

Chapter I develops body and en as one, interactively implying each other: "The body *is* an environment *in which* body-process goes on *further*" (6). The body is going on further in how it just went on.

Implying is not "just anything," but always "precisely this" (the body's feeling). But implying is not already specified.

Chapter II develops body-en implying still further. Bodies have many cyclical processes, such as the cycle of eating–digesting–getting hungry–looking for food–(eating again). No matter where these ongoing cyclical processes "are," every step bodily implies all the other steps, all the body-en occurrings of that cycle. Here we have an interacting/implying that isn't now happening. So this process is generating new forms of time. "Process [has] time implicit in it . . . but not only linear time" (9).

Further, chapter II also delves into body-en implying as "always in living." "A bit of life process is always also the implying of further bits" (11). No matter what happens, what occurs, occurring always occurs into implying.

Chapter II shows how occurring and implying are more intricate than already specified in any patterns or concepts. What we bodily refer to comes before any specific forms. We are always already in a situation that we can bodily feel, even if we don't know how to characterize it in words.

Only in chapter III does it become clear what the objects we live with actually involve. They involve the situation we find ourselves in even before we can say it in words. At first, real objects come only when something is missing, and we have them as the body's continued implying of them. In contrast, "had" or perceived objects come later in chapter VI.

Husserl said, "We don't hear sounds. We hear motorcycles and doors slamming." We can understand that "only sounds" are not what we hear. But Husserl didn't point to what our bodies are implying, in a felt way, beyond "*this* door slamming." He didn't point to the unspecified richness that comes with "all that." "Seeing the couch there," for example, seems to provide the couch as an object. But "seeing the couch *there*" already includes "how it's there-for-me to sit or to lie down on if I want," "how I don't want to bump into it if I walk past it," and many other not-yet-specified interactions.

Chapters IV and V continue in much the same vein, spelling out how occurring-into-implying happens in different contexts.

A Process Model makes the case that an unspecified richness comes as a primal, immediate, and bodily felt implying of "all that": what William James called "the much-at-once." And *this* is what this volume expands and develops—how our behaving, our perceiving, our language, and all our human living comes with, through, and in the bodily felt implying of "all that."

A PROCESS MODEL

Prefatory Note

I shall lay down some terms as if they came out of nowhere. I want to show that this model can look like any other and that it has at least the same powers. After a few pages I will turn to discuss some of its sources and motivations, and more of them in chapter IV-A-d.

Body-Environment (B-En)

Body and environment are one, but of course only in certain respects. Let us carefully define them. The body is a nonrepresentational concretion of (with) its environment. But body and environment also differ in some of their characteristics and doings. Let me define four kinds of environment (en).

En#1 is the spectator's environment, what spectators define in *their* en which may affect an organism. For example, it is en#1 when scientists or hunters define the environment of an animal. *They* define the en factors. They do it in their own terms. Some monkeys live in trees, others on the ground. The spectator defines these en factors as there, separately from the animal. The spectator may also note something (pollution for example) that is about to affect the animal while the animal does not yet notice. The spectators' bodies interact with "the animal's environment," their own environment attributed to another living body.

En#2 is the reflexively identical environment; it is identical with the organism's living process. Body and en are one event, one process. For example, it is air-coming-into-lungs-and-blood-cells. We can view this event as air (coming in), or as (a coming into) lungs and body cells. Either way it is one event, viewed as en or as body. Here we are not calling it "environment" because it is all around, but because it participates within the life process. And, "body" is not just the lungs, but the lungs expanding. Air coming in and lungs expanding cannot be separate. The point is that we need not split between the lungs and air.

Take another example, walking. The same pressure which is the foot's on the ground is also the ground's pressure on the foot. We can separate ground from foot, but not ground's resistance from foot's pressure. The en#2 is not the separable environment but the environment participating in a living process. The en#2 is not the ground, but the ground-participating-in-walking, its resistance. The behavior cannot be separate from this ground-participating. If the body is hanging in air and attempts to walk, its swing will be much wider and it will not move forward; it won't be walking. In deep water "walking" will immediately be thrashing; the motions will be different. The body cannot enact the same behavior without the ground. And the ground cannot be ground-pressure (it cannot be this en#2) without the behavior. Without walking there is still a ground in the sense of en#1, but not as en#2. The en#2 is a function of ongoing living, and exists only in that living.

The familiar statement "the environment is a function of the organism" receives here a more exact understanding. We can clarify what the ethologists mean by saying that there is no single reality, only the reality of each species. It is in the sense of en#2 that each species has a different environment. Of course its species members are different, but so is the rest of the en. Environment#2 and the body are functions of each other. In just this sense there is "no reality" except the various ones that are implicated in the various living processes.

Thus body is both equal and not equal to en! Rather than staying with such paradoxes, we are building distinctions and concepts. We have been able to specify some exact respects in which it is and is not equal.

Body and en#2 *imply* each other—it is basic to this philosophy that "imply" is being defined, but we cannot yet define it from here alone. But we can notice that what are usually called "body" and "en" *look different*, even when we say that they are part of one event (foot and ground, air and lungs). They are not look-alikes. The mutual implying between body and environment is "non-iconic," that is to say nonrepresentational. The muscles and bones in the foot and leg do not look like the ground, but they are very much related. One can infer hardness of the ground from the foot, the leg, and their muscles. In an as-yet-unclear way "one can infer" means that the foot *implies* the ground's hardness. Other kinds of terrain or habitat imply different body parts. Since the body and the en are one event in en#2, each implies the other. They imply each other in that they are part of one interaction process, one organization. Or, we could say, each is a part of a larger organization which includes the other. Each functions as it does only in this wider functioning organization.

This use of "imply" also says that the whole event is already there even if the body aspect or the en#2 aspect are thought of alone.

En#2 is always in some process and identical with the body-in-some-process.

En#3 is the environment that has been arranged by the body-en#2 process. The body accumulates (is) a resulting environment. The mollusk's shell, the spider's web, or the beaver's tree when it falls, these are their main environment, but they are results of the animal's body-en#2 process. En#3 is wider than en#2.

We can set up a continuum of greater and lesser seeming separability. The beaver's tree seems quite separable from the beaver, a bird's nest also; a spider's web is separable from the spider who will live on and make another if we destroy this web. The mollusk's shell isn't as separable yet we think it separate. How about our hair—is it not a product of the body? But our skin too. And the body too!

The body of any creature is the result of its life process. En#3 includes the beaver's felled tree, but also the beaver's body. The environment which the process produces is wider, but it includes the body.

En#3 is another, a different way in which body and environment are one (the body is environment), but since this environment is wider than the body, this equation isn't perfect. How body and en#3 imply is more complicated. (See IV-A-h-4.)

The bloodstream is often called the environment of the cells it feeds. The many processes in the body have various parts of it for their environment. The skin-line is not the great divide. En#3 stretches from the beaver's tree into its body to the cells. En#3 is the environment that has already been regenerated by body-process. It is the web and also the spider's body and its parts and sub-parts.

The life process *goes on in* en#3; it goes on in the spider's web as well as in its body.

The body *is* an environment *in which* body-process goes *on further*.

The body was made from an embryo engaged in process. The body structure is not only made but also maintained by ongoing processes—if they stop, the body disintegrates.

See the lines on a seashell, a small first part is already a seashell, and was the smaller animal's shell; rings and rings more are added on by growth. The shell has the nature of an action track, it is process concretized. The body is also like that, a record, an action track.

When aspects of en#3 get reinvolved in life process, they are thereby also en#2 (both within and outside the skin-envelope body).

The process *is* body-en#2 and *goes on in* body-en#3. But only some results of life become en#3, only those *in which* it goes on. En#1 is what the spectator observes all around the body, but the body also has its own environment which it has made.

But if en#3 affects the body only if it is again en#2, is the distinction only for a spectator? Of course it is one body, not two. En#3 can affect the body only insofar as it reenters en#2. But then it matters very much that *this* en#2 is not all new; it is also already a product of this life process. The process goes on in its own products. Say a different tree is about to crash and hit the beaver—the observer may see that it is about to happen. But en#3 does not reenter the process in that arbitrary way. The very tree the beaver gnaws will not hit it. It will affect the beaver in many ways once it is on the ground, but these will be importantly different from the intrusion of a tree that was not already en#3. The body implies the environment that the body already "is." Life happens largely with environments that life has produced or modified. The process goes on largely in its own products.

The main "environment" of any animal is its species members, other animals like it. These are products of the en#2 process of the species. In that sense they are quite obviously en#3 (and, when something is ongoing, en#2). By far the greater proportion of animal activity is with and towards them. The mother for the infant, female and male for each other, the group for the individual, these are crucial environments. We must not take the physical environment as our basic model of environment, although that too will often already be en#3—already organized by the life process when the current life process draws it in as en#2.

En#3 is the cement you walk on, the mole's hole, the beehive, the anthill, and our bodies and theirs. *The life process (en#2) makes itself an environment in which it then goes on further.* We can call it the "homemade" environment, or the "domesticated environment"—en#3.

The use of the word "in" is as yet unclear (when I say that the process goes on "in" en#3) because we do not wish to begin with any clear notion of space. We have and use our space, of course, but let us permit new concepts of space to arise from our interactional concepts. (We will "derive" the distinction between "external" and "internal" in VII-B.) Many quite different kinds of space can be generated from the process (both conceptually and experientially), as we will see. So let us allow this two-directional "in" to stand.

What "inside" and "in" mean is no simple question. The simple "in" of a skin-envelope assumes a merely positional space in which a line or plane divides into an "outside" and an "in." But the ground pressure is exerted not just on the sole of the foot but all the way up into the leg and the body. From most any single bone of some animal paleontologists can derive not just the rest of the body but also the kind of environment and terrain in which the animal lived. In breathing, oxygen enters the bloodstream-environment and goes all the way into the cells. The body is in the environment but the environment is also in the body, and is the body. We can say that en#3 participates in en#2, or we can say that the body-en#2 process goes on in the en#3.

En#0 is a fourth type. Something may someday affect the life process and be en#2, but is not now. This has never happened, and is not now any creature's en, not even the spectator's. In the seemingly infinite richness of the unborn, something may happen which has not yet, and will then be definable in terms of the process in which it participates. Let us allow ourselves to talk of this now. We don't want to say it plain isn't. Since this has no reality as en#2, and since en#3 is the result of en#2, we need a term for "environment" that has never been functioning in a life process.

En#0 is not what does function but has not been recognized. Vast reaches of the universe are involved in our process; these are all already part of en#2. En#0 is that with which some en#2 might come to be, but has not. (We need not assume that what is, must become en.) If something new enters en#2, it is determined as much by life process as by en#0.

But is en#0 spatially distinct from what is already en? Or may it be right here *in* what is participating? Obviously we must choose the second, if we choose at all, because the space relation is as yet undefined.

In these definitions process is first. We don't assume the "body" and the "environment" and then put them together. Later we will develop terms to speak of "the body." Right now it is b-en#2.

With later terms we will be able to say what part of en#3 is the body.

Body structure is always involved in some processes, or else it disintegrates. It is a structure from process, for further process, and only so.

Body and en#2 and #3 imply each other because each is part of one organization that includes the other. Each functions as it does only in this wider functioning organization. This use of "imply" stems from the fact that the whole event is already referred to, when we think only of the body, or only of the en.

II

Functional Cycle (Fucy)

Let us not begin by simply assuming that we live and think within an old model of time. Although we use linear time since it is inherent in our language and experience, other kinds of time are inherent in them as well, perhaps kinds of time that have never been explicated before. Let us see what model of time develops from explicating the explication process. No explication is ever equivalent to what (".....") it explicates. "Explication" and "process" have time implicit in them, of course, but not only linear time. Let the present, past, and future arise *later* from the process, as we did in chapter I, when we used the words "body" and "environment" to say that they are one interaction process. Then we can distinguish them later with new terms that develop *from the processes*.

In the old model of linear time-bits we would have to say, for example, that a given bit of foot-pressure implies three different ground-pressure bits: one, by resisting, first enables the foot to press; a second is equal and opposite to the foot's pressure; a third ground-pressure is the result of the foot's pressing. The fact that one bit needs all three is an ancient problem with the linear model.

The "body" implies all three, if someone makes bits. So all three were implied when we said (in chapter I) that "the body implies the environment," although only now do we see this.

A whole string of en#2 is implied by the (any this) body-en#2. And it may imply many strings. If an animal hears a noise, many situations and behaviors will be *implicit* in its sense of the noise: places to run to, types of predators, careful steps, soundless moves, turning to fight, many whole sequences of behavior. Meanwhile the animal stands still, just listening. What it will do is not determined. Surely it won't do all the implicit sequences—perhaps not even one of just these but some subtler response.

I say that hunger *implies* feeding, and of course it also implies the en#2 that is identical with the body. Hunger implies feeding and so it also implies food. It might imply the chase to get the food which may be far away. Hunger also implies digesting, defecating, scratching the ground to bury the feces, getting hungry again. These are a string of en#2s as well as ways in which the body will be.

9

If digestion is my model instance, then the process is cyclical. Hunger also implies getting hungry again after defecating and sitting a while. I call this a "*functional cycle.*" In such a cycle any "this" event *implies* all the rest, all the way around. But let us not decide that the sequence is simply predetermined, as is usually assumed.

Also in walking no single foot-pressure-ground-pressure event simply *is*. If there were suddenly such a single is, the animal would fall. Its weight *is* already on the way to . . . (Momentum cannot be expressed as mere change of location.) The "bit" moves the animal over. Or it might be a bit near the beginning, the increasing foot-pressure-ground-pressure with the weight coming onto the foot. Any bit to which one might point implies the whole movement of walking. Any occurring *is* also an implying of further occurring. And each bit implies something different next.

If a spider is taken off its half-finished web and placed elsewhere, it goes on as soon as it can, spinning where it left off. It spins outwardly the rest of the net which thus has a hole in it. Like digestion, its web-spinning process cannot just begin again in the middle. The events cannot follow in just any order. More intelligent animals can re-include feedback from what they did in ways which would let them begin at the beginning of an interrupted action, but even so this involves quite a different sequence than an uninterrupted action. Living cannot well be thought of as unit events related to other events only by position, that is to say single events that one could rearrange in any order. I don't mean that anyone claims that living events can occur in any order. But why this is not possible is thought of only in terms of externally imposed relationships of things in an observer's space. Let us instead allow the spider to generate time and continuity. The spider's own process has its own order. The rest of the web will remain implied until the environment #2 cooperates in the occurring of the rest of the net. Each occurring is also an implying, and this stays the same unless it is changed by an environmental occurring that has *a certain very special relation to the implying*.

Life process is "temporally organized," but here this does not mean only that someone notices hunger coming before eating. It means rather that hunger *is the implying of* eating. And eating? There is that special relation again: if hunger is the implying of eating, then eating is the "....." of hunger. The term we want is implicit in the "....." and when we get the term it will do to our "....." what eating does to hunger. We can try out saying that eating satisfies hunger, that it carries out what hunger implies, that eating carries the hunger into some sort of occurring. Hunger *is* the implying of eating (the "need" for food we say, making a noun out of this implying). Then eating is the satisfaction (another noun). The nouns make separate bits out of the process. But actually it's no fun eating if you're not hungry while eating. The eating happens only with hunger. Eating happens *into* hunger. The bits have both in them. The process is both implying and occurring. *A bit of life process is always also the implying of further bits.* Right here, "implies" means just this well-known and little understood fact.

Time is generated by the sequence. But the further parts of the cycle (all of them, or the next one) do not look like this one. Hunger doesn't look like eating, which in turn doesn't look like defecating. Implying in this sense is again non-iconic, nonrepresentational (as we found in chapter 1).

The whole cycle of ensuing events is, in a way, here now, at one point. We can say that the whole sequence is ongoing. We can say that hunger *is* being about to search for food, find it, and eat. This "is," and our word "implies" (in just this use, here) speak from this relation: all living is an occurring and also an implying (of .....).

Implying has (makes, brings, is, ...) time, but not only the linear, merely positional time. Though far from clear (we are only beginning), we want the sequence to define time for us. We did not begin with a clear notion of time. Let us say that *the relation between occurring and implying* generates time, rather than saying that life processes go on in time. (The latter statement would involve an already assumed time.)

Now a caution: one might be tempted to say that each bit of occurring is what the last bit implied. But this would be only the old linear model. Later, in IV-B and VII we will have developed the terms to derive our capacity to think of time as a linear series of positions (past, present, and future). We have those now, of course, but let us not assume that these linear positions must be "basic," as if everything else must fit into them. In VII we will develop terms for how one can remember something from before, or imagine what has not yet occurred. We will be able to derive linear time as a simpler case from a more intricate model of time from which much else can be derived as well. Our primitive concept of "occurring into implying" will elaborate itself more and more.

From the spectator standpoint we may know what will happen, because we have often observed the same events ensuing. But let us not assume that the process is a sequence of predetermined events. Implying is not the same as what will occur. Hunger is not eating. It doesn't contain a hidden representation of eating. Let us not make the occurring-implying relation into an equation. We don't need to assume that the process consists of already-defined events that the spectator predicts at time one, observes at time two, and remembers at time three. We need not assume that the implying consists of defined units. In nature a myriad different ways of eating have developed, and more may arise. The implicit is never just equal to what will occur.

Implying is a part of occurring, but occurring is also equal to en. It is body = en. The body implies *and* occurs in the en. But implying has a more intricate sort of "is" than en. Occurring has this more intricate order too, but only in regard to the next occurring. All occurring also implies, so implying is part of every occurring. But implying is much more than just the next event which the spectator has observed before.

Although open for further events, implying and occurring are always just so, just how they are, not at all indeterminate (see Gendlin 1997e and 1992b), but implying is more orderly than one set of b-en#2 events.

Implying is never just equal to occurring. Therefore implying is not an occurring that has "not yet" occurred. It is not an occurring in a different position on a time line.

So we see that implying is not what *will* occur. Nor is it ever right to say that what has occurred *is* what was implied. We need more terms to become able to speak from their relation.

So far the word "into" has been used to speak of that relation. We said that the en *occurs into the implying*. Since en is part of occurring, we can also say that occurring *occurs into implying*. This relation will soon elaborate itself. So far it is clear that it cannot be an identity.[1]

In the old model everything is assumed to stay "the same" so that change is explained by tracing identical units that are only rearranged. In the old model the system of localizations and possibilities always remains the same. Instead, let us begin with change. Later we will derive "the same" from change.

Occurring is change; something happens. *Occurring into implying can change the implying*. The occurring sequence is also a sequence of changes in the implying. So the sequence is not determined from the implying in one event.

The process is a changed implying all along the line.

We can go a step further: Since implying implies a next occurring, and since occurring changes implying, therefore *implying implies a change in implying*. It implies its own change. The sequence can be defined as the implied changes in implying. But those are not determined possibilities.

Since there is always an implying, we can say that occurring always occurs into an implying, but it does not always change the implying as it implied itself changed.

But it is misleading to call it "change" as if it simply implied just anything else. Implying implies something so intricate that only a very special occurring "changes" it as it implies itself changed. Anything else may disrupt the body or leave the implying *un*changed—still implying as before. For example, while the animal is hungry something other than food happens. Then the implying of feeding continues unchanged. Or a predator may chase it so that running may come to be implied. Or the animal may be killed. Since there is always implying, all occurring happens "into implying," but not always as the implying implies. We can already say that certain distinctions are coming here. Implying implies an occurring that will change it so that it no longer implies as it did, but not because it was disrupted, rather because what occurs relates to the implying in a certain (not fully predetermined) way. More terms with which to think about this relation will develop.

An Object

Our concept of "implying" has already moved to a second meaning. First we said that all parts of body-en#2 imply each other as part of one whole; then we found that any occurring is also an implying of further occurring (and of change in implying).

But what if en changes in a way that is not part of the process? So far we defined body or en as one body-en#2 event. But if the foot changes so that it doesn't press, then the ground pressure is not there. Or if the ground pressure is lacking, then the foot pressure would not be as it usually is, either. Therefore, if any aspect of body or of en#2 were to be different or missing, then what occurs must be different as well. The walking must stop; the living body may die or go on living differently.

Much of en#2 is constant, air or water perhaps in some cases. Then these are not separate aspects (unless we separate them). But these and other aspects of en#2 may sometimes be missing. The body might have changed so that the food is no longer there for it. Or food may be missing. If there is a flood, the ground-pressure is not there.

If the creature does not instantly die because some process is stopped, then we have an implying that was not changed by an occurring. For example, the animal remains "hungry," that is, food and feeding are implied but do not occur. Now the hunger is not merely the implying into which eating occurs.

Perhaps there is soon some new kind of food, or perhaps a new way forms to do something that changes the implying somewhat as feeding would. But if not, then the implying of feeding will **remain the same** no matter what other events do occur.

For the first time in our model we have derived a sense of "*the same.*"

Now we are speaking not just of the whole body-identical "environment," but of a certain aspect of it which separates itself by being absent. So the feeding process separates itself as well and remains implied. Everything else involved in feeding is here, the animal, the other animals, the air, ground, light, all together. What is not here is only a small but separated "part" of the whole en#2.

If such an aspect of en#2 is missing, we can speak of "a" process that is separated and stopped. Now there is *a* stopped process—*separable from the whole process.*

The part of en#2 that separates itself by being absent plays a special role. It stops a process by its absence. Let us give this part of b-en#2 the ancient name "object" (even though it often means species members, not just things as in the old model). If we do this we don't think of the environment as already consisting of objects, and especially not of spectator-defined objects. Rather, something is an object only if it is part of body-en#2, and also sometimes missing. A creature might have just one or two objects.

Because there is now a stopped process, this missing part of en#2 has attained a startling power: when this small aspect of en occurs, all of that process which was stopped by the absence will occur.

Of course, the process involves a great deal more than the missing part which has now returned. The process which resumes is much more complex than one could guess just from the object. Yet when this object occurs, the whole complex process which was stopped, resumes.

"The animal recognizes the object," says the spectator. "It responds appropriately to the object."

We can now derive the old notion of G. H. Mead that the environment is a function of the organism (Mead 1938, 422). This is not so in every respect. The body and the en have their own reality connections, and this leads to a new sense of our term "en#2" in which we can speak of it separately. The body-process may not be able to determine the object's disappearance or reappearance. (Later we may find processes that can provide themselves with at first missing objects, but that is different.) The object is a function of the process insofar as the process separates this object by not occurring without it, and by resuming if the object recurs.

In a *resumption* the body does not encounter the object as if for the first time. It looks that way, as if living things just happen to have objects, or as if the animal just met the object. If one begins with this, one must remain puzzled by what the animal does with the object, and how it can.

What we call "*an* object" is part of en#2 and part of the functional cycle. It was already part of en#2 but not separated (not "an" object). By being absent it is separate. Now we can say that objects were already part of the functional cycle, although we are only now separating them out. The stoppage has enabled us to think further about implying, to make more terms from it. Because there is implying, and implying implies an occurring that will change it *in a certain way*, which we will become able to define, therefore there can be a stoppage (i.e., an occurring that does not change the implying in that certain way). Then the implying remains the same for a while, and we can feel and think about it. At such a juncture something new might occur and have this certain (to be defined) relation to it, because implying is both more intricate and still open.

Since the next occurring does not immediately change it in a way that it implies itself changed, we encounter the implying "....." as such (carried by other occurrings). But so long as it remains the same it also continues to have the same object in the environment. We can speak of *an* object. But we cannot speak of en#2 as if it consisted of "objects" since most of it is never missing, and never separated and implied as an object. Most of it is constant and not divided into objects.

When people say that objects are "a function of the organism," they sometimes say that the organism "picks out" or "selects" what is an object for it. This assumes all of the spectator's objects. One assumes that the animal interacts with some of what is defined by the spectator. Instead, let us think of the life process as including what is en#2 with it. Some part of that can differentiate itself by being sometimes missing. Then the implying of it stays "the same" as long as it is missing.

In our ***third meaning of the concept of "implying"*** the implying continues "the same" as long as a process is stopped. This leads us to the question: how can there "be" a process that is not ongoing? The next chapter will pursue the question.

We notice another oddity that will lead us further. As far as we defined it, there can be an object for the body only while the object is missing, and the process with it does not happen. As soon as the object recurs, the process resumes and changes the implying so that the object is ***no longer implied***. Objects, so far, are objects ***only as long as they are absent!***

Later (in VI) we will develop terms for how a body can have objects that can be there for it, such as perceived objects, but we don't have terms for this as yet. For example, we have no terms to say that food might also be there for the body while the food is being eaten, and afterwards. So far as we have developed our terms, the food would be an undifferentiated part of the body's whole process as soon as food occurs. The food would be part of the whole en#2 and would not be a distinct object. So we can ask: How does the body come to ***have and keep*** objects in front of itself? How can terms for this develop from our terms?

By allowing our terms to work logically in this way, we arrive at puzzling results that generate further questions. Sometimes we dip into their more than logical implications, but we must also take them logically, quite exactly. It is clear that we have as yet nothing like objects of perception. We have as yet no terms for perceptions, images, or memories. We have devised concepts for something earlier, more primitive, namely how something separate like "a" process and "an" object might come to be in the first place. Before the object was missing it was not an "it" for the body at all.

When the object returns, the stopped process resumes and moves on. Then the object is no longer implied.

Our third kind of "imply" can be used in both directions, although not in the same sense. We can say that the partially stopped body-process **implies** the missing en-aspect. We can also say that this en-aspect **implies** and resumes the stopped body-process. For example, the food implies feeding to the body. To be an object is to resume a process with the body.

Later (IV-A-e) when we have the terms, we will be able to use them to think about an "original implying" that is "resumed" in a process that need not have had a stoppage.

The object implies the resumed process to the body because the body implies that process. Such an en-aspect has a role, a function, we could almost say a "*meaning*" to that body; like a *symbol* it means (implies) feeding. The body "*recognizes*" the object, we could almost say—almost, but this use of the words comes much too early. Below I will discuss this "too early" use of term.

Some Motivations and Powers of the Model So Far

When I say that a missing and implied en-aspect has a role, a function, *a meaning*, that it has the role of a *symbol* to the body, my "too early" use of these terms is deliberate. The too early use is part of the project to create an alternative model in which we define living bodies in such a way that one of them can be ours. We *start from* how we know (feel, are, ...) our own more complex body. From the start, let us develop concepts of "body" and "environment" that can apply also to our own bodies. Since our human bodies have environments including species members and other objects, meanings, and symbols, we know that living bodies *can* have objects, meanings, and symbols. Let us therefore not build the "basic" terms in our model in a way that makes our own bodies seem impossible from the start.

Since we humans are here, we can be certain that we are not impossible. A conceptual model of "reality" that makes us seem impossible has to have something wrong with it.

Human meanings and symbols seem impossible in the spectator's space and time within which we have been taught to think about anything. Therefore, currently, the human world seems to float disconnectedly; human meanings seem added on to a "reality" that makes us seem unreal.

Postmodernists want to reject any conceptual model. I call the rudimentary outlines of a model "basic" not because someone believes that a conceptual model is the foundation of anything, but because the "basic" structure is acquired by all the other terms. The usual "Western" model is widely rejected today, but it remains "basic" not as an assertion, but because it inheres in the structure of most concepts, and seems to be the only way to make new concepts. This will remain so as long as we lack an alternative "*basic*" model. By rejecting all models, the postmodernists make themselves right. But a model ceases to entrap as soon as we have an equally "basic" alternative. Then we are able to devise concepts beyond the old model—*and* beyond the new one too.

We can devise an alternative, if we fashion the "basic" terms from the living bodies that we have (are, act from, speak from, ...). With basic parameters that are "too early" versions of human processes, we can make the later definitions of meaning and symbol possible. We won't darkly announce later on that humans have a symboling power, as is usually done in the currently disconnected social sciences. We want to understand that power and its continuity with less than human processes. We are not pretending to be without or before language. Of course we are devising concepts from some aspects of how we are and live. The usual mathematical "reality" is also derived from human processes, of course. Nothing is more exclusively human than mathematics.

We can speak from living, and we can make rudimentary concepts from speaking-from, and especially from focusing (Gendlin 1981) and from the process of explication. Since these are possible in reality, they can lead us to an alternative set of "basic" concepts of a "reality" in which we would not seem impossible.

Our rudimentary model will develop into a connected matrix of concepts with which we can "derive" human behavior and symboling.

Then it will have the concepts with which to speak **about** itself (VII and VIII).

It is known that symbols and rituals have deep bodily effects, but there is no way to think how that can be. We are building a way to think from and into those effects. And of course we spend much of our lives speaking. The old notion that symbols "stand for something" never opened this relation. It is left like an external relation. What lets symbols be "about" things? We are told about "signifiers and the signified"—but the signifiers float. The old terms about language and signifying do not internally explain themselves, nor do they relate to living bodies. Even our little primitive model with its few terms is already further along than the usual model. With body and environment making up one event, and with the concept of "implying," the body implies its participating environment, as well as special objects that can be missing and can resume a process.

What makes something a symbol is usually said to be that it "stands for something." Our definition so far is not yet of a symbol, also not yet of an object that is present and perceived by a body. So far the "object" disappears as soon as it recurs. And yet it already "stands for something," namely the process it resumes when it recurs. But "stands for" comes from the old model, as if symboling were an external relation. I say instead that the body "implies" the object by implying the process which the object resumes.

Our rudimentary model can already say quite a lot that needs to be said and cannot be said in the old model.

We also have terms to say that an object (and later a symbol) involves a whole implicit complexity even though it can look so simple and single. Like the missing en-aspect, the effect of a symbol cannot be accounted for by examining it alone. Our rudimentary model provides a way to think these dimensions without assuming representations. The body does not imply the object by having some kind of copy of it. Nothing in the implying or the body's process looks like the object. Secondly, the implying of the object is not a "reference" as in the old model. What is really implied is a further body-process, not just the object. Explication is never representation, always itself a further process.

Later we will derive terms for cognitive processes (the kind that carry the word "of," such as perception of, symbol of, etc.), but not by making a fresh start as if humans cannot be part of the world studied by science.

But, of course the too early use is not yet how we want to use the words "meaning" and "symbol."

The Body and Time

IV-A. A Different Concept of the Body, Not a Machine

(a) The body (when a process stops) is what continues; it is the other process. As soon as we have more than one process, the body is the other process, the one that is not stopped.

We will now define a stopped process. If some aspect of en#2 is missing and the body does not die, it continues in an immediately different way. Some of the usual process will not go on. A distinction has been created. There is the stopped process, and some *other* process which does continue.

The body is the new process which does continue.

Until now we had no way to speak about the seemingly separable thing that we ordinarily call "the body." Now we have defined the "body" as separate at least from the stopped process.

But in what way does a stopped process exist, since it is not going on?

Let me first say that not every change is a stopped process. The changed occurrences *might* very well change the implying as it implied itself changed. Implying is not a determined occurring; it is not some single way. But if the new occurring does *not* change the implying as it implied itself changed, the implying will stay the same in those respects, and the stopped process will continue to be implied.

What continues is *different* than if there were no stoppage. In section (e) we will be able to discuss these differences. Right now we can let them define the sense in which the stopped process exists as an occurring. Since it is stopped, it does not exist as itself. *The stopped process exists insofar as what does continue is different.* Now it continues alone without what is stopped. We can say that this difference in the ongoing process *carries the stoppage.*

A stopped process is an unchanged implying carried by a changed occurring. It is *carried* by the process that does continue, by how that process goes on differently.

The differently ongoing process includes some unchanged implying which implies the object (the missing en#2 aspect which would resume the stopped process). *The object is implied by the carried stoppage.* It is carried by the respects in which the occurring is different and by the respects in which the implying keeps on being the same. (Of course, these "respects" are not separated. Only the continuing process is separate from the stopped one.)

The carried stoppage is *the body-version* of the missing object. I put it this way to remind us of the old representational way of thinking, so that we can notice: *a carried stoppage is nothing like a copy or a representation.* For the same reason I also want to call the carried stoppage the "*schema.*" In the old model the term meant a kind of picture which enabled a body to "*recognize*" an object. Here the carried stoppage fills this role, so that the missing process resumes if the object occurs.

I have already said that "recognize" is used "too early" here. This resuming can happen even with plants and simple animals. We want terms for this widespread recognizing, so that we can later build more elaborate terms for more developed kinds of "recognizing."

We are setting up a new conception of the living body, one in which the body means or implies. So far we have defined three ways in which the body implies: within body-en, the next occurring, and the stopped process and object. We will now develop a fourth: when there are many processes, how they imply each other.

If the stoppage is new, what continues has never occurred that way before, alone, without what is stopped.

Were there "two" processes before one of them stopped? "They" had never occurred separately before. The spectator can always divide in many ways. But let us give a different status to a division between occurrences that can occur without each other.

What continues would not be new if the *two* processes had already been distinct. In that case the one that continues would continue unchanged. But we think of the process as undivided. What continues has never happened without what is stopped. So the division is new, and what continues is a new whole.

We can also see novelty developing, if we consider this: when the stopped process resumes, it will do so into a changed organism, one that went on in new ways during the stoppage. *So the resumed process won't be as before either.* When it resumes, there will be *a new whole.* The whole process won't be as it was before the separation from what continued.

What continued was different during the stoppage and is changed further by being together with what resumes the stoppage.

Are there still *two* processes in the whole once the stopped process resumes? This question is in the old model: *either* one *or* two. Our result is more complex.

If there are many stoppages and resumptions there will be many processes, i.e., many newly organized occurrences, ways the whole body is. For many processes (perhaps all) there will be phases when "they" occur *only together*, and other phases which tempt us to think of them as separate processes.

This *result* is what most people *begin* with: coordinated process*e*s. Instead, we *derive* the fact that there are many processes, and that they become many in such a way that they *are already coordinated*. Let me show this:

In our new model the processes are *originally and inherently coordinated*. In phases when a process is resumed, the rest of the body occurs *only together* with it. Whenever that process is stopped, the rest of the body lives without it. So the other processes have phases during which they are always together with this one process, all one with it, not differentiated from it, and other phases during which they have gone on and formed without it.

The processes may seem independent along their whole sequences, but they are different processes only during phases in which one went on without the other. When a process goes on, it goes on together with a lot of other processes. Each phase of each process developed only together with some, but only without some others. All the phases of each process developed during the stoppage of some others, and only together with some others.

Therefore how any one of them is, at a certain moment, is part of the bodily whole that includes just certain phases of the others. We can now say:

The exact way a process is in each of its phases implies how the others are. This is a fourth sense of "imply."

It is an empirical question whether all processes imply each other in this way, or just which ones do, or what shall be considered "a" process. We are not saying that two processes cannot be independent, even if our model so far does not formulate such independence. The empirical intricacy can always again exceed any conceptual model. Once we know this, we can use many models.

When one defines separated processes or bodily "systems," their interactions can be puzzling. They are often much more coordinated and affect each other mutually in more ways than one can account for. Then "holistic" medicine seems to be outside of science.

Once a process has become differentiated by not going on during some phase of another, one is tempted to trace them as if they were separate even in the phases in which they occur *only together*. But let us not assume separate processes when they are not separate from each other all along their way.

The spectator could formulate complete and distinct strings of separate processes, for example, digestive, respiratory, reproductive, etc. These are not separate all along their way, nor are their subprocesses at the microscopic level.

The illusion of separate processes arises also in studying social change. For example, one traces changes in work patterns over time. Then, separately, one traces changes in family patterns, in health patterns, in economic patterns. Different terms are developed in these different studies, as if these lines of development existed separately over time, when in fact they are often merged in each event that people live through.

If one assumes separate events, processes, or systems, one must then add their coordinations as one finds them, as if unexpectedly. Currently science is only slowly finding more and more kinds of them.

As simple as this model is, so far, it gives us another way to think of coordinated processes.

Many processes and their resumptions happen only during certain phases when others are ongoing, or only during stopped phases of others. They will seem separate but coordinated. But they are not separate during phases when they occur "*only together*." Those stretches need to be considered a unity that has never been divided.

They are separate in the phases when one occurs without the other, but even so not simply separate. Rather, the stoppage of one happens *only together* with certain occurrences in the other. As we saw above, when one process continues on by itself, it becomes different just because the other is not happening. That is why although they seem "separate," their phases are coordinated.

There seem to be separate processes which "interact." It seems they are first many; then they inter-act.

Instead, let us use the *type of concept* I call "*interaction first*." The interaction process may exist long before they become differentiated. "Their" *interaffecting precedes* their being many, and continues when they have become many.

Above we defined the body as the process that continues. Now we can define the body from the viewpoint of any one of these coordinated process*es*:

For any one process, the body is the other ongoing *processes—and also this one in those phases in which it is ongoing.*

One usually says that a process happens *in* the body, but this "in" is only an observer's space-location. Without as yet having a space, "in the body" can be defined for any one process. A process goes on in the body insofar as it goes on in the coordinated interaffecting with the others.

The body is always the other ongoing processes—and also this one when this one is ongoing.

Any one process goes on in the others.

Let this intricate relation stand as it is, so that it can help generate our further steps with all the logical force it is capable of having. We need not artificially make the concept sharper and more separate from the development in the midst of which we are here. On the other hand, we won't let its subtlety fall back into a merely vague wholeness. Let us keep and name just this pattern which has emerged so far. How shall we name it?

"Interaffecting" and "coordination" are words that bring the old assumption of a simple multiplicity, things that exist as themselves and are only then also related. So we need a phrase that does not make sense in that old way. Let us call the pattern we have been formulating "*original interaffecting.*" This makes sense only if one grasps that "they" interaffect each other before they are a they.

We can also say that the processes are "*coordinately differentiated.*" They became differentiated in the first place in a coordinated way, and are "separate" only in this way, with their phases implying each other.

(b) There is only the whole implying.

The body's implying is always all one implying, but to make this clear let me raise a rather technical question:

When a stopped process resumes, does *it* then imply the rest of its own sequence? Or is it still only the other processes, the whole body, that imply this one's further continuance?

It might seem to be an odd question. If the whole process with which we began implies its sequence or cycle, and we call the resumed one "a process," it seems that it must imply its own further sequence. It seems odd that the other processes would imply this one's continuation, and it would not imply its own continuation.

Let us not unthinkingly transfer our concept of "the whole process" to each of the coordinately differentiated process*es* singly. *The whole process implies the next occurring of the coordinated processes*. But, let us not just assume that each of them does its own implying of its string of further events. We saw just above: *they are not separate strings*.

To let new concepts emerge, we must permit exactly what has emerged, and we must tell ourselves carefully just how we have it so far. We see that we have used the singular whole "process" (and "the rest of the process") somewhat differently than the use of "processes." The process*es* imply *each other* in the same occurring. When one is stopped, the whole other process(es) (the body) implies the continuation of the stopped process. When resumed, still the whole process implies each. But now we are not sure if *a* single process also implies its own continuance, or if only the whole process does.

We are sure that the body (the other processes and the resumed one) implies the coordinately differentiated next occurrence and the subsequent occurrences. We have it from II that the whole process implies its further events. But we have to say that a resumed, coordinately differentiated process does not imply its own continuance; only the body—the other processes—implies this one's subsequent events. Of course, the body is now the other processes *and* this one (if it has resumed); so it is part of the implying of further events, *but only together with the others in the whole process.*

So we can also say that *the schema* is the whole implying.

Implying is always one implying. This is an important principle for our later understanding of how the body can, in one felt meaning, imply so very much.

When a baby lamb can first walk, it will not stop before a cliff. It walks right on and would fall, were it not for the experimenter's glass plate. After a certain number of days when "the perceptual system" has developed sufficiently, the baby lamb will stop at the edge of the cliff, even if it has never seen such a drop before, indeed even if it has been blindfolded since birth and has seen nothing up to this time. Since it stops short of the cliff, the spectator says that the lamb "recognizes" the difference in the spatial relations which constitute the sharp drop, and so it stops. When the en does not carry the implying forward, the sequence stops! We will have concepts with which to explain this in VI when we have built them for (from) behavior and perception, but we can say even now that if a perception that can be what "was" implied does not arrive to carry the sequence forward, it stops. The implying remains the same implying. Without a perception that "was" implied at every step, the walking stops.

But there is another finding which is my reason for telling the story: When a baby lamb has been separated from its mother at birth, and raised carefully away from her until it is of the same age as the lambs that stop at a cliff, it will not stop. And this is so even if the lamb was never blindfolded. That is to say, if it is separated from its mother, then even with much experience of spatial perception it will not fully develop its normal "perceptual and motor systems."

"Impossible," commented a lot of people at first. "The perceptual-motor system is separate from the reproductive system." They knew that a lamb raised apart from its mother will not develop a normal sexual instinct in adulthood. This was understandable since adult sexuality and early mother-infant relations were understood to be part of the same functional system. The mother forms an "imprint" in the baby, and this controls its sexual choices in adulthood. But it was not possible to trace how being with the mother in its early days affects its perceptual and motor processes. Nevertheless, this was the finding. I don't know if it has been widely replicated or not. But it is a good illustration of the point here.

At a given stage of science not all interrelations have been traced in spatial mechanical terms, nor need they all be traceable in that way. The body, as we are defining it, is not only a filler of mathematical space. The coordinately differentiated processes are together not just as neighbors that can affect each other in space. How the body (all the other processes) occurs is not only how it is rendered in the flat terms of spatial diagrams and mechanics, although what is so rendered is highly useful. We can retain all the advantages of the usual reduction to space-time-fillers as far as they go, but we are also becoming able to think about the body always as the whole bodily occurring.

So it is a logical implication of our concepts that a resumed process does *not* imply its own continuation; only the process as a whole implies it.

This is not the simple either/or of unity or many, but rather a new type of unity and many: just these phases of the new processes occurring "only together."

By implying the whole process, each implies the others and in this way it thereby also in a way implies itself, but only via implying the whole process.

The implying is thus always the whole body's, one implying. This will also be important in many ways later, for example for focusing (see Gendlin 1981 and 1991b). The processes are not separate. How each would imply just itself is not how it is implied by the others-and-it, that is to say by the body's one implying.

(c) The body is the subprocesses; they are body-en#2 and #3 all the way in.

Just as there are not simply separate processes (as we just found), so also there are no simply separate parts of the body. The spectator can divide the spatial body-en#2 identity in many ways. For example, there are also obviously important divisions into organs like heart, liver, and intestines, and many tissues and cells that are involved in processes that define them as parts. But the coordinated differentiation of the processes is such that a great many processes are always going on in any given part. There is never only the processes that define and separate that part. Any part is involved in many processes and in many ways. In some of them it is indeed this part, just as itself, but in other processes it is only a part of a larger whole, while some other processes set up only some sub-part, while other of its sub-parts are happening within different wider and smaller processes.

There is no single set of bodily parts. In some process some "part" acts as one, but what we thereby spatially distinguish may not be one in other processes. It may be only together with more, and within it many subprocesses may involve only sub-parts of it.

As we said of the whole body in I, a part changes and may disintegrate if the processes (subprocesses and larger processes) in which it is involved stop and never resume. Parts of the body are derivative from process events.

We arrive at the concept of a layeredness (although no single system of levels). The body isn't one body and one environment. Rather, body and environment are interspersed. Some part is "body" in some process (and identical with its en#2 in the events of that process), but it may also be many different en#2 aspects for many other processes with other body-en#2 identities. In one process it is body with an en#2; in another process it is en#2 with some part of itself (or in some wider part of the body). The body consists of b-en#2 process events all the way in. We can now develop this conception further.

In chapter I, we had no distinction between body and environment. We were not putting together two things which had been separate. Now also, we cannot divide body from en in these body-en#2 identities, all the way in. So far we have defined the "body" only as "the other processes and this one." In what way can these layered subprocesses give us a definition of "the body"?

The body is usually considered the stuff within the skin-envelope. But we are not assuming that the spatial distinctions in the spectator's space are the basic conditions of reality. We can use them, but *within interactional terms that are wider*. (Later we will derive space of another kind, and still later also the spectator's space, as well as the way in which these work in concepts and language.) "Environment" does not mean, for us, what is "out there," "external"—except in the spectator's sense of en#1. What then does "en" mean? Those en#2 aspects which are sometimes absent (we called them objects) were the first environment that is separable from body-process. The subprocesses and parts happen in many larger systems, not just to those within the skin or the skin-demarcated body. Therefore what we call "the body" is a vastly larger system. *"The body" is not only what is inside the skin-envelope.*

If we follow the logic, we notice that there is no single order from wider to narrower: some sub-sub-part of a part might be coordinately part of a process that is vastly wider than that part. We must not assume some classification system according to which parts and "particulars" are "subsumed" or totally determined "within" or "under" or "inside" some categories. A part of a part can be (in) a much wider event than the part.[1]

The subprocess of some process *may* go on entirely in relation to this process, but most subprocesses are involved in other processes as well. This always remains an empirical question. Just what functions as a whole and what does not, should not be obscured by some general holistic principle that everything in the body is a whole. The happenings themselves determine what the whole is. What we actually find will always supersede inferences that seemed to make it impossible. But we find more every year. The superiority of the empirical applies only to what has actually been found. It does not follow that one can deny what has not been found (this year), or cannot be found. From a lack of finding nothing follows.

We need different kinds of formulations, not just one. We don't lose the others by adopting this model. There are also reasons to expect that the usual logical models will be understood and employed more subtly if considered within this one. (See Gendlin 1997e.)

Spatial parts can be defined in many ways. Also, many spectator spaces are possible, not just one geometric space.

All the way into the skin-envelope, there is "body" in the sense of "*other process(es) and this one*" (any specific one, when it goes on). There is no body separate from process. There is no stuff that is the material of only one process, or no process, just stuff. It is process through and through and also concrete through and through. "Concrete" here just means "occurring," the environmental sort.

With our additional terms we can now *derive* the body in the sense in which processes go on "in" it; I called it "environment #3." This concept of the body is laying itself out more complexly. A process happens *in* many other processes and subprocesses. They are many insofar as they are distinct by sometimes going on and sometimes not. Now we are finding in what way the body is not just a structure in space and time.

The body or any part is never just environmental stuff. Because it is organized in many processes, it is never just there in one glob, as if it could be fully definable as filling up a piece of space-time. Nor is any part of it there in that way. *The en#3 body in which* a process goes on cannot be environmental stuff as a single space-time structure, because stuff and process are not divided; the body is not all process in one sense, while being all stuff in another. It is b-en also in all the parts. In IV-A-a we said that the body is always the "other" processes, but now that includes the subprocesses and their en#2s. At any level (however one defines a set of levels) a part of the body is also partly en#2 for subprocesses with parts which are again both en#2 and parts.

We have now in a rudimentary way **derived** the concrete palpable body made of environment. We also have more detail on how the processes are in each other, and may include some of each other's events. The body always occurs as a specific whole.

(d-1) Symbolic functions of the body

The concepts we have built explicate (speak from, make broadly applicable, ...) how a body-process has **its own** continuity and its own **internal** relations between events. The process is not only an occurring but also always an implying.

Implying is a rudimentary kind of symbolizing. A symbol is something which "stands for" something else, something other than itself. In such a view there is no inherent connection between the symbol and what it stands for. Instead, we want to understand the living body's own indicating, own implying, own way of being now or here and also being something that is not occurring now or here.

We can group our concepts in terms of how the body does that. The first three are a horizontal sort of implying within one occurrence: the whole occurrence is implied by any part of it.

(I)   Body and en#2 are one event; each implies the whole event.

(IV-A-a) Differentiated process*es* imply each other. Each implies that the others are a certain way.

(IV-A-c) Any body-part (anything that is "body" for one process, or part of anything that so functions) is involved in and maintained by many other processes, but as a different part or parts. *It* implies the others, but not just as "it." In implying the others *it functions not as itself,* but as functioning-in that implying.)

The next three implyings bring (generate, are, ...) time, as we will further see below (as well as the horizontal implying).

(II)   Any occurring is also an implying of further events.

(IV-A-b) Each of the process*es* implies the whole next event and sequence of whole events.

(III)   How a process continues differently **carries** any stopped process and implies the object (en-aspect) which would resume it. (The missing body-process is implied, and since it can happen only with its en#2 object, that remains implied as well.)

(d-2) Some requirements for our further concept formation

Sometimes I stop in the midst, and turn to discuss the strategy employed in generating the model. These discussions can be taken out—to show that the model can stand alone—and they can also be put back so as to show what else is involved in arriving at a model. We can open the whole arena that is usually kept implicit when one formulates a model. Therefore we need to discuss the strategy, and also be able to take the discussion out.

Our concepts stem from the intention to put **interaction first**. We began with body and environment as one event, and only gradually developed certain limited ways in which they are separable. "Interaction first" comes from many sources. I will now cite a few of them.

A great deal comes from *Experiencing and the Creation of Meaning* (Gendlin 1997a). Focusing (see Gendlin 1981) is its application. Some instances and stories from focusing can move us on. From the process of any kind of explication we say (know, feel, wait for, ...) how the body always implies its next bit of living process, and thereby also the environmental objects. But we have no specific terms for any of this as yet.

The model is intended to differ from mathematical-perceptual kinds. The few concepts we have so far generate an odd kind of time and space.

For example, two people in a close relationship may find the following pattern: "If she were a little bit better or more loving (or different in this and this way), then I could be so good (or I could be in this and this way .....). But I can't be. Why not? Because she won't let me. She isn't that little bit better. And why not? Because of the way I am. If I were a little bit better then she could relate to me the way I need her to do, so that I could be a little bit better, so that she could."

Individuals are commonly thought of as separate originative causes. In a relationship between two people, each is said to "contribute some of the trouble" and carry "some of the blame." On the other hand, family therapists say about a troubled family that "the system is sick." They rightly consider the interaction as a single system. But there has been no way to conceptualize this so that we could think much further about it.

If one person could begin to be different, and stay steadily different, then the other would change. But as often as one tries, one is soon pulled back into the interaction pattern. Perhaps if both could be that little bit different at the same time, they could leap out of one interaction pattern into another. But it would be a leap; there seem to be no steps and no way to think from one pattern to another. To think further, our model begins with concepts that begin with interaction.

My example and those to follow show that *one* occurrence can consist of two or more people, and that the occurrence can assign them their character in the interaction (much as an interaction in quantum mechanics defines the particles).

In the West people are accustomed to think in units and nouns, and to attribute causality to individuals. "There is a boy over there" is an acceptable sentence; it is optional information whether he is running, or sitting. But one would not easily accept the sentence "There is a running over there," adding only later that the running is a boy. Nouns can stand; verbs cannot. Similarly, it seems we must first have a boy and a girl. Then they can interact. It seems we cannot first have an interaction.

The very word "interaction" sounds as if first there are two, and only then is there an "inter." We seem to need two nouns first. We think of two people living separately into adulthood; then they meet. A good deal of their interaction is explained by their antecedent lives. But not all of it. To an important extent it is their interaction which determines how each acts.

It is commonly said that each of our relationships "brings out" different traits in us, as if all possible traits were already in us, waiting only to be "brought out." But actually you affect me. And with me you are not just yourself as usual, either. You and I happening together makes us immediately different than we usually are. Just as my foot cannot be the walking kind of foot-pressure in water, we occur differently when we are the environment of each other. How you are when you affect me is already affected by me, and not by me as I usually am, but by me as I occur with you.[2]

We want to devise concepts to capture this exact aspect of "interaction first": *what each is within an interaction is already affected by the other*.

This will also lead to a new way to think of time. Usually one traces cause and effect separately one after the other: "She affects me and *then* this makes me act so as to then affect her." In our model they cause each other by "original interaffecting" and "coordinated differentiation." One need not precede the other in time.

For example, a therapist described a difficult therapy relationship with a man. He traced the trouble back and found that it was already there in the first hour, and even at the start of the hour. But he was so used to attributing causality to individual entities, and to find causality always in a time before, that he could not imagine that the interaction itself originated the trouble. Finally he said about the client: "I must have been affected by the sound of his walk when he came down the hall before I saw him." To explain something seems to require showing that it was already so at an earlier time. But such an explanation does not get at the interaction, the system of the two together as one event. Instead of "the sound of his footfall" (just him), we need to be able to think how one event determines what each is with the other.

Two requirements for our concepts are: interaction first, and a new conception of time in which we can explain something, without having to show that it was already there in a time before. The usual type of explanation and the usual concept of time deny novelty. They deny that anything actually *happens*. Instead, we show that it was already so, and needed only a bit of rearranging.

A third requirement is to include structur*ing* or pattern*ing*, rather than only structures and patterns. If everything must be thought of in terms of existing patterns, then even if an interaction precedes, there seems to be no way to arrive at one that is differently structured. We would have to *jump* from one interaction pattern into another (or wish that we could).

For example, Piaget thinks in terms of interaction patterns between knower and known (called "child" and "object"). But he cannot show how the child develops from one interaction to another more developed one.

Here is a fourth requirement: for us an interaction (a process, body-environment) *implies its own changing*. It has to be *non-Laplacian*. Laplace was the man who said, "If I knew where all the particles of the universe are right now, and the speed and direction at which they are moving, I could tell you the whole past of the universe, and predict all of its future." What he did not recognize is that this assumption was built into the good old mathematical concepts he was using. He might as well have said that if he knew 2 + 2 he could know its future. We would never want to do without mathematical concepts and logical inference, and we use it in building this model, although we use other powers as well. But we require concepts of something happening, something that cannot be found already there before, as one must always do in mathematics.

Already in II we said (but did not show) that the body's implying is non-Laplacian—the implying of the whole sequence changes at each point.

Let me use another ordinary example to specify this requirement of novelty and non-Laplacian time sequences.

How people experience the present has to do with their past. If I hadn't gone through this and that, I would not perceive what I now perceive here in this situation. If we had not had those years together, we would not understand each other as we do now. This has some degree of use and truth. But the explanation from the past experience is often puerile. One explains a present by what was already so in the past—but one doesn't explain how that sort of thing could have come about in the past, for the first time. So one fails to explain how it could happen at all.

According to the most common theory of communication, it is impossible for you to understand me unless you already have all the meanings to which I allude. The theory dodges the question of how you can acquire new meanings. But if you must have them from the past, how could you have gotten them in the past? If there was a way to understand something new then, why wouldn't there be a way now?

This has often been remarked before. Why then does this kind of explanation continue to be assumed? It is because it is indeed a very powerful kind—the mathematical kind, also the kind used in constructing anything out of preexisting pieces. But we need other kinds. Everything is not reducible to preexisting units, nor is everything something constructed. When something is constructed, each constituent is first alone, and is therefore conceived as capable of existing alone. When "it" enters a combination, "it" is "the same one" as before. It acts as itself. (See Gendlin 1997e; we will derive "human making" in VII-B.)

If something new can ever happen, then something new can probably happen now too. So we need not assume that to explain an event must mean to show that everything that makes up the event was already there before.

Past experience does not alone determine present events, yet it does function in some way, now.

Sometimes the role of the past is viewed along the lines of Freud's transference: I am not "really" perceiving and feeling you, just my father. In revolt against this view, many current psychologists emphasize the "here and now." But these notions of "present" and "past" come from what I call the "unit model." The present is supposed to be just itself, as if the past is just another thing. They are placed in successive *positions* along a line. Then one seems to have to choose between them.

Instead, we need a new conception of time, to speak from how we experience the present, but experienced (with and through and by means of .....) the past. Let us enter into this more closely.

Obviously I am not experiencing the past as such when I experience the present, or else I would be thinking and feeling the past events, and my images would be of those incidents. If that is happening I am missing what is going on in front of me. This happens when I daydream or relive the past. But the past does play a role when I am fully in the present. Obviously, the present wouldn't be what it is, if it were not for how I have lived up to this point. I experience the present, but my past experience is part of what makes up my present.

My actions and thoughts come out of me from out of my body. I don't know a great deal about how they come. Mostly they are new; they belong now and have not been heard, known, or felt before, but although they are new creations they obviously involve what has happened before.

The past and the present cannot be understood if we think of them only as two different things in two different positions on a time line. The present is a different whole event. The past functions in every present.

If we can develop concepts for this, we can then differentiate the different ways in which the past can function now, for example so as to force the present to repeat it, or so as to become part of a fresh new whole implying, or in many other, more intricate ways. *Our actual experiences cannot be understood very far with a merely positional conception of time.*

We can apply the concepts we have built so far, and say that past and present are both occurring now, and the present goes on in the remains of the past, and lives them forward. As we said, en#3 is a kind of past *in* which the fresh body-en#2 process goes on. And en#3 is altered in being lived further by the process. Yes, there is a past that is now, and this past is being altered now. Of course this is a different past than the dead and gone past which was recorded on someone's video, and functions no longer. For some purposes we will want to keep the usual notion of that all gone past which happened long ago. But there is also the past which is inherent in any present experience, and which can function in it in various ways.

What I now do, feel, and think comes out of my body. This may sound odd, but where else does it come from? The mind? To separate mind and body deprives "body" of certain vitally important characteristics of living tissue. I am not referring just to the famous mind/body problem on the abstract level. The problem involves a way of thinking, a type of concept, which removes implying (and as we will soon see, also meaning and symbolic functions) from body. For us it is vital not to miss the fact that living bodies imply their next bits of life process.

The usual conceptual model deprives *everything* of implying and meaning, not just living bodies. It constructs its objects in empty positional space and time, so that everything consists of information at space-time points. The space and the objects are presented before someone—who is not presented in the space. It is rather someone who connects the space and time points. The connections come to the points only externally; they are added by anonymous people called "the idealized observer."

The observers are living bodies; they are us! The connections which they supply are inherent *internal connections*.

Shall we now study the observers (ourselves) by positing still another set of observers to connect us in *their* spectated space and time? Concepts that consist only of external positional relations are too poor to enable us to think about what living bodies can do, even plants and certainly animals, let alone ourselves.

Instead, let us think-from and speak-from how we experience the present with the body, and how the past is in the present and in the body, indeed how the body is a kind of past, a past that is now involved in experiencing the present.

If you attend to the middle of your body just now, you will find your intricate (more than defined) body-sense-of *the present*—which consists of my words and also a vast amount more. Language is always implicit in human bodies, so that a present body-sense always leads to the formation of fresh phrases if you allow it. Even before those come, you can sense the past that functions in this moment, much of your thinking and reading (more than you could explicitly remember), your reasons for reading this, what you hope for, your curiosity, excitement, perhaps even disgust at some of what I am saying, but also what else went on today that allowed you the time for this now, what your alternatives were, perhaps what you wanted to avoid, perhaps what you are always good at in philosophy, also what has often been hard for you, many past events bearing not just on this reading but on what else is going on in your life just now. These are my words. You would first find only a slight seething body-quality (often just ease or unease) which can open into your version of "all that."

Suppose you are talking with someone and you would like to say something funny. Not much you can do about it! At other times a funny remark *comes* and even slips out. When you examine it you might find that it has beautifully integrated certain unlovely traits of the person and certain background facts in the situation, often quite a number of them. If you can rein it in you might prefer not to say it, just because it is "so true" in so many ways. You can observe how the past has functioned in the production of this snide remark which is a novel present creation.

Let us be guided by this more intricate past which has at least the kind of role we find.

These many past experiences are *now* functioning within one new experience. This is not the past as it was then, but as it is here now, relevant now, involved and being lived, participating in the experiencing that your body implies and enacts—now. The past comprises many events, but the present is only this one. Many experiences participate in one. We will want a concept for this way in which an as yet unseparated multiplicity functions in one fresh formation. That is a fifth requirement for our further concepts.

We find a pattern I might call "*many making one*," in which the many and the one *mutually determine each other*. "The past" which now participates in shaping the present is not what happened long ago, but *a past that functions in this present.* The unseparated many are *in interaction first*, and only then specifiable one by one. What each is, has already been affected by the others which were already affected by it. There is one implied next step which *many facets have shaped in one fresh formation* that is not deducible from an antecedent pattern or set of units, but from which new units and patterns can be generated.

Can there be such concepts? In what we said, we have them already, but as leaps. I call what we have been saying "leap concepts." They speak-from experiencing. We tell a story, or we say "we need a concept that is like such and so." But "like such and so" is already a concept. In saying "many into one, like a snide remark," the incident has already "applied" itself to other situations; it has *implyingly crossed* with them. A kind of "concept" is already in action, but we have not yet formulated a concept as such. That comes later. There is not yet an internally articulated concept, but this "naked" use is actually more intricate than an articulated concept (see Gendlin 1992b, 1997f). The intricate crossing cannot be *equated* with an articulation, but we can *articulate from it*. (This odd phrasing avoids the error of equating.) In articulating from the crossing, we gain the power of a few more complex patterns, and we can always return to the incident for more.

In stories and in odd sentences we first let the concepts work. Then we can enter and explicate (some strands of) how they have worked. We articulate some of their internally differentiated linkages and sharpnesses so that they acquire the power of logical inference. We must therefore let them stand as we have them so far, and protect especially the ways in which they are odd and not immediately amenable to logic. (When our terms are more developed, they will enable us to say more about the process in which they are now arising. The role of "like" is discussed in VII-A-c and VII-A-j-4. More is shown in VIII.)

We can explicate from how we went. Backwards, we can *generate a new set of units* with which we can then locate where we began, and move from there. But the naked sense-making is not determined in advance by units that last across. Such units are made from how the whole is changed by the move.

A sixth way in which our model will differ is that we do not assume a given set of units. Units are generated from interaction, from making sense. They can be newly generated and regenerated, both in regard to their number and what they are.

This is like saying (as we did just above) that an interaction process is not determined by the antecedent participants. Our rudimentary conceptual model already says this.

If one looks directly at the assumption of units, one may not wish to hold it, but it is a silent assumption that inheres in the structure of most concepts. If we ask someone whether they assume that everything comes in already fixed mathematical bits, particles, time units, space units, chemical units, they may say that the assumption is simple-minded. But this assumption is nevertheless built into how most concepts function when they are used to *explain* something. The explanation consists of an assumed set of fixed units, pieces, elements, constituents that remain the same and are traced through. Such explanations are highly useful, but need to be considered within the larger context which is not reducible to them, and in which other units can be generated.

Looking back over two centuries from Kant and Hegel to the present, notice that nature, life processes, and animals were given over to mathematical mechanics, time and space units, graph paper, deterministic logical necessity, Laplacian uneventfulness. Only humans were thought to have events, and even this was a puzzle.

Even very recently, still, human bodies seemed completely determined by logical mechanics, so that creativity and novelty were possible only in art, which was to say only in "illusion." Novelty-making had to hide in "transitional objects" (Winnicott), "ambiguity" (Empson), or bizarre exaggerations (Bakhtin, Bataille). So convinced were thinkers that nature is graph paper. How odd! Logic, math, and graph paper are quintessentially human creations—nothing natural comes in equal units that can be substituted in logical slots. Every leaf and cell is a little different. Only humans make graph paper. Where do you ever see it in nature? The larger process is creative, and generates among other things the wild and world-shaking production of graph paper.

So we surely need not give nature and bodily life process over to fixed units and logic—however powerful their use is. We need not think of nature as artificially constructed out of separate pieces, although it is useful (and dangerous) to construct and reconstruct them.

We have as yet no good conceptual model with logical links that does not assume fixed individuated units at the bottom. I do not mean to slight much elegant work which is moving in the same direction as we are here. On the contrary, I hope to contribute to it. I am only pointing to a difficulty that is often in the way. It helps if one recognizes the assumption of units directly, so that one can let what makes sense stand, even if it does not assume such units.

We also need to recognize the way time is assumed in what I call the "unit model." At time one (t_1) some set of basic elements have to be already there, so that t_2 is a mere rearrangement of them. In such a system of thought nothing can ever happen. When something happens, it is an embarrassment and an anomaly.

In our new model, process is happening. An occurring is a change. We are devising concepts for real change, not just rearrangement. So we forego the type of explanation which requires $t_2 = t_1$. (The latter can be derived as a special case.)

When the past functions to "interpret" the present, the past is changed by so functioning. This needs to be put even more strongly: The past functions *not as itself, but as already changed by* what it functions in.

Our next concepts will need to formulate what is said by this odd phrasing: "not as itself, but as already changed by." The concepts we have built so far do already imply it. Of course, I developed them from stories such as the ones I told here. My stories will let us develop our concepts further.

Our sixth requirement is: rather than a fixed set of units being determinative, we need concepts to think about how units emerge, and can reemerge differently.

Our concepts will retain logical consistency, but they will also require:

(1) Interaction first. The interactional event determines the individual entities (or the "slots" for individual entities). Each functions "not as itself but as already affected by."
(2) A model of time in which a past and an implying function in the present
(3) Process events
(4) A non-Laplacian sequence
(5) Many factors shaping one event
(6) Units emerge, and can reemerge differently

(e) Everything by everything (evev)

Let us now pick up the thread and develop more concepts with the requirements we just formulated. In IV-A, a–c, we built concepts for a sequence of whole events. In such a sequence each bit (any this) is a specifically differentiated whole. Let us now develop more exactly how *original interaffecting* and **coordinated differentiation** produce differentiated wholes.

A stopped process is "carried" by **the differently ongoing process**. Now we want to understand more exactly how this new whole, a newly **differentiated multiplicity** ("all the differences"), forms itself as the continuing process.

During stoppage the new whole (the next event) forms from how the process*es* interaffect each other, the phases where some subprocesses stop or resume being together. In this way they become differentiated into many process*es*. Therefore I called their relation "*original* interaffecting."

What continues during phases of stoppage is new and becomes separate. When the stopped process resumes, some of its phases occur *only together* with a phase of other processes, or only without some of those. In this way they become differentiated.

So the specific differentiations are determined by what occurs together as a whole, and how this differs from what occurred earlier as a whole.

In each new whole there are new internal differentiations between processes.

In IV-A-b we found that implying is always the whole body's *one* implying rather than that of separate processes. They are one coordinated multiplicity rather than many really separate sequences side by side. So each process and subprocess is the implying of the same whole next event. The same implying is thus in many parts of the body.

A change in one of the processes implies changes in how the others are implied in the one implying of the next bodily event.

Even a very tiny process in some microscopic location implies (is also the implying of) the larger processes of which it is a part. The various processes each imply the continuance of the others *as the whole process*, and thereby also its own continuation.[3]

We also said that any piece of the body occurs in many processes and subprocesses, and is not the same piece in them. Similarly, what is "a" process different from the others is determined in each occurring.

If something different in one of the process*es* makes other process*es* different, and we don't assume a single identity of our first process, then the difference *it* makes in the others also depends on how the other process*es* affect and differentiate our first one. *That is to say, the first-mentioned difference in our first process is itself already affected by the differences it makes.*

A process or part does not function as itself; it does not function as an individuated "it"; rather, it functions as already interaffected. What "it" is (and its effect) has already been affected by the differences it makes in the others which affect it.

Let me develop this more specifically: from one multiplicity the whole process moves to a somewhat different multiplicity. How have the members of the first multiplicity functioned to bring about the second altered one? In coordinated differentiation and original interaffecting there is a change in the numbers and identities of the members of the multiplicity.

If we have introduced the change externally, we think of "it" as what we know we did. The old model assumes that what we did (from outside the system) is distinct from the differences it made (within the system). But for the system the event is just those differences. The same relation exists between one difference and the rest of the differences. In the old model, the difference one thing makes in the system is an event in its own right (outside of the rest of them). But for the rest of the differences the first difference is not a separate event, but only how it affects them. If we consider the first difference as within the system, what it really is will include how the others affect it. In the old model one assumes that there must *first be* "it" as one unit, separate from how its effects in turn affect it. But such an "it" is an event only in the en#1 observer's process. In the process we are looking at there is no separate "it," no linear cause-effect sequence with "it" coming *before* its effects determine what happens. So there is something odd here about the time sequence. How can "it" be already affected by affecting something, if it did not do the affecting before it is in turn affected? Let us appreciate this problem. It will solve itself below.

With the old assumption of fixed units that retain their identity, one assumes a division between *it*, and its effects on others. (This "it" might be a part, a process, or a difference made.) In the old model it is only later that the difference made to other units can in turn affect "it." And only still later can how it is affected also change the difference it makes to other units. If we must think of the changed difference-making as happening at the same time as the original difference it made, this would be called an anomaly.

But in the old model the unit-event has been separated from the differences it makes; these differences must occur before they, in turn, can affect the first event and thus change the differences which the first event can only then further make (now that it has in turn been altered).

If we do not assume these separations, then some well-known anomalies dissolve. In the model developing here, what *occurs* is the result of how the effect of each process, part, or difference is changed by how its effect on the others affects it.

Why is this so?

The separate differences made do not occur. Only the result occurs.

Our model moves from one differentiated whole of multiple aspects to another. Instead of leaving it at a gap, we can make concepts for the process in which a newly differentiated multiplicity forms.

We assume neither independent units nor a mushy undifferentiated whole. In a coordinatedly structured whole, no aspect exists just so without the others being just so (IV-A-a). Each is also the further implying which they all are (IV-A-b). The material "parts" are relative to the processes (IV-A-c) and not as if they existed identifiably apart, and only then entered into processes.

The single occurring includes all the differences, and the differences made to each other by these differences, and again by the differences they make. Occurring is an interaffecting of everything by everything (evev).

The interaffecting or difference-making goes on just as far as it can, which is not indefinitely (we will ask why) so that there is an occurrence. (Why there is then still another occurring we will also ask.) All the differences that interaffecting can involve already make all the differences they can, so that no more differences are made.

If we want to imagine this happening in linear time (differences occurring one after the other) I can tell a story: When I was in the Navy, I learned to repair and tune the radio receivers of that time. They had several parts called "IF cans" (Intermediate Frequency), each of which had a screw on top. I had to turn the screw on the first one to the point where the signal is loudest. Further turning diminishes the signal again. Then I would turn the screw on the second to its maximum. But this would make a difference to the first. I would turn the screw on the first to what was now the loudest point. But this would affect the second, so it had to be turned to its loudest again. Now this altered the first again, but only a little. After going back and forth a number of times, both are at their loudest. Now came the third, and then each time going between the second and the first again, second and first, second and first, between every tuning of the third. And so with the fourth, where one must return third, second, and first, second and first, between every two tunings of the fourth. Eventually all differences all of them can make to each other, and all the differences that makes to all the differences, and so on, is taken account of. (In section f I ask about how "loudest" works here as the direction.)

The point is that there is a result. *All* differences having made their differences, the result is what it is. It is the result of *everything interaffected by everything ("evev")*. But in our model the differences do not occur. Only the result occurs.

There is no single set of separate things that could be "everything" or "all." What happens remakes "all" parts and differences. Implying is more ordered than a structure of parts, processes, or differences; occurring redetermines its multiplicity. (In Gendlin 1997a, this is discussed as the "reversal of the usual philosophic order.")

In the story of the IF cans, each new tuning takes time. But *everything x everything does not take (or make) more time than the occurring itself.* The differences which each makes in the others, and they in it, are not actual occurrences, nor actual time-spans.[4]

Differences are results of comparing or measuring. Unless someone does something, differences are not actual events. In the old model "reality" consists of universal space-time comparisons which are not events. Newton showed that the water in a bucket at the end of a twisted rope climbs up the sides when the bucket is rotating, and not when it is not. This showed that motion is not just a change in the relation of the bucket to the earth. This showed that there is something utterly different and empirically independent when a thing moves. But Newton continued to think of motion as a change in space and time relations. So he concluded that the space and time relations (which are really just passive comparisons) have to be considered "objective" and must be given primacy over actual events. The comparing process became "absolute." Einstein modified but did not alter the claim of mere comparing (localization) to overarch and determine actual occurrences.

Relativity theory limits the greater number of solutions one could write for quantum mechanics alone. Physics is slowly moving past those restrictions. Mere comparative localization would no longer have a status equal to interaction (Gendlin and Lemke 1983; Gendlin 1997e). Only interactions, for example measurements that affect the process, are events in it. The space-time localizations are mere comparisons by a merely spectating observer. Comparisons are not occurrences in the process.

Differences are comparisons; they do not occur.

"Eveing" is a way we can think of the formation of implying and occurring. We have to keep in mind that implying is always orderly in a more intricate way than an occurring. The concept of "eveing" is a way of thinking about implying without assuming the differences as such. In forming a new whole, all differences "*implyingly cross*" with each other (the concept of "crossing" can derive from here) in such a way that each acts on the others not as itself but as already crossed.

We need to ask about time: everything by everything makes it seem that everything happens at once and takes no time. Time might be said to be the fact that *everything does not actually happen at once.* But why is the implying eveing carried forward into an occurring? And, why is there then still another occurring? There is another and another, because occurring changes implying into a new implying. But why does the change within eveing (which takes no time) stop so that something occurs, and what is there about the kind of change which is made by occurring which is not part of the eveing (the crossing of all the differences which takes no time)? What makes an occurrence an occurrence?

The answer is of course that implying never happens alone, but always along with occurring, both from occurring and into occurring. And occurring is body-*en*; it occurs in the environment, or we can say that the en occurs into implying. Therefore implying implies the environment, since implying implies an occurring and that is always body-en#2.

So the implying (the eveing) does not go on forever because a body-en occurs, and changes the implying in a way that does not happen within eveing. So the question of why eveing does not go on forever is the question: just how is the implied occurring related to what is occurring?

We said at the start that implying (or implied occurring) is never equivalent to one occurrence. Implying is always more intricately organized and in that sense more precise than any environmental occurring can ever be. Our concept of "eveing" is a conceptual way to speak from this intricacy. (A concept does not represent; it speaks from or carries forward.) Eveing happens in the implying; occurring and environment is not eveing, but occurs-into the eveing. More concepts concerning this will soon develop. Just keep in mind that occurring into eveing is not eveing. Chapter V will make this difference quite clear.

We also said that the process goes on largely in en#3, that is to say in an already life-organized en which speaks back to the implying as, for example, the beaver's tree is already the one the beaver felled. And even if the en is not already modified by life, it is already implied by implying as the en#2 that is part of any life process. So there is more than a new and accidental relation between implying and body-en-occurring. But although the en is already implied, it must still also occur, and that is not determined by the implying alone, both because implying has a more intricate order and because occurring is the actual body-environment.

The question why eveing doesn't continue forever concerns the relationship between implying and occurring, or between the implied body-en and the body-en that happens into this implying. IV-B and V will develop terms from and for this.

In terms of linear time we would ask: how is implying related to what has occurred, to what is now occurring, and to what will occur next, but this division cannot be accepted as the frame of our discussion. Neither can we insert implying between the last and the next occurring, as if the implying took up its own time between occurrings. We will return to this question in the next section.

But now we have developed two ways in which the implying can change—either the original carrying-forward change which the implying implies, or by an eveing during a stoppage (if it doesn't die). **But can we still distinguish these two?** In stoppage we found the development of many coordinated processes in phases of many stoppages and resumptions with many objects. What decides whether the life process has developed and is being carried forward, or whether the whole development is still a version of stoppage? Rather than this either/or, more distinctions will develop in V. There are at least two different ways in which the life process is carried forward by this coordinated development.

I–IV is only a general model, an alternative to the old one that now inheres in most concepts. We have not distinguished tissue process from behavior and perception, nor these from culture, language and action, let alone from what goes beyond these.

In VI we will find that behavior constitutes a still further way in which the regular life process can incorporate and regularly exhibit stoppage (with its implying of objects) and resumption.

In our general model here, shall we still maintain a simple original carrying forward of a single process, the stoppage of which produces the development of many processes and many stops and resumptions? Or should we think of every bit of every process—if it is being carried forward—as a kind of environmental resuming? Of course, there is not eveving until there are many differences, and *many differentiations among processes and objects*, but even the simplest known living things have many. The development we have been discussing has already occurred. So we need not take the development as a history beginning with something simpler than we find. We can also take it as the development of our concepts. In that case we can consider all carrying forward as carrying eveving forward, even though we developed eveving from the simpler general model of carrying forward. Carrying forward is an occurring that changes the implying in a way which it implied itself changed, so that it is no longer "the same" implying.

"Stoppage" has now become derivative from carrying forward (and we can say that we now see that we used the conceptual pattern of "stoppage" to get at carrying forward, and that the concept was altered in functioning for us in this way).

Just as we spoke of processes that affect each other and then find *original* interaffecting (and an unseparated multiplicity), just as we first think of differenc*es* that cross, and then discover that they are *already* crossed, so we are discovering that carrying forward is an *original resuming*.

Eveving and original resuming might be due to an earlier stoppage, or a stoppage might be due to an eveving that makes the usual process impossible.

But the concept of "stoppage" must keep the function it has been performing in our model. It marks a juncture where the usual process cannot happen, and a new development arises. We need not assume that the development comes from the impossibility of the usual process due to some unaccounted-for change in the body or the en (as I said in II). It is equally likely that a development makes the usual process impossible (see Gendlin 1987b). As long as we are clear, we can proceed with both of these two schematic alternatives, unless at some point we find them making a difference we need to pursue. (See Gendlin 1997a, chapter 6, on the functional equivalence of alternative concepts.)

For now, "resumption" is both derivative from, and explanatory of "eveing" and "carrying forward."

We can now apply the concepts of "schema" and "resumption" to every bit of life process, just as if every bit were a stoppage and a resumption. But of course we still distinguish "carrying forward" (resumption) from events that leave the implying unchanged. Since implying is more intricately organized than an occurring, it is only from the occurring that one can say if it was something that can be what the implying implied. Only the carrying forward determines what can carry forward. (See "reversal" in Gendlin 1997a.) See also a very different instance of the reversal, the concept of "reinforcement" in B. F. Skinner (1953).

Events are a life process's own only if they carry it forward. We will be specifying many kinds of carrying forward, although never a single list. Occurring can happen *into* implying without carrying the process forward in any sense, and some of those can make for stoppages. Of course, we retain the vital distinction between the body's own process and other events that happen to it. And, of course stoppage as such must be distinguished from carrying forward (or stoppage-and-resumption).

Our concept of "eveing" is an expansion of the concept of "implying." Eveing implies further occurring, and occurring involves the en, so of course eveing implies the en, but it is still only the implying. How en actually occurs into the eveing will be taken up in V. For a while now, let us pursue the eveing.

(f) Focaling

In my story about tuning the radio, the direction was given in advance by my desire for the loudest, so that I could receive distant stations. The purpose of a machine (or anything we make) remains in the designer. But how does it arise in the designer? If it must be brought to the designer by still another designer, how could they ever arise? So we need to ask: *how do purpose and direction arise from within a process?* For lack of this question today, everything is treated as if it were a machine, and moreover a machine that had no designer. Our purposes are left unthinkable within our science (which is nevertheless influenced by many purposes).

In retuning each IF can, the differences became smaller and smaller and reached a stable result. But without a purpose or direction, how can the eveing arrive at a result?

In our model the occurring brings and changes its own implying of the next occurring. The body's own implying is the *focaling* of the many processes, the many parts and differences into one implying. Purpose and direction are aspects of the process. The purpose is not something added on. For example, in human events what we call "purpose" already inheres in what a given action is. Or, as Dilthey argued, every experiencing *is* already inherently also an understanding (Dilthey 1927). The plant doesn't need a separate purpose to turn to the sun. To render purpose as a separate, added thing is artificial. It is usually artificial to say what "the" purpose is.

Many "purposes" and many possible actions are focaled into *one*. Only one action occurs next. Our concept of "focaling" develops from this relation of many into one. It develops from this function at this juncture in the model, and from many experiential instances. For example:

"Wouldn't it be sad," I ask students, "if you had exactly the same values now as when you were fourteen? But wouldn't it be even sadder if you simply lost the values you had then? So we are sad if they are the same, and sad if they are different. What do we wish? Obviously we are looking for a more intricate relation, something like more developed, more complex, differentiated, realistic, from a deeper human level, more understanding, ... —something like that. In other words, we hope that your values continued to play their role in how you lived, but that they developed by playing this role."

When an artist draws an exactly right line in an unfinished drawing, no aim exists in advance to determine the line. The artist feels and says that the unfinished drawing "needs something." Not the drawing alone, but the drawing and the human body together imply something more. But of course, the artist has no finished drawing already in mind. The aim and the direction develop from the process.[5]

The artist does not try out and then reject all possible wrong lines, and does not "select" the right one. In geometry one can say that a plane contains an infinite number of lines, but those lines do not exist, nor does the line that will eventually be drawn. That line does *not* exist on a blank sheet. The already drawn lines (and much more) participate in the formation (the eveving) of the "needed" line. When it comes, it changes the interrelations of all the lines so as to carry this one implying forward. Neither the aim nor the line exist in advance. The artist's one implying is an eveving of the relationships of all the lines to each other. The artist *focals* the right line.

Another example: a new theory can expand science in a way that does not follow logically from any earlier theory. When you think forward, *you can observe the focaling process at work*. You pursue unclear but possibly rich edges. You sense more than you can as yet think clearly. Once you devise a new theory, you can specify what has changed. In advance you cannot. (What dialectical logic can do is similar; Hegel could arrange the history of thought behind him in a neat dialectical progression, but this could not generate even one step forward.)

The direction and result of focaling comes from implying. Eveving (each already affected by its effect on the others) *is* focaling; it arrives at *one* implying of a next step.

(g-1) Relevance

We can also formulate this point in terms of "relevance." In *Experiencing and the Creation of Meaning* (Gendlin 1997a) I showed that the many meanings are always already involved in any one. Here we are just coming from the many meanings (everything by everything). We have really already said that relevance is eveving and focaling.

What determines which factors make a difference? Obviously they first make whatever difference they make, and so they determine themselves as having been relevant.

When a process is carried forward, all that is involved in forming the next event was "relevant" to the previous event. But there might be an objection. (See Williams's objection in Williams 1997). It might seem that just any event whatever would be relevant by our definition. But consider: *From itself, a process does not form "just any event whatever."* The next event will be relevant, not just by definition, but by carrying the process forward. We will be able to see how the preceding event has functioned in the formation of this one. We can define "relevance" more exactly: it is the function performed by (the role played by) the many in the formation of a given one (the next one).

Many factors are indeed relevant, and do indeed have a part in the shaping of what occurs. But in participating in the next formation, they open and cross. They do not do it as themselves, but as already crossed with whatever else participates in shaping the next event.

It is just my point that a process differs both from arbitrariness and from logic. From the next step we can specify how it is relevant, why it carried the process forward. But to formulate this will constitute a further carrying forward. The terms in which we can do it must first be derived from understanding the steps of the process. But this is nothing like saying something is relevant just because we say it is. Most anything that might happen would not be relevant. Even totally "free play" makes sense (usually new sense) when it is enjoyable.

A process is a relevanting. This verb says both that a process occurs relevantly, and that the relevance is made by the process. What occurs makes itself relevant. So we cannot use relevance as if it were on another level from which one can predetermine what will occur.

Implying, eveving, focaling, and relevanting are "forward" relations; they are made by "carrying forward." Retroactively one can specify them (in various ways). *But we do know something of great importance in advance: we know that the process will form relevantly.*

But nothing is lost if we give up the pretense of determining what is relevant in advance. One always finds the relevance retroactively, even if one's conceptual model demands that one read it back as if it had been determined in advance. Wittgenstein and Merleau-Ponty struggled against this pretense.

Events that "were" in no way implied and do not carry forward can impinge on the body. As we will see, even such events happen into the ongoing relevanting, sometimes with a new but highly organized result. But irrelevant events are not produced by the body. Even with all your human capacities you are unable to think of something that is in every way irrelevant. Right now something irrelevant would be a relevant example in this discussion. But at other times when you think of something irrelevant you can usually trace how it came—quite relevantly—in that situation.

Do we not lose what is called "technical control" with this reversal which puts the process first, and makes the seeming "determinants" retroactive? No, we lose nothing, but our model enables us to think differently about technical control. We badly need a better way to think about it.

We lose nothing because technical control is always obtained only retroactively after many repeated observations. Only then can one predict. Then one can change something and observe again. One may predict the effect of the change, but perhaps it will do something different. Only from seeing a regular effect many times, does one gain technical control. We are not altering this. But should we say that what we retroactively formulate are "determinants" that existed in advance? If we say this we belie our actual procedure, and lose the capacity to think about nature altogether. We need to think about the fact that our scientific formulations change every few years. Neither the last set nor the next set of "determinants" can possibly be what actually determines nature.

To read our formulations back as predetermining nature pretends that nature has the sort of order that our formulations have. Actually it is quite obvious that nature has something like the sort of order that *the progression of our formulations* exhibits over the years. Nature is capable of being carried forward by all those formulations—and so it cannot possibly be equivalent to any of them.

We are building a model with which we can think about that kind of order (see Gendlin 1997e). Of course we can still use any of various logical models within our wider model. With our model we can also conceptualize a great deal that cannot be conceptualized by the old model. But we will not read our model under the occurring processes as if the model determined the processes.

Implying and occurring (carrying forward) is an eveing, a focaling, and a relevanting.

(g-2) Old and new models: some contrasts

For us the same units do not need to last through a change. If they do, it is a narrower special case. In the old model, events must occur within a static multiplicity of space points, time points, and particles. A particle alone is "this one," "the same one" that was earlier there and is now here. In the new model the occurrence forms its own new multiplicity. If a space-time-particle grid is desired, it is determined from the occurrence. Nothing in the new model forces us to lose anything from the old, if we want it. But with the new model we do reject the assumption that occurring must be determined and necessitated by the units of previous occurrence.

Certain processes we will derive later do form structure, but nothing is actually necessitated by imposed structure (the origin of which then remains puzzling).

The old model has only explicit structure, "information" that is attributable to space-time positions. Most of the parameters of our sciences are structured in just this fashion, so that it is no use denying these assumptions themselves, since they are not only general; they also inhere in how everything else is conceived and written down.

In the old model something (say a particle or a body) exists, defined as filling space and time. Then it *also* goes through some process. Or it does not. It is defined as "it" regardless of the process "it" goes through. "It" is separate from a system of changes and relationships that are "possible" for "it."

Let us reconsider the terms "possibility," "constraint," what "can" occur, and what "cannot." The old model assumes a fixed set of possibilities. What actually happens cannot change the set. It simply fills out one of them. One of the possibilities makes good, so to speak, like the one sperm that gets into the egg. It is as if there were no real difference between what occurs and these possibility-units, except for some indefinable preference that one possibility attains—without changing the fixed set of them.

Instead, let us allow the word "possibilities" to be used in two different ways: before and after eveing and occurring. We can say that "a" (determined) "possibility" *participates in* eveing. So it came *before* eveing and enters into it but does not determine or limit the eveing and occurring. Looking back from the event there may have been a different set of antecedent "possibilities" that were (re)-generated from the event.

In quantum mechanics the space-time and particle systems may not last across an interaction. The set of possibilities which "explain" the results of the event in retrospect is not the same set as those which appeared to be there in advance. Although frequent and important, these cases are considered anomalies. They must be written in a very cumbersome way, and with odd particles thrown in and taken out again, to make them conform to the consistent localization of relativity theory.

Can we conceive of a model in which *actual occurring could change the system of possibilities*? Of course, we would often employ a static set of units to formulate predictions. But we would not require that they be read backward.

In practice, of course, scientists revise their theories and systems of what is possible—and they do so retroactively by seeing what occurs. In practice there *is* a relationship between one version of such a theory, and the next improved version. Instead of sameness, we could take *that* wider type of relationship as our model instance.

The issue goes to the heart of the question: how shall we think of an occurrence? We are thinking philosophically, that is to say we are rethinking some basic assumptions of our concepts.

Why limit our model with the assumption that nothing ever really happens? Or can we sufficiently develop a model in which occurring creates (re-creates) order and possibility, rather than the reverse?

(h-1) Crossing, metaphor, law of occurrence

What have been considered the antecedent "determinants" that shape what happens are themselves shaped by participating in this shaping.

We see this easily in the case of a metaphor. We grasp it immediately. Then, to explain it to someone who did not, we can generate many explanations, many similarities which we (then) say it is based on, and many differences which it did not mean. We can say that all these "were implied" in the metaphor, but they certainly were not there as such. We have to take time to think and work to generate them from our immediate grasp of the metaphor.

A metaphor is an eveving, a focaling, a crossing.

How one devises (and understands) a metaphor can be used here as a metaphor for this point: It was long said that a metaphor is "based on" a preexisting similarity between two different things. In our model it is the metaphor that creates or specifies the similarity. By speaking of A as if it were B, certain aspects of A are made which were not there before as such. The metaphor does not "select" this trait from a list of existing traits of A; there is no such fixed set. Nor does the metaphorizer go through the endlessly many traits which A might acquire by being compared to B.

We reverse the order (see Gendlin 1997a) or, more exactly, the old model reversed the order and we are putting it right again, as it occurs for us.

Order comes *from* implying and occurring. Occurring doesn't just fill out an abstract order. The word "possible" needs a more intricate use. What is possible in implying and occurring is not predetermined. Of course what occurred, could occur. Since it occurred, it was possible. We can reverse this and say: *what could occur at the given juncture, did. I call this the "law of occurrence."*

We must notice: *this introduces a distinction into the meaning of "could."* Everything that "could" happen enters into eveving and occurring, and is (re)generated. Looking back from the occurring, the word "could" *could* only say what the implying (eveving) and occurring could in fact do together. The system of possibilities which the event (re)generates behind itself in linear time may not have been possibilities that entered into the event. No abstract set of possibilities determines what "could" carry the implying forward—this is not determined, neither in advance nor in retrospect.

Since eveving takes no time, we can say that whatever could participate, did. Whatever aspects could be relevant, were relevanted.[6] *Now*, if we retrospectively specify them, they are aspect*s*. The "could" and the "they" are determined along with what occurred rather than being an antecedent scheme.

In "Crossing and Dipping" (Gendlin 1991a) I have shown that a metaphor does not cross two situations; rather, the one new situation crosses with the whole use family of a word (see Gendlin 1997a and 1991a for a developed theory of metaphor). All language use is metaphoric in this respect. What after Wittgenstein we can call a "use-family"—our felt sense of the many situations in which we can use the word—crosses freshly with the topic area or situation in which we speak (see Wittgenstein 1953). In crossing they open each other and generate more than could possibly follow logically from either.

If we can understand the metaphoric nature of ordinary language, we can move past the "postmodern dilemma" which seems to make it impossible to say anything without falling into metaphysical concepts. Wittgenstein showed very well how such concepts mislead us in philosophy, but he also showed that language is not determined by them.

Derrida shows quite rightly that there are only metaphorical uses, no so-called proper ones (Derrida 1982). But he is quite wrong to argue that the old theory of metaphor reestablishes itself around each metaphor. As Wittgenstein has shown very well, word use is not actually determined by the concepts that philosophical analysis reads back into it (Wittgenstein 1958). Nothing requires that we reassert the traditional requirement for originally literal propositions, or come to a dead stop because those are impossible.

Instead, we can notice that computers can neither interpret nor generate metaphors. This shows that ordinary language and actions in situations have an order that is more intricate than logic. Notice that ordinary language does not generate contradictions unless one first seeks to reduce it to logic.

There are several kinds of truth in metaphor. We can use any word in any situation, but it says only whatever meaning the crossing makes, there (if any). *We can use any word about any other thing but they cross only as they can cross.* What we get from their crossing is not arbitrary. A crossing has a certain kind of truth.

Nothing arbitrary happens when something is changed and opened by functioning in the formation of something else. Crossing is very precise and generates only just what it generates, although it opens the logical determinacy of the meanings that are schematized by participating in schematizing something.

For example, you can cross toothbrushes and trains. Then you might say, "Yes, I see, a toothbrush has only one 'car,'" or you might say "They both shake us," or "It would be great to have my personal train." There are always a great many results from a crossing, but they are never arbitrary. *Two things cross only as they truly can.*

The bad repute of metaphors comes from the fact that one can be led to unwarranted conclusions in the new situation *if one does not know the new situation well*. For example, if someone tells workers they have to accept the bitter medicine of a pay cut now, rather than an even worse one later, or that the government is cutting "fat" out of the economy so that it will be healthier and produce more jobs, this might be believed by people who have no direct knowledge and experience with the economy. Just as medicine might be unpleasant, but saves us from worse trouble, so a given policy *might* be unpleasant but save us from worse trouble.

For someone who knows economics, the metaphor might bring out something from that knowledge *or it might not*. A knowledgeable person might reply either "Yes, the deficit gets worse because interest payments exceed tax income," or "No, taking money out of the economy will lead to fewer jobs, not more. If people can buy less, then production and jobs cannot be increased. Loose money will have to go into something else."

If I tell you that George, whom you don't know, is an "elephant," you cannot know what I mean. You might expect that he has a heavy-footed walk or great size. But let us say we have been discussing George Washington. Now what emerges might be how Washington seemed to be above the squabbling parties, his own prestige so totally established that he didn't need to squabble.

Of course, it would be nonsense to say that of an elephant! So we see that the metaphor generates new traits, and does so on both sides of the comparison.

We must notice that "our knowledge of elephants" and "our knowledge of George" both function *pre-conceptually*. The example can show what "pre-conceptual" means in my use of it. There could not be new traits, new precise effects, if the word were used only in accord with a defined concept. Instead, we see that word and situation do not function like defined concepts do, although all human experience involves a welter of implicit concepts. But language use is "pre-conceptual" in that we can derive new concepts to explain it only afterwards. Wittgenstein showed this with hundreds of examples. No metaphor or fresh use of words would arise at all, if the implicit concepts didn't open in crossing. If they functioned like explicit concepts—they would keep all subsequent steps consistent with themselves.

We notice it most when a word is used in a new way, but of course it always means *this* precise effect, which saying it just made in *this* situation.

Our model *is and is about* explication, this relation between pre-conceptual and conceptual, or between implying and explicitly occurring structuring.

(h-2) Degrees of freedom

In using eveving to think about metaphor we overturned another basic assumption of the old model: the assumption of limited "degrees of freedom," the more determinants, the less room there is supposed to be for novelty.

In the old model there is only limiting or indeterminacy. To say that the artist's line "could" occur on a blank page meant only that no determinant prevented it. The old model doesn't take account of how such a line comes about as an *eveved* effect. Determinants do not only delimit; they also cross and participate in implying something new.

In the old model, order is only a limitation on what can still happen. The more order, the less can happen. But we are making concepts for the order of implying, which is neither structure nor indeterminacy, but more intricate than explicit structure. We think of it here in terms of eveving. The effect of all determinants is more finely shaped than any of them.

The old model has only two terms: indeterminacy and limitation. But implying is neither of those. As we have seen, it is *more* determinate than explicit structures, but in a different way.

In the old model, the more determinants, the less is left for novelty. When something is fully determined, *no* "degrees of freedom" remain.

We can use "eveing" to say why (as shown in Gendlin 1997a) the more determinants, *the more* creativity may happen. Explicit determinants make lowest common denominators. Eveing is implying. In eveing, if there are more determinants, they cross and produce more novelty.

It should have been realized long ago that *more* structure makes *more* variety. We see it all about us. Higher animals show more variety than simpler ones, and humans even more. The more a person has understood, the more complexity is brought to the next event. Something new will be understood more quickly, and more new ideas and avenues of exploration arise. We understand this if we think of understanding as an eveing, a crossing between what we bring and what is to be understood.

The more different people we have known well, the more easily we understand the next person, even though the next person will be different from any we have known. We can explain this. It is because the more complexity we bring, the more can *cross* so that the other's meanings can generate themselves out of ours.

The more philosophies we have understood, the more easily we will understand the next one we read, although it will be different. The more complexity I bring, the *more precisely* can the new meanings be precisioned in an eveing with what I bring.

For example:

In biology Howard H. Pattee (1973) tries to deal with an anomaly: "In a control hierarchy the upper level exerts a specific, dynamic constraint on the details of the motion at lower level, so that the fast dynamics of the lower level cannot simply be averaged out" (77). "The interesting problem . . . is to explain how such ordinary molecules . . . can evolve such extraordinary authority as members of a collection" (78). Pattee seeks a kind of "constraint, which does not simply freeze-out degrees of freedom, but imposes new functional relations between them" (106).

Now note the example with which he thinks about this: "As isolated individuals we behave in certain patterns, but when we live in a group we find that additional constraints are imposed on us as individuals by some 'authority.'"

The underlying model assumes individuals that are complete in themselves, and antecedent. When they enter a group, there are "additional" patterns put on them, conceived of as constraints.

Sociologists would deny this, but since their underlying model is the same, their denial leads to the opposite error. Pattee thinks of society as an addition to individuals, but it has long been recognized that the individual individuates in a collective matrix, so that group-relations are deeply inherent in what an individual is. But currently this is misunderstood as if social and cultural determinants functioned like explicit concepts—as constraints. So it is assumed that the individual cannot exceed the culture.

Actually, the cultures provide paths for living—always insufficient and always further developed and changed by any individual who lives them forward into developments that could not possibly follow from them as patterns. Individuals differentiate themselves in and with the patterns that the group offers. The patterns function in eveing together with implying intricacy which has never been structured or separated.

The point is not to attack Pattee's illustration, but to carry forward what he points to. He seeks a "concept of control (that) involves a more active dynamical role than simply limiting the available space in which matter can move . . . such constraints . . . can lead only to fixed structures . . . *The general difficulty is that we need to find how to add constraints without using up all the degrees of freedom*" (1973, 82–83; emphasis added). Of course, the puzzle is due to the model, not the molecule that acquires more functional relations. (See Gendlin 1997a: "The more factors delimit a next step, the more creativity they also enable." See note 3, chapter IV.)

One ought to leave room for eveing or crossing even when the old model seems to work quite well. (See Gendlin 1997e.)

(h-3) Schematized by schematizing (sbs)

I want to set up a term for the relation between two things that cross with each other in eveing. I say that each "is schematized by schematizing the other," or *sbs*.

Sbs means that the two do not function as themselves in relation to each other; rather, each functions as altered by affecting the other.

When two things cross they do not do so alone, since they occur as part of some eveing and some event. The next event may look as if it were only "their" crossing, but actually there is aways an eveing of the whole mesh of experiencing. (See metaphor and relevance in Gendlin 1997a.) There is no line dividing the two that cross from all the rest because each moment and each "thing" is (involves, brings, functions as, means, ...) an intricacy.

(h-4) The two directions of sbs

There are *two different ways* in which two things may schematize each other and be schematized thereby. We do not get the same results in the two directions. This is difficult to grasp. Let me illustrate it and then say why it matters.

For instance, if we are writing history and using the elephant as a metaphor for George Washington, that's quite different from using George Washington to help us say something about elephants. In one case the elephant is available for anything it can help us to say about Washington. (He pretended to be an elephant as if he were so far above the squabbling parties that he didn't even see them, but usually he did what Hamilton wanted.) In the other case we have just lived with elephants for two years in the bush, and we are writing our report. Now anything from George Washington (and anything else) is available to help us to schematize our elephant-experience.

Is it apparent that in each direction the crossing will bring out new aspects of both, but different ones in the two cases?

Let me now use "past-present" and "sbs" instead of "George Washington" and "elephant." Let me first use the concept of sbs to schematize the relation of past and present, and then use that relation to schematize sbs. I am taking the very term sbs and putting it into an sbs relation with "past and present."

Can sbs help us to say something about past and present? Yes, the past functions in the formation of the present. So we can say that the past has a role in schematizing the present, and by doing so the past also becomes schematized (what from the past is relevant, or functions *now*). What it "is" can be defined only backwards from the present, since it is by schematizing the present that the past is itself schematized and becomes relevant. If someone has a past event on video, it doesn't change, but (the sbs relation can help us to say) how the past is still now at work in our bodies—this past is changed in the present. This can lead further: the way our past still affects how we live can be changed in the present by living and acting differently.

We can now say more about the way body and en#3 imply each other. We left this relation in I. There we said that the life process **goes on in** en#3; it goes on in the spider's web as well as in its body. Now we can say that life process sbses en#3 and goes on in the sbsed en#3 (not in an en#3 that is past and not here anymore).

We have already gone in one direction by using the sbs relation to speak about the past-present relation. Yes, past and present schematize each other and are also both schematized thereby. Can we now do this in the opposite direction? Can we use the past-present relation to help us explicate more about sbs? To do that we would cross them again, but this time to use the past-present relation to say more about sbs.

If our theory were already closed, and if we used it only logically, we should get the same thing, just as the road from Athens to Thebes is the same as the road from Thebes to Athens. But since we are forming the concepts (and since even finished concepts can always be used experientially), what we know experientially about past and present may be more than we have used so far. What might emerge if we use this experience to think about sbs?[7]

Of course! Now it pops out. How could we not have seen this before? The two directions are very different in the case of present and past. In fact, now we see that sbs cannot apply in the other direction at all.

It is very well to say that past and present schematize *each other* so long as we mean that their crossing creates aspects of both. So we can *say* both "the present schematizes the past" and also "the past schematizes the present" but these are both still only the same direction and the same thing. The present is the essay we are writing about George Washington, and both acquire new aspects as the past participates in constituting the present.

But in the reverse direction the past would be going on now; it would be the essay we are writing now. The present would only participate. The past would be happening, going on, occurring.

The past may intrude on the present to such an extent that one loses track of the present, but it remains the past even so. There are odd times when one does indeed relive the past, but that happens in the present even so.

We can say that past and present sbs each other, but still only in one of the two directions. So, yes! We can use past-present to schematize the concept of sbs itself. We learn something about both, which we did not find the first time, when we used sbs to schematize past-present. Now we can say that in an sbs relation one term occurs (like a present occurring), it happens-into; it goes on in. The other term is gone on in (like the past). If we write about elephants then that functions like the present, and George Washington functions like the past.

The words "schematized by schematizing" cannot express the difference since both happen even in one direction. But now we can use time to define the two directions:

In an sbs relation one term functions in the presently ongoing formation of the other term. The result of sbs differs depending on which term is the one that is occurring, and which term is not occurring but only participating in the other's occurring. For example, the present is occurring and the past is not, but participates in the occurring of the present.

Let us take what we just saw about sbs and the past and present with us to the next section.

IV-B. Time: En#2 and En#3, Occurring and Implying

To develop our model of time, we have to relate *occurring* and *implying* to *en#2* and *en#3*, and the *body*, so that time can emerge from these. It may seem that the present is in the term "occurring" and the future in "implying." The present also seems to be in "en#2," and the past in "en#3." The body is each of these in some way. Present, future, and past will be quite different than in the old model, if we conceptualize time from these terms.

Let me first repeat that I-V is our *general model*, an alternative to the one that seems to inhere in most current concepts. Later, in VI–VIII we will develop specific terms for behavior, perception, and human processes. Since thinking and model-building are human processes, of course we *use* our human processes to build our model. Mathematics is a very human process, but we have not chosen it to begin our model. I have shown that such a model must drop out much of what is most important to living things. Let us choose something else from our human process to begin with. Here we *chose* to put occurring and implying first in our model, and we will derive perception and objects from these. We put occurring into implying (carrying forward) at the start, and these will inhere in all the other terms. Space, time, and perception are derivative from them. The body and its environment as one *interaction* is prior in our model. From this we can derive separate individual things and units.

So far we do not have terms in our model for a space in which objects *appear* in or to the process. Of course, we who are building the model have space and perceive objects. We have chosen to build our model so as not to begin with these, knowing that we will later develop terms for such objects, since we can speak-from our own having of them. But in our basic model there are objects only while missing. When they occur and carry the process forward, they are no longer objects. The process *has* as yet no representation of time in which it appears to itself to be going on. Of course, we could say that carrying "forward" involves linear time. But linear time is a thin and simplified derivative from process. Many aspects of humans, animals, and modern physics and biology cannot be thought about at all if everything is considered to happen in simple linear time. Instead, let us see what more intricate kind of time we can derive from our model and from our familiar human process.

In the old model everything only *happens to* something; nothing has a process that it implies and enacts. In our model we have emphasized the kind of "occurring into" implying which carries the body's own implying forward so that it enacts its own sequence. Of course, we also made room from the start for events that "occur into" implying without carrying it forward (e.g., the tree that falls on the beaver). For us the primary distinction is between the carrying forward and not carrying forward. This determines whether the events are the body's own process or not. It makes no difference whether the spectator would say that some event is the environment's action on the body, or the body's action on the environment. For example, the responses of other species members or the arrival of food may seem to be something that **happens to** the body, but our model says that these are the body's own process and carry it forward. On the other hand, the animal might trip and fall, which might seem like the body's action, but we would deny that it is the body's own occurring-into-its-implying.

Since there is implying, we can ask whether what occurs into it carries the implying forward or not. All occurring **happens into** an implying, but only some of it carries the process forward. What the spectator would consider a surprising new event may also carry the implying forward. Implying is more finely organized than any one set of occurrences.

We do not begin with living bodies as separate objects in the (spectator's) environment. For example, many body parts have internal environments. On the other hand, a newborn infant's body implies the mother's breast, and the mother's body implies the suckling infant. If the infant doesn't come, the breast becomes impacted and has to be pumped. The single nursing sequence requires actions by each of them to carry the implying forward. Each is the en for the other; both are "the body" and "the environment." In our model there is as yet no space for separable already-built bodies (en#3) apart from their being-gone-on as the ongoing en#2.

Although the spectator thinks of most sequences as repetitious, I have argued that repetition depends on someone comparing the sequence to a previous one. Internally the process occurs freshly. Occurring into implying is a change. From the change process we can derive sameness and repetition as a special kind of change.

Implying is always part of some occurring; occurring always includes an implying. They cannot be separated. We have to take all occurring as occurring into implying. "Occurring into implying" is a single term. It may carry the implying forward. "Carrying forward" is a single term too.

Implying and occurring are two strands of bodily process. Notice, please: they are not three. Don't add the past. Implying may be some sort of future and occurring some sort of present, but let us allow our conception of time to develop from these concepts. Then we will see that these are not the usual kind of future and present, and we will also see that the past is something else (although it functions in these two).

But since implying is part of occurring, it seems to follow that what is implied must be occurring. But it does not occur; it is only carried or carried forward by what does occur. The imply*ing* is part of occurring, but *what* is implied is not occurring.

What is implied is not the next occurring either. Implying is more intricate than any one occurring. Therefore implying is not "the future" in the sense of what will occur. It is more intricately ordered than an occurring can be, and yet it is also incomplete. As with the lamb at the cliff, *the body's own sequence carries the implying forward if the body-en-occurring "was" implied*. But there is no separate record of what the implying "was." Internal to the process, the implying does not stay; it does not become past. Implying cannot become past (except on someone's record).

In the linear model the past, present, and future are determined by their *positions* on a time line. Except for their position the three are the same. From how an event is described and defined in the old model photo you cannot tell whether it is past, present, or future. (Kant said that the time of an event is not written on it.) In the old model past, present, and future differ only in regard to their position. In the model developing here, past, present, and future are very different.

We are serious about *deriving* present, past, and future from how they *function differently*. We are not taking them *primarily* as positions.

Something is past, future, or present depending on how it functions in occurring into implying. (This past and this future are the internal continuity of a body's own process.)

The implying doesn't become past, as we might think if we assume the linear time in which someone might remember. Within our model the implying is changed if the process is carried forward, but it always remains a part of the ongoing occurring.

If there were no *ongoing* implying, there would be nothing about an occurrence that had to do with *other* occurrences. If each occurrence were purely present, it would be just only itself, without *its own* continuity, order, and connections. Of course, this kind of pure present is artificial. All its internal connections are taken out. Then they are lodged in an external observer. As Kant said, an observer must relate events by remembering and bringing the past *to* the present. If you didn't remember the last "1" when you count, you would not get 1, 2, 3, 4 but only 1, 1, 1, 1. So we see that if we make linear time prior, we artificially cut everything into positional units and we make it impossible for anything to have its own activity. Perhaps not everything does have its own activity, but why decide from the start to adopt a model in which we shall never be able to think about anything that has its own activity?

"Its own activity"—that means it has its own implying *into which* it occurs. "Its own activity" means "carrying forward." It is our starting distinction between events that do and those that do not. "Its own activity" is always both occurring and implying.

If we live with plants and animals, we can see that some things have their own activity. We tend to fall into a city philosophy, just humans and stones. Then it can seem that only the "speech community" "assigns" meanings to meaningless objects, as Brandom characterizes "enlightenment thought" (Brandom 1994, 661n54). But since we find ourselves in the continuum of living things, we cannot avoid noticing that other creatures also "assign" (feel, are, imply, enact, ...) meaning and generate time (and that we feel, are, imply, enact, ...) like them. So we have every reason to build a model in which we can think about something that is its own activity. Later we can limit some things, if we find some that do not.

If we let our model be the wider one first, we can generate terms for behavior and human processes, as well as for fossils that are now in the rocks, the kind of time that paleontologists tell us about. We will generate terms to say how humans *have* (project, feel, live in, ...) time in a way animals don't, and how animals feel afraid in ways plants probably don't. But let us first permit a time that is not an imagined future or a memory of the past.

So for example, there is a past in a plant not because someone remembers it, but because what occurs includes (incorporates, employs, regenerates, lives) its body-en#3 which is the product of what we (in remembered or imagined time) call its "earlier" process. But the en#3 body in which the plant lives is not a separate and remembered past. It is the regenerated body now. We have both kinds of past, but in us also the capacity to have memories depends on our bodies being our regenerated past. Our memories are not floating pictures or separated records; they can form for us only because *our present human bodies are physically also the past*.

If I have amnesia because someone hit me on the head and stole my wallet and identity cards while I am visiting in California, and if I make a new life there under a different name—what determines that I have not lost my past?

The past *is* the body. It carries the scars of my childhood cuts. It has the hangover from last night. It has (is, ...) my past experiences and those of the race and the species. With similar people I would make life-mistakes similar to those I make here. Bodily processes do not occur only "in" the body (one says) as if it were a static receptacle, an old stage for new events. Most of the body must constantly be regenerated freshly. It begins to disintegrate the moment circulation stops. Hair and bones last longer. There are various degrees of preservability of various parts in artificial environments without bacteria, like alcohol. In living the body keeps being regenerated. From death on, a different kind of change no longer makes it "the same."

Our concepts of process can derive how something is made to stay "the same," seemingly just lasting in time. The changing body generates the time in which it remakes itself as "the same." The body does not only last in a remembered and compared time. It does not simply last. It does so first and foremost in the time which its own changing generates.

The past is gone on in, as one might go on in a situation, in an argument, or in a play. It can only be done by taking the past along and changing it, like the present sentence or an action does. The past is in a present occurring; it is a change of the situation *in* which one acts. En#3 is not only the body but the whole homemade environment. When we act in a situation, we remake it, but not into some other situation. No, a good action "saves the situation." It is still that "same" one, but not because it hasn't changed. Rather, like a human institution (for example, the University of Chicago since 1890) it keeps being the same, although with new people who are newly and differently doing "the same" functions. And this is true also of the buildings which are maintained by the janitors, and rebuilt periodically.

We saw that there are degrees of separability of en#3: the beaver's felled tree, the university's buildings, the mollusk's shell as long as it lives in it, our hair, a person's clothes and house. But right now in our merely "basic" model we do not as yet have terms for these complex things, just a process that generates the kind of time in which they will be possible.

As en#3 the body must be lived on as en#2. Its "past" cannot be separate or static. Unlike a machine such as an automobile, the body cannot be kept dry and oiled on four bricks in a garage without running. If the body doesn't "run," it dies and disintegrates. Without an ongoing process you don't have the body either. This remarkable fact tells us that present processing remakes the body as a product, and that this is different than something we *make* for example a machine or a chair. If we are fixing the car or reupholstering a chair, we can either finish the job, or stop in the midst. We can leave the chair half done for a while. *The life process for which we are building a conceptual model cannot stop for a while.* Human making is a very different kind of process.[8]

En#3 is *constantly* regenerated; the body cannot be only en#3. It has to be changing—it has to be an existing thing, a concreteness, a kind of present.

This last can be said also of the chair being reupholstered—the past is here as the existing chair, and it is being reupholstered and changed. *But, in the chair, these two aspects can fall apart.* The upholsterer can stop working for a time, or indefinitely; the chair will last. In the living body these two aspects stay together, and if they don't—if the present changing stops—the past's product also disintegrates, or changes very greatly. *The past en#3 body disintegrates if it is not gone on in as en#2.*

We want to develop the concepts of en#2 and en#3 so that this remarkable fact will emerge clearly. We want to develop them so that it becomes **derivable** from them. We can say that present process goes on in the body, and also that the body is in process. (As we saw earlier, the word "in" can be used in either way.)

The present process goes on in the en#3 body which it has regenerated and altered. That is why in h-3 we said that the present occurs in the sbsed past, not the already-gone past. A process is a regenerating en#3. It goes on in its en#3. We say the same thing, but it sounds odd, if we say: the process goes the en#3 on. "Going on" is a transitive phrase; it means going it on. The process goes the en#3 body onward. It sounds all right if we say that the present goes on "in the context of" the past, but we have to mean the context it regenerates. *The process goes on—not in the context that was (and isn't here to be gone on in)—but in the context that is changed by it.* This principle will have many uses.

For example, reflection and explication are often considered as if they were a mere looking back, as if the past remained there to be looked back to. Later we will derive memory, but of course memory is possible only because of the occurring body. So it is possible only because the actually occurring body is a regenerating (or going on) what it was. This understanding of reflection and reflexivity will often turn out to be quite vital.

The other direction of "in" comes to the same thing: The past body *functions* in the present. "To function in" means to be changed. Something changes when it functions in the formation of something else. We saw this in the case of metaphor. "Sbs" was our concept for it (IV-A-h). It does not function as itself, but as already schematized by its role in shaping the present. *How the past can function in the present can far exceed what it was in its linear time position or on someone's record.*

The pastness of past experience is this kind of functioning. Therefore en#3 is not just the past, not gone, but *gone on by* a present process; (not the past context but the one that is regenerated by the present process that goes it on.)

The present process goes on in the en#3 body, but it would be foolish to say that the present process goes on in the past! The en#3 body is the one that is gone on in the present.

At the end of IV-A we spoke of a "past" that is *sbsed*. Sbs requires no record. The sbsed past does not occur separately, not even on a record. It is only the fact that what does occur would not be as it is if the past did not *play a role in the formation of what does occur.*

For example, many strands of your past are part of what is happening now, quite without memories. The past is always involved in the very texture of the present. It is the *now-sbsed* past. If the past is considered only as the unchangeable events of the linear past, one cannot conceptualize many important human phenomena. The presently gone-on-in past is capable of much more than the fixed-photographed past on a record. No, we need to derive the linear recorded past from the body's own process (of which it is a simplification).

En#3 functions as *a past in the present*. We are going to need this concept. And implying is *a future that is in the present*. But if past and future are in the present occurring, we seem to have concluded just what we didn't want: the present is complete and self-sufficient so that really there is no time, only certain aspects of present functioning. It might seem as if this present has no connection to the future that is not yet, and to the past that no longer exists.

No, there *is* a connection. Later we will develop the ways in which a body can remember and can have those connections. But before more terms develop, we can assert the connection only from the outside, as spectators. What is no longer happening is connected to this very different newly sbsed en#3-past which functions as part of the ongoing body. And what will happen—when it happens—will happen into this ongoing implying. But what will happen is not the implying, and what no longer happens is retained only as it functions now.

For example: what a historical event really *was* becomes retroactively determined by how subsequent events develop its significance. The Bosnian war is part of what the fall of the Austrian Empire "was." The event of its fall is sbsed by current events. Somewhat differently, we need our model to let us think about how our present living can change the past; we need to be able to ask: what sort of living changes the past, and what sort does not? How a person's past is sbsed is not quite how historical events do it. And our model develops retroactively in still another way. But all these differ from how the *Soviet Encyclopedia* does it—by lying. These distinctions require later specifications, but we will be able to make them because our "basic" model is capable of a past-in-the-present, rather than framing everything within the kind of time that consists only of cuts between different linear positions.

The en#3-past and the en#2-present are *interlocking terms*. An event (an occurring) involves both; they are not two events together. The body is both en#3 and en#2, but not by being two bodies together. Going-on is not half an event; it is already the whole event. What is gone-on (the sbsed en#3-past) is that very same whole event.

This defines "interlocking terms." Clearly when two terms are interlocking, they are not the same. They are two different strands of one interaction process.

The en#3-past that is gone-on by life does not last in the way that an empty seashell lasts. It may take years to dissolve in the ocean, but this is a time which the shell does not generate. The slow water wearing holes in the shell is not the animal's own change. There is no implying of these holes in the living mollusk. A past alone in alcohol does not generate the animal's time. How inanimate processes generate time is different, but they too generate time. Our model has greater capacities for new concepts concerning those. (See Gendlin and Lemke 1983; and note 6 in chapter IV.) Let us not assume that they can happen only within the already generated static positional time of observers.

We have been discussing the interlocked past and present.

The present also has an interlocking relation with the future (the implying), but we have already shown that implying is not the linear future that is about to be the present, and then becomes the past. The implying is not the occurring that is about to be, and it does not become an implying that was. We derive a more intricate future from how implying functions in the process.

When occurring carries forward, the occurring is a change in the implying.

The body that occurs *is* this changing of the implying. So we cannot say that the implying will be *carried out* (enacted, occurred, ...) by the next occurring, but rather that it will be **carried forward**. Occurring changes implying into a different implying. Since the whole sequence is implied in any occurring, and since it is implied with a different "next" at each point (as in the example with our spider), the sequence is new at each point, however many times the spectator has seen it.

The findings of modern physics show that *actual happenings can generate their own space-time system and their own new system of "antecedent" possibilities "retroactively" from the event* (see Gendlin and Lemke 1983). There have been no good conceptual models for this. The concepts we are developing may help with this problem.

Later we will generate the observer patterns, but our model must first let us think about how a process has its own implying of its own changing sequence. In such a sequence events (interactions) cannot happen singly. Occurring *is* a happening-into the *changed* implying of which it is the changing. This is a different kind of continuity. Mathematical space has no gaps either. But its continuity is made by the mere fact that any two points no matter how close still have an infinity of points between. Yet each infinitesimal point is supposed to sit by itself, without its own relations to other points (the observer adds the relations). Only momentum is the parameter that gets at the active continuity of the motion, but momentum is what you can measure only if you give up on a space-time point-location system that stays the same across the change.

From momentum we can see that inanimate processes also have a continuity of occurring, and a kind of future that functions in the occurring, and is not merely the continuity of predefined positions in an imagined space or time.

In the old physics it was said that a moving body "has" momentum. The body could stop and be the same body without momentum. Currently in physics this does not work. In our model, the body *is* an implying that its occurring is changing, so it cannot stop and be the "same" body.

· We already saw that the process cannot stop as if the body could just be the en#3 body. The en#3 body is interlockingly one event with its occurring. Now we see that the body's occurring is also interlocked with the implying into which it happens, and of which it is the changing. Occurring is both, but let us be careful not to merge and identify the two interlocks. They function very differently and we are deriving time from how they function.

The body occurs in and as the en. The sbsed body-en#3-past is the environmentally occurring body. On the other hand, the implying is not = en, not what occurs (it is only carried or carried forward by the occurring).

For example, hunger implies something like feeding. But the feeding is not occurring. In hunger the feeding is not occurring in some implicit, hidden way. Hunger is not hidden feeding. Hunger is an actual occurring, but it is quite different than feeding. If it goes on for long it involves large changes (belly swelling up, for example) which are nothing like the changes that constitute feeding. The sbsed en#3 body is the one that occurs. The implied body is not. The implied body is both much more than any occurring, and also not what occurs.

When we come to derive concepts for human processes, it will help us that our model can conceptualize even dramatic and ugly-looking pathological conditions (like the belly swelling up in hunger) as the implying of a missing process-resumption that would be quite healthy. Pathological occurring may carry a quite positive implying (which it keeps unchanged).

What is implicit can never be the same as an explicit occurrence. Implying is never what explicitly occurs. Implying has all the intricacy of occurring, all the intricacy of what has ever occurred, but it is *more intricate order*. Since it is carried by the occurring, we can also say that occurring is always more intricate than what it is explicitly. Since it carries implying, more is happening than what has happened.

What occurs is a new formation, whether familiar to the observer or unusual. Eating is familiar to the observer, but intravenous feeding also carries the process forward. A wonderful variety of modes of feeding is found in nature. *The implying implies "some way" of carrying forward, not any one way.* What carries forward in the "usual" process is just as new to the implying as intravenous feeding. Implying is always open, and what occurs into it does not equal it. The spectator's usual observation makes the implying seem poor. When something healing and creative happens, we may quite rightly say that this is the implying *"was,"* than the usual occurrence.[9]

From this we can see again that *what* is implied is not just one occurrence. "It" is not a single it, but a more intricate order than what can occur in the en. But implying is always unfinished. The novelty happens as en happens into the implying. The new step is indeed implied, but it does not exist in the implying.

The new step does not exist in the implying. It does not exist until en happens into the implying and carries it forward. It is generated only as en carries the implying forward.

What functions as we just set out can be called "the future." It functions more intricately than the linear future. By simplifying we can easily derive the linear future from it, later when we have terms for remembering and imagining, and for *having* time.

Carrying forward changes the implying so that it is no longer implied because *what "was implied" has occurred.* But since implying is not the occurring, we had better say: there is carrying forward when what has occurred "was" implied. The implying is not the occurring which "was implied" until the en happens into it and carries it forward.

One major distinction has been with us all along: much can happen to a body that does not carry its implying forward. The tree that the beaver gnawed down can be distinguished from a tree that falls on the beaver. The latter is like the ocean water wearing down the seashell—it is not implied by the mollusk's body. Unless such an event kills the animal, it does not change the implying. What was implied as the next event will still be implied as the next event.

We call it carrying forward when what occurs changes the implying so that what was implied is no longer implied because "it" has occurred.

Occurring regenerates the body-en#3 and it is also a change in the implying. How the en#3 body functions is the past. How implying functions is the future. *Occurring changes the past and the future.*

Even if we were tempted to put linear time around all this (instead of within it), we could not say that there is a bit of implying between each occurring and the next. We have also already shown that implying as such does not take up time. So implying is in the occurring, not between occurrings.

In terms of linear time we would ask: which implying is "now" being occurred into and changed? Is it the "previous" or the "next" one? In positional time the implying would be viewed as if it were itself an occurring that happened before each occurring. So there would be a distinction—a positional distinction—between a previous implying and this one, and again between this one and the next. Occurring would occur into the previous to change it into this one, and another occurring would happen into this one to change it into the next implying.

That would lose the whole point of the concept of implying, since it would function like a present, and nothing would function as a future.

The continuity of time cannot first be made by things next to each other, because such a continuity is passive; each bit *is* alone, and must depend on some other continuity to relate it to what is next to it. So the implying of the next event cannot be just before the next occurring; it cannot be merely next to it. The implying must be *in* the occurring event. But someone is still sure to ask: Which implying is in the occurring, the last or the next? Or this one?

But now it is clear: *in the time of carrying forward it is a wrong distinction to want to divide between the last and the next implying.*

This is also the relation when we say that explication is not a representation of what "was" implicit; rather, explication carries the implying with it and carries it forward. An explication does not replace what it explicates. If one divided them, one could try to divide between what is new and what is from before. Then one part of the explication would be representational, and the other part would be arbitrary. But explicating involves the continuing function of the implicit, carried (forward) by the explication. To explicate is to carry the implying forward, and not just once but on and on, through cycles and series. An occurring that carries forward is an *explicating*. It is neither the same nor just different. What is the same cannot be divided from what is different. The present cannot be divided off by itself alone. Time cannot be divided off from events, as if abstracted time relations subsisted alone, and events only accidentally happened to come into time-relation. Time is an aspect of events. "The present" means the occurring into implying and the going in en#3. It cannot be divided from them.[10]

We see this as "retroactive time" if we begin with the linear order. But the occurring need not go *back* in linear time to reach an implying that "was." It is only the scheme of linear time which leaves the "previous" implying behind at an earlier position, so that the occurring has to go back to it, in order to go forward in it. But the implying is not left behind in a linear series; it is always the future that is now.

In terms of linear time the "line" seems to move *both* forward and back behind itself, like the Greek letter theta (ϑ).

If we put several thetas in a row so that each flows into the next, then for each one, points A and B occur at the same linear time point. Linear time would be going both forward and back behind itself to bring the last implying forward.

B   B   B   B

A   A   A   A

But if we put the successive cycles contiguously, they become a stripe, a rod, or a pipe, so that the points on the spiral seem to occur at a linear time point.

BBBBBBBBBBBBBBBBBBBBBBBBBBBBBB

AAAAAAAAAAAAAAAAAAAAAAAAAAAAA

When it looks like a pipe one can consider it as a straight line. But that would cover up "occurring into" and "carrying forward."

From our point of view time is not retroactive—it is an aspect of the carrying-forward process. We can derive special models for linear time, repetitious units, various kinds of logic. We can suit specific models to specific empirical contexts; their narrower scope need not limit us if we derive them within our wider model.

In *Experiencing and the Creation of Meaning* I show that "temporal schemes are merely one group of very many kinds of schemes that can be aspects of experience" (Gendlin 1997a, 157–58). I must refer to that longer discussion, which requires that whole chapter. Here I will just assert that time is not necessarily the prior condition that so many philosophers have considered it to be. The priority comes to time and space because most philosophers have considered experience to be primarily perception. Then percepts seem just to be there, with space and succession as their prior conditions. But even perception cannot give just one *scheme* of time.

Our conceptual model has developed this scheme of time (derived from carrying forward) before we derive perception and the kind of time a sentient creature can *have* (feel, project, sense itself in, ...).

The terms "implying" and "occurring" together have led to "recognize," "carrying forward," "feedback," "eveing," "sbs," and we could use them to talk about "metaphor," "comprehension" (Gendlin 1997a, 117), and "crossing," and as we will soon see, much else.

Our alternative "basic" model needs one more section. We need more terms for how the environment occurs into the implying. We turn to this now, in chapter V.

V

Evolution, Novelty, and Stability

V-A. Intervening Events

I hope my reader is now hungry for "had" space and objects, for how our primitive terms can generate a way "the process" can register what goes on around it even when this does not carry the whole process forward.

This chapter concerns two questions. Before I ask those, let me first ask: with our new model, can we develop concepts for the theory of evolution? Currently the theory says that new forms just happen by "random" change. Natural selection only explains why adaptive forms are saved, but not how new forms come about in the first place. There are many indications that the random theory isn't right. The random creation of endless numbers of forms among which some are saved—that is a very old speculation (Aristotle quotes Empedocles holding that view in *Physics* 2.8, 198b29). If we look closely we can see that the old model is forced into this old speculation because of the basic way order is understood in that model. Order is only an arrangement of parts. Throw the parts up and how they come down is random. If they happen to have an order, it is not inherent in these parts. Order is only external relations among them. The parts are no different by being thrown up, no different for being in one order or another. In our new model there is no fixed set of parts. Therefore order or form is understood quite differently than as an external arrangement of unchanged parts.

If we conceive of process as we have done (in I–IV), we can think about how new forms evolve. In doing so, more explicit new concepts will evolve from the ones we have. Especially, we will see how environment and living process change together. When the environment changes, the body does not simply lose its organization so that it must select another from among randomly given new ones. *An organized system can give a new organized result in response to an impact on it*. Let me show more exactly how this can be thought about with our concepts.

The first of our two questions is: how do new and more elaborate events form? The second question is: how does a stable environmental context develop?

The first question can also be phrased in another way. How does the organism develop new sensitivities to the en? It is the same question, since new events are also new sensitivities to the en. Occurring is always b-en; therefore new ways of b-en are new ways of engaging the en, new ways in which the organism effects and is affected by changes in the en.

The second question arises because so far we have no stable object, only the process being carried forward and changing. In a stoppage the body implies the object (the missing en-aspect; see III), but as soon as the process is resumed by the object, there is no longer an object for it. As long as other processes go on somewhat differently because one is stopped, we call the differences the "schema," a bodily version of the missing en-aspect. But when it occurs, the process moves on and no longer has an object. The organism never has the object when the object is there! Obviously, somewhere along the line we must develop the groundwork for something stable—for a way an organism can have an object even when it is present (not only when it is missing). But nothing so far in our concepts is of anything lasting, except stoppage, that is, absence.

(a) Let us first consider how major new events may develop in the other processes.

We spoke (in IV) of a stoppage in one process interaffecting other processes. We spoke of this as if the differences are likely to be slight. But now I want to add that these differences could be major new events.

As one process is stopped, others are affected, and these in turn affect still others. What might seem to an observer an unnoticeable difference in one process could result in major new events in another process. For example, a tensor muscle made tense as one difference could result in still another process in kicks, or foot tapping. A very tense, frightened man trying to write something may find his hand jerking off the page.

We have added only that the differences in the other processes could be major new events.

(b) New events might develop in what we called "the stopped process" itself.

A process might just stop when it cannot continue, but it might also develop new events. This might occur in two ways:

(b-1) At the point where the process cannot continue, the last bit which can happen repeats.

This is frequently found. We can also think of this repeating bit as the first bit of the process which cannot go on. Only this bit can, and then it repeats over and over. How can we think about why such a repetition occurs?

We can conceptualize it this way: there is always an implying, not only an occurring. Each occurring occurs *into* the last implying and changes it. This *changed implying* is the last bit's implying. It implies the rest of the process. However, process is a continuity (we put the θs so close as to make a stripe; see figures 1 and 2 at the end of IV). There are no "bits" in the process. The stoppage forms such a "last bit," or "first bit." Now, if the process had continued, it would no longer be implied. Since occurring did not change the implying, the rest of the process is still implied. But only this "bit" could happen, and did. Hence the process is still implied, so that whatever part of it can happen, will happen, and that is this "bit." So it happens over again—but a little differently, since the occurring did change the implying somewhat.

If the process originally came divided up into bits, this could not explain anything. The bit that happened would change the implying exactly so as to imply the next bit which cannot happen. But since the interruption forms such a bit, the change in the implying is a new one. The bit as it "repeats" is not literally the same. The process keeps being implied, and yet a new occurring sequence occurs, consisting of such "first bits," each a little different.

This "leap concept" of a new kind of sequence is a new kind of carrying forward (see IV-A for leap concepts). As new kinds of carrying forward, and other new concepts, arise for us, we will regularly view them in terms of the concepts we have up to then, yet we will also recognize them as not reducible to the old ones. Explication involves more parts and distinctions which cannot be reduced backwards, nor need there be total gaps (as, for instance, with Piaget). There is a continuity between implicit and explicit.

"Intention movements," as they are called in ethology, are often observed—for example, when two male monkeys that would normally fight are separated by a glass wall, the fighting sequence cannot occur. Instead, there is a long series of fight-starts. (Later we will discuss a further development in which they become what are called "threat gestures.")

Nature shows many instances of similar bits reiterated over and over, never quite the same. There are pulses of the heart, eye blinks, nerve impulses, and also structurally: our concept of "subprocesses" of the organism (IV-A-c) lets us think how this is reflected in body structure, such as pores of the skin, hairs, and leaves on a tree. I will make such intervening occurring a verb, and call it "*leafing*."

We have *derived* rhythm, the many body-processes which are leafings.[1] It will be seen later how many of the organism's further developments are against the backdrop of rhythm, of leafing.

It is important to see that the new sequence is not exactly the first bit over and over. The first bit changes in character. For example, if you know you will stop, your first move in beginning to run is not really the same first bit as when you lean into a running that will go through. If you suddenly stop after the first bit of real running, you will fall forward. Similarly, a threatening gesture of raising a balled fist and waving it back and forth in the air differs from a swing into hitting. The implying of further change is different. The repeated first bits constitute a different sequence, *a new type of sequence.*

The insect hits the windowpane again and again, beginning to fly out to the light only to hit the glass painfully. But after a while it makes little tries, bzzz, bzzz, bzzz, bzzz, but these are no longer those awful first few hits when the bug smashed into the windowpane as its body implied flying out to the sun. Now they are little rhythmic starts, almost continuously, along the window surface, as if exploring, maximizing the chance of finding an opening if there is one.

We see that the first-bit sequence is different in kind. We also notice that it provides more opportunity for something new than the original first bit did.

Consider a macabre example. During the Cold War the U.S. Strategic Air Command kept bombing-ready planes in the air at all times, "just as if" they were on the first leg of a bombing mission. A new sequence called "being in the air" developed—it wasn't really the same as the first part of a bombing mission. The fueling problems, the long times, the round-the-clock shifts, all this was not part of a mission. Many parts that would lead to an actual mission were not done; other aspects of a mission were done.

We shuddered to think what might happen with so much bombing-ready time in the air. The chance for some unexpected occurrence during this phase was much greater than in the first few minutes of a real mission.

By leafing, the organism stays in the field of the stoppage. It remains at the spot, and under the conditions, of the stoppage. It would have spent only a moment there, if the process had not stopped. Now new events might form with the environment, which could not have formed before the stoppage.

(b-2) A second kind of new event may occur in the so-called stopped process.

As an example, say a walking animal falls into the water. Walking in water immediately assumes an unusual form since the movements do not encounter ground-resistance. So there is also no foot pressure. The movements will **therefore** be much wider. We call it "thrashing." The example shows that when the usual events cannot happen, what can happen may seem like quite a lot more.

Thrashing is a new sequence. It is certainly not unorganized. It has the organization of walking but in water. The movements are **immediately** wider because there is less resistance from the water. In addition, these movements also splash water toward the eyes so that there is a shift in posture to avoid the splash. There is also the shock, the faster circulation and all that goes with it, plus a host of other new but organized bodily effects. All this is immediately part of the next events that form upon falling into the water.

We could phrase it this way: when the implied further walking "bites into" the changed en, neither walking nor chaos results. Rather, a new organization results. Or, to use our more careful terms, when the en is different, what **occurs into the (unchanged) implying** is different. It is still an occurring into the implying.

A process is more than just the explicit arrangement of explicit parts that an observer sees. When the usually observed process cannot happen, a different but orderly process can newly form.

Let us be clear that this new formation is not a mystery. In our simple example we can see how implied walking plus water makes thrashing. The implied walking never occurs. If we are too literal we will ask where the walking is, since it doesn't occur in the water. It is in the thrashing, but not literally, rather as an implying. An implying is not a specific explicit form, we said. Now, in this simple example, we can see that clearly. **The implied walking participates in the formation of thrashing, yet the walking does not occur.**

When what is implied cannot occur, it can function in the formation of a new organization. What happens may be much more and involve larger movements than the usual process would.

If either the body or the environment changes, the process will go on differently.

Another example: if a chemical that damages the cell wall is introduced into the solution in which certain living cells exist, the cells produce a new chemical which exactly repairs the cell wall damage.

The cell does not need to adapt itself to the new chemical over millions of years. The very first time it ever forms in this chemical, it forms in a differently patterned way.

It is not that we "explain" this finding; rather, we are devising concepts that are consistent with the finding. When there is a change in the body or in the environment, the usual process of a living thing *immediately* has a new organization.

With these concepts we can think how it is that when the environment changes (in climate, other species, etc.), the living things change along with them. How the body functions, how it makes and remakes its structure (en#3) changes along with en#2. Although changing, the animals remain "adapted," as it is called. And, as we see here, *they become more elaborate*, as in evolution.

What determines the form of such an intervening event? It was not in the repertoire of the animal. Merleau-Ponty (1963, 39) cites such a case: if one cuts off the lower half of the legs of a beetle, it will still walk . . . but not as it ever has before. Its movements are odd, and much more complex. Different gravitational pulls affect it. Now its whole body sways and other parts move to compensate for this. Yet this odd walking has never been in its repertoire.

The interaction between body and environment is such that if either of them changes, their interaction forms differently. The beetle's changed body engaged the en differently. *A change in the body makes for a change in the en#2.*

The beetle doesn't take time gradually to develop the new walk from the old one. The new walk occurs, as our law of occurrence states, as it can. The new series of events forms immediately.

I call this kind of new events "*intervening events*." When the usual process is stopped, such events may intervene.

But can we still call it "stoppage," when not only other processes, but the supposedly "stopped" one seems also to go *on?* We might call them "stop/ons," since they are part of the process that cannot go on as usual. But is there still a difference in kind between the old process that cannot go on, and these stop/on events? Let me postpone this question for V-B.

Let me first try to show that these novel developments are likely to continue and to multiply. If there is even one bit of change, many new events will occur and proliferate.

Two avenues of novelty: *there are two avenues of further change*:

By interaffecting the other processes a stoppage or stop/on in one process will make the others different, and these may interaffect still others. A slight alteration in one may lead to dramatic developments in others. But interaffecting is not the only avenue by which a change can engender more changes.

By altering the environment shared by other processes, a change can make for further changes. Since events consist of both body and environment, the new stop/ons engage an altered en#2. This may change the en#2 of other processes since they may share that concrete en (or if the reality circumstances of the new en#2 are such as to bring along other en aspects that affect the en#2 of other processes).

For example, by splashing water in the eyes, thrashing may affect the en of the eyes. A new sort of walk might stir up dust and thereby affect the en of breathing. A rhythmic swaying in one spot previously gone through quickly might expose the animal to many new environmental influences.

The other processes may be affected by a changed en (eyes may close, dust may be inhaled, etc.). Changes in these processes may affect still others via the en. Dust coughed out or moving with eyes shut may involve further new en aspects that can affect further other processes.

Meanwhile, as we said, through also interaffecting in the body a change in one process may affect others.

A change along either avenue can lead to further changes both by interaffecting and by how a changed en is differently engaged.

If change came about only by interaffecting, the difference would be made and novelty would end. But since it also changes the en#2 of other processes, and these changes interaffect other processes which bring about more changes in en#2, the series of novelties can develop indefinitely.

Of course, the subprocesses and their ens similarly affect each other and elaborate the body structure.

Let me more exactly explain why both avenues are needed for continuing novelty: the question is the same as why ev × ev goes to a stable result.

We saw in IV-e that everything × everything is just the occurring: the many differences do not *occur* and then make further differences that again occur and so on. One occurring forms.

Therefore, if we think of the bug, its new walk occurs *immediately* upon the change. All the differences the change makes go into forming the very next occurring.

Similarly, if there were only the shared en changes, novelty would come to a stop. Every difference made to the en of all other processes would be made in one sequence, and no further effects between the processes would happen on that account.

These are two *kinds* of change: one is part of *the formation* of one event; the other happens after something occurs as b-en.

But why is this so? Why can we not say that interaffecting also changes the en#2 of other processes which are immediately different and also interaffect still others, and so on? Then all novelty would form in the very next occurring.

The question is the same as why everything does not happen at once.

The answer can now be clear: when we say that there is immediately a new organization, this "immediately" refers to the eveing in the formation of the next event. *Another set of changes arises because that event has occurred.* The change via the shared en happens only as the event actually occurs.

Both interaffecting and shared en happen in the formation of each event. But the changes due to the shared en are those that happen only in an occurring, as implying "bites into" or "engages" the en in one occurring.

For example, let us say you are typing. By interaffecting you are set to type some Freudian slip and your fingers move to letters that express something more than what you are thinking about. This is an interaffecting change. But suppose some previous change has moved the keyboard over with a slight jerk. Then even the "wrong" letters will not be typed as implied, because your fingers will land on different letters. That is the second kind of change. You don't first type the correct letters, and then the wrong ones, and only then the displaced ones. Only the last occurs. Then the occurring may have further effects on either or both avenues.

Let me emphasize that the displacement of the letters on the shifted keyboard is *not eveved*. The displacement is not due to an interaffecting. *The shifted keyboard happens into the eveing.* Because of the eveing only certain letters will be typed, but because of the en-shift, the typed letters are different than the implied ones.

Thus the existence of two change avenues enables continuing change, as each makes for more change on the other avenue in any occurrence.

"Everything" does participate in forming one event, but its occurring involves en#2, and that changes the implying. Now it is a different "everything," and that again engages the en in another occurring.

A change from interaffecting alone does happen in the formation of the one event, and so does a change from the shared en alone. Say both happen in one event. The implying may include changes from interaffecting and it may also have bitten into an en that other processes have changed. So the occurring may be doubly different. *The changed occurring* may newly interaffect other processes (which might change the en), and it may also make for *new* changes in an en that other processes share (which will make for new interaffecting changes).

So a change in the shared en can make new interaffectings, and new interaffectings can make new changes in shared en. These are two different avenues of change. Both produce something new *immediately*. They may (or may not) generate an unending chain of novelty.

Let us recall that what participates in eveing does not occur. Many past experiences function in shaping one present; these past experiences don't occur. Similarly, the difference a process makes in the others and how this in turn affects it, do not occur. Only the eveing occurs. As I put it, eveing doesn't take any more time than the time of occurring. The many lines the artist might draw, and the various effects these lines would have, enter into the artist's sense that guides the right line. But all those other lines and effects don't occur. They are only part of the formation of a single occurring (see IV-A-e). This is basic to what an implicit order is. Nor does it require time to produce the novel organization due to a changed en#2. If the implying bites into a changed en, something different occurs. *The process will not first occur as implied, and then differently*.

We have now answered our first question. We have derived an *increasing capacity to be affected by the environment* or, as we also put it, the body's engaging the environment in ever new ways (en#0 becoming en#2).

There is an important implication here for the theory of evolution. To provide for novelty and development, the traditional evolutionary theory uses mutations. These are supposed to be random, with natural selection providing the selection according to which only what is adaptive will last and be reproduced. But this is an ancient question, not at all merely the modern theory of evolution. Students of philosophy recognize the mutation theory as an application of the ancient question of whether order can somehow come by chance from random chaos. (See Aristotle's discussions of Empedocles in *De Anima* and *Physics*.)

The theory argues that mutations account for evolution, not because adaptive mutations have often been seen (students of actual mutations, as in fruit flies, report that they are always stunted forms and not novelties, and paleontologists have dug up nothing like the billions of odd forms), but because the theory needs a source of novelty. The old model cannot *explain a formation* of structure. This problem instances the difficulties of the old model. New organizations must drop in from heaven, so to speak. They must be externally "imposed" "somehow" or "gradually," because the model of fixed parts makes novelty a mystery.

Once there are new forms, natural selection can explain why some are kept and continued. There are quite good empirical corroborations of this; for example, the bird species that can no longer fly because the wing they spread for sexual attraction has gotten so large. This example also shows that selection is not always adaptive.

Might the change we just derived be adaptive? We have not shown that it would be useful to the animal, or that it would help with resuming or otherwise surviving a stoppage. That is not certain, but let me show that it is likely:

For example, if walking is stopped, does thrashing or eye-closing help get out of the water, or adapt to it? If a given process is stopped, does it help to do the first bit before the stoppage over and over?

It would be far too much to say that it would usually help. At most we could say that many new developments occur during a stoppage of one process, and that these developments would engage new aspects of *the environment during the stoppage*. The animal would become more sensitive to the circumstances of the stoppage. The intervening events engage the environment as it is during stoppage, and so they are likely to involve factors that are at least pertinent to the stoppage.[2] So it is not certain, but it is likely that a way of carrying forward would develop.

While an elaboration leading to adaptation is likely, it might not occur despite a great many new developments. Then the animal might die; the species might become extinct.

If an intervening event turns out to resume the stopped process, or if all the changes and new en-engagements enable a resumption to occur, the intervening events that lead to resumption would become part of that functional cycle. It would be an elaboration that has become a part of the cycle. The erstwhile intervening event would now carry the process forward in the same sense of "carrying forward" as any other stretch of the process.

What about the other intervening events—the ones that do not lead to a resumption of the process? They would still occur where they have developed, but they would not be part of the functional cycle *in the same sense*. But we will soon see that they do acquire an important role.

In IV we saw that what eventually resumes a stopped process might be very different from the originally missing object. The intervening events are all changes in how the body occurs. The changes may enable the body to be carried forward by different en-aspects than erstwhile. I called the difference a stoppage makes the "schema." Now we have seen that via occurring, such changes can continue and proliferate. The intervening events can be thought of as the specifics of the schema, further developments of the schema, often quite dramatic new events and elaborations.

This development will have made a great difference even if the resuming object is the same as before, because now it occurs along with a lot of additional environmental interactions. So the resuming event is more complex and more differentiated than before the stoppage. An observer might pick out only the object, which might look the same, but to the process the object occurs together with other en-aspects. After the development of intervening events, the object occurs *in the context of* (in the midst of) these more elaborate engagements with the environment.

V-B. Stability: The Open Cycle

A process might be stopped, even though a great many intervening events and leafings are going on. The animal might die. The species might become extinct. This might happen swiftly or slowly. Many new elaborations might develop, and yet the process might remain stopped and implied. Despite all the new intervening developments, the animal might still die out.

The intervening events are thus a *new kind of carrying forward*, since they are a carrying forward in the stopped process, and yet they may not resume it. The intervening events are in a sense a carrying forward, in another sense not. They *are not* the carrying forward of the stopped process because that process is still implied. They are a new or special kind of carrying forward. I called them "stop-ons." This contradictory tag says that they are further events that widen and proliferate while the main process aspect is still stopped and still implied.

The leafings are a sequence of *versions of the stoppage*. Each bit is a slightly different version. Other kinds of intervening events are also versions of the stoppage, although less obviously. The leafings reiterate the stoppage.

A change in en or in the body may also change some of these reiterating leafings. This might happen because of interaffecting among the bodily processes, or because a change has an effect on the en which in turn affects the leafings.

Therefore the leafings (and the other intervening events) have made the body more "sensitive." It can be affected by more aspects of the en than it could before it developed these reiterating leafings.

We recall that some intervening events are also new body structure.

Leafings are bits of process occurring only just as far as it *can*, which is each time again the first bit. This will happen also in the subprocesses (IV-A-c).

The leafings and other intervening events are not themselves functional cycles. They are all part of the one implying of the whole body event (IV-A-b), not new implyings of new processes with their own ensuing sequences. These new elaborations are not themselves going anywhere. Or, we could say, they go *into the blue*. They are *like the fingers of a river* that is stopped and spreading out. They go as far as they can; they occur and reiterate since the stoppage remains. So they are again implied. They occur again insofar as they *can* occur, but slightly differently for having just occurred.

Whereas our functional cycle in II was a circle (we took digestion as an instance: feeding, satiation, defecating, resting, hunger, food-search, round and round), this new reiterating cluster is not circular. Instead, this reiterating context is *open*. Like the fingers stretched out on a hand, they go as far as they go and stop. Since it consists of fingers of the functional cycle, I will call it the *open functional cycle (opfucy)*, or simply the "*open cycle.*" I also call it the *reiterative context.*

"Open cycle" has a contradictory ring. The reiterating context is part of the implying of the functional cycle, but it is open; there has never yet been any completion for it. It implies "into the blue," and yet it has the functional cycle's completion-implying.

We can interpret the term "functional cycle" itself functionally, because what matters to us most is not that it comes full circle, but that it has a further implying. So do its open fingers—they have the functional cycle's own original implying. Yet they are open. We have derived something that is not only stable (in reiterating), but is open to novelty.

From the start we said that implying is for any carrying forward, not just for one specific course. The functional cycle itself is open for novelty. The intervening events are in fact bits of novelty, new carrying forward.

The open cycle provides a stability that is new in our model. Until now we had only fresh carrying forward or new carrying forward on the way to resumption. Now there is a cluster of pulses that isn't going anywhere else. It would occur further if it could, but since no "further" can occur, it reiterates. It is not a new source of implying. It is only a special open part of the functional cycle.

"Open functional cycle" is a schematic concept. Its usefulness remains in doubt until it is used, so that much else (empirical data and practical instances) is formulated along its lines. In VI this concept will enable us to formulate behavior and perception very differently than is now done. It enables us to build the process-relation between *implying and occurring* into the earliest notion of something stable.

We have a great stake in seeing exactly how we derived something stable and constant from our basic concepts of change. The old model attempts (and fails) to explain change from more basic concepts of statics and sameness. Let us clearly trace how we are deriving the seemingly static from process, that is to say from reiterating pulses of change. These may seem to be a static condition to an observer. For example, seeing seems like a simple constant being affected, a steady receptivity, but actually it is a continual rhythmic scanning. Many constant body states are really made and maintained by one or more processes occurring roughly repetitiously.

The concept "The body generates a context *in which* it then goes on further" was already what we said of en#3. Our new context generated during stoppage is part of en#3.

If the stopped process is now somehow resumed, the resumption goes on **amidst** all the intervening events which would also be going on. The resuming occurs **in the context of** these many new environmental interactions.

The leafings are like fingers the river made, but they are not *that* finger which became its new bed. The finger which *is* the new riverbed is *among* these, it occurs **in the context** of all of their occurring.

The intervening events **form in coordinated differentiation** along with other changes, and they too happen only **together with the rest of the body event**. In this respect they are simply **part of the whole event**.

But, insofar as the leafings form a constantly reiterating b-en, that is to say a sector of b-en which keeps being "the same," the changing process *goes on in* this "stable" context. This is a new meaning for our phrase "goes on in," and a new kind of en#3.

Whenever I move to a new stage I will always do something like I just did. I will give the new kind of carrying forward both as simply part of the kind we had, and also as itself a new kind (in different respects, of course). In certain respects the new development is simply understandable as part of what we had, while in other respects it forms something new and is understandable only as we let further concepts form. We must take both respects along.

The leafing is a new stable context in which the process now goes on, but it is also part of each b-en occurrence.

The intervening events are interactions with the en, of course, like any other processes. Since the leafing events reiterate, they give the organism a constant (that is to say, repeating) interaction with the en. Within this repetitious pulsing, changes in en would make differences. For example, when hungry, the leafings might be different than when satiated, even though the leafings would go on throughout.

Many (not all) body-processes will be in an original interaffecting relation with open cycle, and will occur only in certain of its time-spans. Or we could phrase this as: . . . will occur only along with certain aspects of the environment which are reiteratingly engaged in the open cycle. Thus en is different when it is light or dark, warm or cold, not only as en#1 observer defines these and finds them related to what happens, but also now as the organism is "sensitive to" many new aspects of en, that is to say reiteratingly interacts with many new en-aspects as part of each new whole body event.

We now have an open cycle: a "stable" context of reiterating en-interactions which are part of body events, part of evev. Many phases of many body-processes (not all) will be *coordinately differentiated* (IV-A-a) with it and will occur only with certain of these reiterating en-interactions. When body and en change, this "stable" context may register some of the changes. But the word "register" is too early here; the word implies something to which, or someone to whom, something is registered, and that is not the case here. Now that the body has an open cycle sector, many more changes in the en can affect the body. That is all.

If the process is carried forward after all, this is quite likely to be *by*, or *with*, one or another of the many intervening events. This might happen either because some new aspect of the en, with which there is a leafing reiterating bit, turns out (perhaps after some versions) to cf (i.e., "carry forward") the main process. The leafings lead the body to some new aspect of the en which does carry forward. Or the changes due to interaffecting may change the body enough so that a resumption of the stoppage becomes possible with some en-aspect with which it could not happen before. Or both.

When a resumption occurs "in the context of" the "stable" leafing context, the resumption would change the leafing open cycle context as well. Similarly, a change in the open cycle due to the process continuing would become part of the eveving of the next process events. The open cycle is not separate, but part of every body occurrence, part of evev.

As these concepts meet the next topic, they will become more precise. Let me say a little more about how we ourselves are *going on in* the concepts we have formed up to now.

In III we discussed stoppage and this enabled us in IV to say about II that carrying forward is an original resuming. Now here in V we developed intervening events, a kind of novelty, and then saw that these are really the schema, i.e., how what does continue during stoppage is different than without stoppage. We emphasized that it may consist of major and dramatic events.

As we develop new concepts, we find that they apply backward to enable us to elaborate our earlier concepts. *Not that we "apply" them flatly backwards*; rather, the newer concepts also become further distinguished as we apply them retroactively.

One way I proceed, which I now want to set up *as a concept in its own right*, is first to develop something and then to *go on in it*. This is again a movement like the Greek theta (ϑ). First the theta's line makes nearly a circle, but then, instead of completing the circle it goes back in a wider movement and forward through the already made near-circle. It is the diagram I presented at the end of IV. It means that the process generates for itself a context, in which it goes on further. En#3 is like that, and now the leafing open cycle is a new kind of en#3.

Now we turn at last to actual things. We will let our concepts apply so as to develop further terms to derive behavior, perception, objects that stay put, feeling, motivation, and memory, which will let us think about the kind of space and time a process can "have." We will further develop concepts in terms of which culture, language, and thinking can speak from themselves not only as has been the case up to now, but with terms that will let us enter into our intricacy.

Behavior

VI-A. Behavior and Perception

According to the usual way of thinking, perception is a kind of intake along the lines of photography or radio reception. This approach does not work out very well. Not only has it led to many controversies (see Gendlin 1997e and 1992a), but most importantly, the old way of thinking does not enable us to relate perception clearly to behavior and body-process.

Perception is always a part of behavior, and behavior is a special kind of body-process. When these connections are missed, then studies of behavior seem to form one field, and physiology another.

In the old model everything is conceptualized as time-space events connected by externally imposed laws. The old model renders body-process, behavior, and human symbolic actions along the same lines, the only way it renders anything. This omits many important characteristics (life, motivation, consciousness), leaving what remains within science rather truncated.

In our model derived from explication, *occurring is into implying*. From the start a vast implicit multiplicity functions in the formation of occurring. A process has its own continuity.

We just developed the concept "open cycle," a reiterating ("leafing") sector of body-environment interaction. As more and more of these intervening events—these leafing interactions—develop, the en can affect the body in more ways. A change in the body or in the en may change this reiterative sector. It is a second environment. The body can now be affected by the environment not only as body-en, but *also* in its reiterative open cycle sector (which is one part of body-en).

The leafings are part of the body, but since they reiterate, they also supply a kind of background within which the body-process now occurs. We will take this background up more exactly below.

As we said at the end of V, the increased affectability is not yet perception. We need to devise concepts for how perception is more than merely being affected. Anything, say a stone, can be affected. But we do not say that the stone perceives. It is the observer who *perceives* the change in the stone. The observer also perceives the type of change in an animal which we do call "perception." Thus far we have not got a hold of the difference. The question is, how can the living process itself perceive (rather than being affected only, so that the observer does the perceiving)?

In V we saw how novel developments might continue indefinitely between two change-avenues. Any body-change might (by interaffecting) make other body-changes, and might (by shared en) change the en of other processes. Any en-change might (by shared en) make for changes in the en of other body-processes which could (by interaffecting) change the body.

All this applies between all body-processes long before a reiterating open cycle has developed. Now that the body has a reiterating sector, the whole body and this subsection can interaffect each other, as well as change each other via their shared en.

Let us now move a few steps further with these concepts. If the open cycle is highly developed (many reiterating en-interactions), the changes along our two avenues (interaffecting and shared en) would be considerable.

A change in the body might change the open cycle both by interaffecting how the body implies the open cycle from inside, and might also change it via the body's changed en#2 so that the body would engage the reiterating en-interaction somewhat differently.

A change in the open cycle might change the body by interaffecting, and because some shared en-aspects may change the body's en#2.

Any of these changes might bring any of the others in turn.

We recall that we wondered why eveving doesn't include all the changes at once, then realized that eveving (or implying) is always part of en-occurring. Change on both avenues occurs at once, but the further changes which result from these happen only in the further occurring.

Now suppose a stoppage in the body-process makes large changes in the open cycle. If the leafing interactions are very different, this "registry" of the body's change in turn (by interaffecting and shared en#2) affects the whole body, which changes how the body registers in its reiterating cycle, which in turn changes the body.

A new kind of sequence is happening. The change in the body (b-en#2) registers as a change in the open cycle, on either or both avenues and this change changes the body and its en#2, which makes again a change (on both avenues) in how the body interacts in the open cycle.

The body is going through changes in how it is in its en#2, and these changes are changing how the body is in the open cycle sector. Each open cycle change changes the body further, and this again changes how it is in its open cycle.

The body is pulling itself through a sequence of a new kind of b-en changes brought about between the body and its own reiterative sector by the registry of the change, and the change made by the registry.

The body has two environments: its en#2 and its reiterative sector. The body makes and responds to these changes in a feedback relation between itself as a whole (b-en#2) and the changes in its own homemade environment, the leafing open cycle.

The body changes itself and moves itself through these changes.

We have derived behavior!

More exactly we have devised a kind of concept. If we think of behavior along the lines of this concept, we may be able to do behavior more justice than with the old model. It is of course only a scheme, a conceptual structure, but probably a better model for making concepts about behavior than the current one.

What are the advantages, the special characteristics of this new concept, this new kind of sequence?

As with the intervening events in V, this new development might be adaptive. Of course, it might not be. But the organism is moving. What is missing and implied during the stoppage is more likely to be encountered if the animal moves. Or, another way to put this: now the body and the en are not just one fixed way during a stoppage. Rather, the animal runs through a whole string of changed *versions* of "the same" stoppage (or "the same" implying). What the body implies is thereby more likely to develop or be encountered. But it might not. We say only that the new sequence is always pertinent (see note 2, chapter V) to the stoppage.

With our concept we can also understand the well-known fact that body structure develops in accordance with behavior. What was shown in V would still apply: behavioral events are a special case of new intervening events—new tissue process. They *are* new bodily developments and interactions with new aspects of the en.

But is the new sequence just a case of the one we had in V, perhaps only speeded up? Or is it different? Both. We can think of the behavior sequence both as intervening events of the same kind we had in V (which they are), and also as a new kind of change that happens against the backdrop of the reiterating cycle which developed as earlier intervening events.

For example, we might think of the reiterating along the lines of a TV screen. The TV tube projects a beam at the screen. This beam very rapidly goes back and forth horizontally, forming very thin regular lines that are always the same. The picture is made by letting the signal from the antenna affect this line-drawing beam so that it registers the picture-signal as a change in those lines. Now we could say quite rightly that the picture consists of the same lines, merely pulled out of their usual course.

The picture is only a special form of those very lines. Or we could say that the signal is something quite different, which registers **against the backdrop** of the reiterating lines.

The TV beam's regular lines do not occur insofar as the picture pulls the beam out of its regular lines. Therein the TV differs from (for instance) graph paper, whose lines remain underneath what we draw over them. Open cycle is like TV in this respect, not graph paper. The open cycle does not occur as usual, but with a new shape on top of it, like the graph paper. Rather, it forms only as changed.

Another example: a motion picture consists of a series of "same" frames, each only a little different from the previous. We see the movements because the differences stand out against the reiterated aspects.

Still another example: have you noticed that the wind is visible in the grass? And of course, we see it in the leaves and branches of the trees. We could not see the wind except for its registry in some otherwise stable context within which the changes are the wind.

In our new sequence the body pulls itself through the changes made **by the registering** (via interaffecting and en). This differs from our examples. The wind is not propelled by the grass registry. But we may take the notion that an existing reiterating context can register changes by staying otherwise the same, so that the changes stand out within it.

When a new kind of sequence develops in our model, it is always both a special case of the earlier, and also a new kind of sequence altogether. It forms as the old kind, but finds itself having a new kind of carrying forward within it.

We note that there is a new kind of carrying forward internal to the behavior sequence. In III, I had a too early use of the word "recognize." I said that when a missing en-aspect recurs, the whole stopped process resumes. It looks as if the body "recognizes" the missing object. We could now reuse the word in a second (still too early) sense. The body *recognizes* the next bodily occurring as carrying forward what it implied, but it now also *re-recognizes* the next occurring as the registry of the body's own move which also constitutes its next move. Now we have a doubled "recognition," since there is a doubled implying. We still have the usual kind of bodily implying and occurring (behavior is always part of a bodily event), but we also have the new relation.

But so far we have not said that the body implies how it will register when it moves. But if it had implied its registry, then the actual registry would occur into that implying and would carry it forward. But the second implying is not there when the sequence first forms. The new sequence forms as intervening events, but then it *finds itself carried forward* in this doubled way.

Once the body-process finds itself doubly carried forward, and the sequence becomes part of eveing, the registry which is also the next move is part of the single bodily implying (IV-A-b). The bodily change is also the implying of its registry and the further move that the registry makes. We can say that the body recognizes the open-cycle change as its own change.

Now we have derived why the lamb stops at the edge of a cliff although it has not seen a cliff before. Since the implied registry did not come, the movement sequence stops. At the cliff the registry is not that which the body's move implied as its registry. The lamb does not re-recognize the cliff drop as implied by its own motion, so it stops.

But this use of the word "re-recognize" is still too early. "Cognition" involves something more which we take up in VII.

Behavior is a new, doubled kind of implying and carrying forward. The body comes to imply its open cycle registry.

Let us go further.

The body moves further as the effect of the registry of how it just moved. It moved and is then affected by re-recognizing what it just did. Each bit of the sequence includes (is made by) the bodily impact (the registry) of how it just was. We could say that the body feels its own doing! Let us try to call this "feeling."

Currently, like most concepts, "feeling" is internally opaque. There seems to be no good way to think about what feeling is, why "focusing" on it (see Gendlin 1981) leads to information about a situation (the environment), and how it could "contain" information at all. It is also puzzling why feeling brings change—for example in psychotherapy. One speaks as if one could ask: "What good can it do me to feel all that stuff I have avoided? I might find out more about it, but how will it change?" Of course the answer is more complex (see Gendlin 1996, chapter 11), but feeling is itself a change-process. It should be thought of not as a noun but as a verb—a sequence.

With our new model we can explicate the implicit environmental information and behavioral origin of feeling. Later we will develop the way a feeling might seem to happen without overt behavior. But it is always part of some kind of behavioral sequence—it moves the body by the impacts made by the rendition of the body's own moves, the impacts of how the body just was. What we are calling "feeling" has (is) doubled information. It is a bodily change. It also is the rendition of that bodily change in the reiterative environment.

A bodily move now also implies its rendition which makes the next move. Therefore feeling is a series, not one rendition. We have to modify what I seemed to say, that feeling is "the" impact of "the" rendition. Feeling is *the series* of changes made by the impacts of the renditions of how the body was.

Later we will think about feelings that seem to happen, without overt behavior. Right now feeling exists only in behavior, as the series of bodily re-recognitions. Let us call it *"feeling in-behavior"* to remind ourselves of this.

What I call "re-recognition" enables us to understand how feeling locates into itself. In feeling, the body "feels itself" but not as if it were an object along with other objects. Rather, the body feels its environment by re-recognizing what it just did. Feeling is the series of impacts of what the body just did. *With feeling the body not only is, but feels the impact of what it "was." This is sentience.*

We have derived consciousness!!

That is the grandiose way of putting it. We don't want to reduce consciousness to any simple scheme. We have derived only a concept with which we can think about one aspect of consciousness, namely its self-registry.

But notice, this is not the concept of "consciousness" in the Western tradition, something like a mere light shining on something given there in advance. With our new concept "feeling" is the behavior; it is the series of bodily impacts *of* the body's own doing in the environment.

Let us go a little further before we discuss this relation called "of." It will develop further.

So far we have only considered the bodily side of behavior, the series of bodily impacts of the open cycle versions. But these also form a series that is part of the behavior sequence. The series of registries in the open cycle (the home-grown environment)—what is that?

Aha! *The series of open cycle renditions is perception!*

Again I must quickly add: when I say this series *is* perception (or sensation), I mean only that we have developed a kind of conceptual structure with which to speak-from and think-from perception (to think further and better than one can with the current kind of concept).

Again I must point out that this differs greatly from the traditional concept of "perception" or "sensing." In our concept, behavior, feeling, and perception are internally related and inherently linked.

Later we will think about a kind of perception that happens without overt behavior. The perception we just derived occurs as part of behavior. Let us call it *"perception in-behavior."*

Perception is felt. Feeling is *of* perception carrying the body's implying forward. The single sequence in which they appear is behavior.

A behavior sequence involves two special cases of the present-past relation, two cases of "goes on in"—our theta (ϑ). With the rendition *the body goes on in* what it renders. Or, to put it transitively, the rendition goes the body on further. The body goes on in its sense of what it did.

Perception is not just an in-take, a reception, a still photo. It is the going-on-in the en that is being perceived.

Feeling is not merely a sense of what is. It goes on further. It is the going-on-in how the body just was.

To re-recognize is to change, to go on further. (This will be important when we come to symbols. They too are a going further, not just static copies.) When we see, hear, or say what we did, we explicate further. Only by carrying the body further is there an open cycle rendition of how we just were.

The body now moves by its own doing. It moves in the en because the part of its en#2 which is its doubled reiterative en moves it further and thereby registers how it moved. Now we can say that the body *perceives*, because it isn't merely being affected but has a doubled re-recognition. The bodily implying (which is always one holistic implying, see IV-A-b) is doubled. The bodily implying also implies perception and feeling.

A better word for "re-recognition" might be "expression." Expression is an external rendition of what one just did or was, *such that* the external rendition has a special impact, namely the sensing oneself as one just was, sensing this in terms of the external rendition. But the word "expression" needs to belong to VII. Let us save it for VII although its grounds are derived here. The bodily carrying forward first creates what is then the doubly implied sequence in which the body re-recognizes its expression as its own. ***The doubled "self-locating" is already inherent in the most primitive kind of sentience.***

Behavior (feeling and perception) is always a body-process, albeit doubled. We built a concept of behavior as a body-process that has a doubled implying. Now we have derived feeling and perception within this doubled self-locating

In the Latin medieval tradition Aristotle's theory of sensation was said to be "reflexive" of itself, which seemed to mean that sensing has itself as an object. But in that version one could not think a few steps further into this. One was supposed to accept as obvious that something affects the sense organs and makes a sensation, but that sensing senses itself seemed a puzzling addition. That whole tradition assumes that experience *begins* with sensation, as if it were our only relation to the environment. It omits the fact that the whole body *is* an ongoing interaction with its environment. A plant's body physically consists of environmental interactions quite without the five sense organs, and we are at least plants.

Without the bodily process that constitutes conscious (aware) sensing, it seemed that consciousness is a floating additional "reflection" like a ray of light shining on what would be there in the same way also in the dark. This has given the very word "consciousness" a bad reputation in philosophy.

In our model the body's movement and its self-sensing develop as one sequence. Just sensing, without overt behavior, is a later derivative which we have not yet developed.

In recent research it was found that sensing does not develop normally without movement. When a newborn animal is blindfolded from birth but permitted to move, it perceives normally later on, when the blindfold is removed. But if the newborn is restrained for some time it does not later perceive normally, even though it was permitted to see everything including the motions of other animals. This is a puzzle in terms of current theories.

Feelings similarly develop only in-behavior. In current psychology feelings are still considered merely "internal." Then one ignores or puzzles about why feelings contain implicit information about what is going on. It seems only a superstition that the body is "wise" about one's life and situations.

In the history of Western thought, perception was thought to be our only connection with the world. Feelings were not taken to contain valid information. They were considered mere "accompaniments" of perception or worse, as misleading distortions. One finds them discussed only in back sections of philosophy books. The important questions were considered without them. We were assumed to feel only emotions, as if our bodies did not thickly feel our situations and what we do and say.

We need to change the "basic" model along the lines of our concepts. One can certainly question and reject these concepts, and better ones will surely be devised. We need not feel sure of our new concepts, but we can be sure that some concepts are needed to perform *the functions* which our concepts perform. We see some of these functions here: the concepts must enable us to think how perception is felt, and how feeling is *of the environment*.

Notice that there is as yet no distinction between the five senses.[1] Thus perception is not visual, nor is it the combination of five separate senses distinguished from other bodily sentience (currently one calls the latter "visceral"). The whole bodily change series is the *feeling of* what we term "perception."

We do not split the bodily changes away from what they are the sensations "of." What perception is "of" is sensed by (with, via) the bodily changes that are the feeling *of* that. They are feeling and perception only because they make up one self-locating behavior sequence. This single sequence is feeling and it is also perception.

The feedback to itself is the moving and the sensing and feeling of moving. Linear time is violated again. The open cycle is (a versioning of) how the body just was. Its impact is also the body's move. Continuity, as we saw in IV, is not just bits pressed close or contiguous, but the functioning of each *in* the last *and* the next. The open cycle both carries the body *forward* and just thereby, not earlier, feeds *back* to the body what it was. In linear time the point on our theta seems like one point going both backwards and forwards (see the end of IV-B, and the figure here).

B B B B

A A A A

Is it the open cycle that registers the **last** move, or the one that is the change and registers **this** move? The feedback to this move has the next move as its impact. In linear time the open cycle seems staggered, and both ahead and lagging behind. But linear time is too simple. We saw that if our thetas can be reduced to a stripe, one point moving along a line.

Instead of cutting between past, present, and future, our time model leads us to cut between interaffecting and the shared en effects. If there were not **that** difference, everything would happen at once, or nothing would ever happen. There would be no differences between implying and occurring.

VI-B. The Development of Behavior Space

(a) Motivation

Once a behavior sequence occurs, the sequence is implied as a whole. This is not a new implying just of behavior, but part of the body-process in which the behavior is **a detour**, a string of **versions** of the stoppage of some body-process. The whole sequence is implied since the body implies the resumption of the body-process (which happens at the end of the behavior). We have derived "**motivation.**"

No amount of just behaving (versions of stoppage) will keep an animal alive for long; at some point it must resume the body-process, feeding, copulating, and so on. Eventually it must ingest and digest, it cannot live just from tracking food. Behavior must return to the body-process in which it is a detour. This return is often called "consummation." The consummation is that event which is both behavior and the body-process resumption.

Consummations are not only those bodily events that existed before behavior developed. Behavior elaborates the body. Some behaviors now lead to consummations that didn't exist before behavior developed.

For example, if the relevant context for certain special behaviors never occurs (say the animal is in captivity), these behaviors will go off anyway after a time (see fixed motor patterns and vacuum activity in Lorenz 1981, 107–52). This does not violate our rule that behavior is "motivated" by a body-process stoppage. It would be better to say that as behavior elaborates and rebuilds the body, stoppage develops from some behaviors.

We might be tempted to say that a familiar consummation defines the motive of a familiar behavior. It seems that the consummation defines the sequence, but as with all implying, the resumption need not be what it was before. What turns out to be consummation is determined by the motivation, the implying, the eveving, the stoppage-resumption itself. It is always the carrying forward that defines and generates the sequence.

Since eveving is part of occurring, carrying forward is an occurring into eveving. If a changed sequence leads to a new consummation, they have become part of evev. Eveving is always the body's implying—but with the en occurring into it.

(b) Cross-contextual formation

We saw (in IV) that eveving does not occur and make or take time of its own. The environmental occurring occurs into the eveving. If a sequence is implied but cannot happen, and the animal doesn't die, some other body-process immediately forms instead.

In the case of behavior, since it is not implied alone but as part of an implied body-process, when a focally implied behavior cannot happen with the en, the bodily implying may continue without any behavior. Or, a different or changed behavior may form

The formation of a behavior involves both the body's implying and how the en occurs into it. The eveving is both, since it is part of occurring. As we said all along (and in the two change-avenues), the actual eveving is a result of the en-happening-into how the body would have implied its next step. Eveving is a crossing of everything by everything (IV-A-e), and in it the en also crosses with how the body would have implied the en if it had not occurred into it differently.

If a new behavior forms, it will be by the open cycle occurring into the implying of the sequence that cannot form. The new sequence which does form is therefore an eveving which would have formed the other sequence, but with this en, forms this new one. In other words: *the old sequence is implicit in the occurring of the new one. The new one happens into the implying of the old one.*

This means the old sequence now has the new one implicitly, and the new one has the old one implicit in it. The next time that the old sequence becomes implied, the new one will also be implicit. Both will be part of the eveving along with the environment at that point. The sequences are not separate. They are implicit in each other. They form a context. *Each sequence is a string of versions of the "context" in which the other sequences are implicit.*[2]

Bodily process (including behavior) is always a fresh formation, whether an observer has seen it before or not. Now we can add: an observer might see only the same as before, but this time it might have one or more new sequences *implicit* in it.[3]

When a sequence functions implicitly, "it" is not quite the same "it." But this is true of any kind of "it" that may function implicitly in the formation of something else which may then, in turn, be implicit in "it." "It" functions insofar as "it" participates in shaping what occurs, hence differently in each new sequence.[4] And, how "it" participated is part of how "it" is eveved at that point, and from then on.

The bodily implying includes a whole context of mutually implicit behavior sequences, eveved and focaled with the actual environment happening into it.

The actual environment includes the body's en#2 and the leafing interactions of the open cycle sector. In eveving this crosses with the body's implying of the open cycle (now the "context" of mutually implicit behavior sequences). The two systems cross in the eveving that is part of any occurring.

If the actual open cycle happens as the body implied it, the usual sequence occurs. If not, something else results in the eveving in which the implied behavior-context crosses with the actual open cycle, which we can call the "environmental behavior context." I say that behavior forms *"cross-contextually."*

The word "crossing" could be freshly derived here, as it is used in this "cross-contextual" formation. (The word can speak from many kinds of "crossing.") Here two systems of crossed, mutually implicit behavior sequences cross in a single eveving and occurring. What occurs is their crossing.[5]

Let us now permit our concepts to develop this formation of the "behavior context" of mutually implicit sequences.

(c) Behavior space

Once many behaviors have occurred, each sequence consists of a string of evevings of them. Each implicitly involves the others in its formation. Each *is* a way of carrying forward a mesh consisting of the others.

Therefore each behavior sequence is a string of changes in how the others are functioning implicitly. A behavior sequence **is** a string of versions of the behavior contexts of all the mutually implicit sequences.

An occurring sequence also changes how the others would occur if they were to form after it. For example, let us say the occurring sequence stops and one of the others commences. The latter would form somewhat differently if the first sequence had gone on longer. How other sequences would happen, if they did, would also be different. Any occurring sequence *is* a string of changes in how any of the other sequences would occur.

Since the behavior context consists of how each sequence would occur if it did, we can think of it as a space, a mesh of possible behaviors that the body implies in all sorts of directions and respects.

It can be called "*behavior space.*" Let us develop it further.

For example, an observer sees an animal make a simple movement in human empty space. Even in that space we can grasp what it means for so many sequences to be implicitly changed by the one that occurs. Having moved, the animal is no longer in the same spot. From the previous spot many other movements might have been made. But now, from this new spot all those movements would happen differently. The animal could still go to that tree, but along a different path. It could now go to that boulder over there, but no longer around it as before, when the bolder was right in front of the animal. *Every conceivable movement—and there would be vastly many—was changed at once by the move that did occur.*

This example is positional. We think of the animal merely moving, pure locomotion in empty space. But empty space and pure change of place happen only in human empty space. It develops later, and will turn out to involve symbols. Behavior space is not empty; it is, so to speak, "full." It is the mesh of implied behavior sequences (not just movements).

For example, the implicit sequences might include chasing a bird up a tree, and eating a bird. If one of them can and does occur, it *is* also a change in how the other is implicit. Obviously this would be more than just a change in position.

A behavior always occurs in the midst of other implicit behaviors, and as a change in those. The whole mesh is carried forward. The bodily implying of the consummatory body-process also implies the whole open cycle context of implicit behaviors and it is carried forward as the actual en interacts with the doubled implying. Different body-process detours develop and imply different contexts of implicit behaviors.

In the old model one begins with bits of perception: a patch of color, a smell. We are far from saying that experience begins with such percepts that are then related into a sequence. The reverse: the perception is a whole-bodied carrying forward; the chain of open cycles results from the sequence.[6]

(c-1) Had space

We don't want to say the body "projects" space, as if that mysterious word were an explanation. We now have a schematic structure of concepts internal to this "projection" of "space" in front of and all around the animal body. The body implies and carries forward the eveved open cycle, with its implicit behavior sequences. As part of this bodily carrying forward the body feels and perceives the whole context of implicit behavior possibilities.

Behavior space is **had space**, that is to say, felt and perceived space. It is not the external observer's space within which an organism might be viewed. Rather, it is a process's own space, the body-process's own implying of behavior sequences.

In V our concepts only went as far as the development of a reiterating sector which could be affected by changes. For example, a plant might bodily grow toward the sun.[7] I cautioned there that this is not yet a space that the body-process feels and perceives. Now our concepts enable us think about how a body-process **has** a space.

As the doubled bodily-behavioral implying is carried forward, the organism feels and perceives the space (the mesh of the implicit sequences). Any occurring now **goes on in** (is a carrying forward of) that space (that context of other sequences).

We say that behavior space consists of "behavior possibilities," but we must keep in mind that only the occurring one "was" really possible. It is not as if any of the implicit ones could have formed just as well. The one that occurred was focaled in eveving with the actual en.

Although a behavior may concern a special object, it takes account of the other objects in the space. For example, the cat runs after a bird, but takes account of the boulder which is in the way. The cat runs around the boulder and does not run into it, nor jump up on it. **Here we see and could derive eveving**: each sequence **is** an eveving of the others. The boulder is also an object in implicit jump-up sequences and hide-behind sequences which do not now occur. (We will soon return to discuss this boulder, and how objects form.)

Behavior space is a new home-grown environment, a new kind of en#3. The body goes on in it, changes it (goes it on), and as with any en, is itself part of it.

The body implies it, and is self-locating in it, as it occurs into this implying.

(c-2) Had space and time

One always hears of "space and time" together, but what is their **inherent** relation? Why are they always together? Were they born separately and then introduced to each other like two strangers?

Could one just as well have three, perhaps time, space, and causality? What is **internal** to each that links it to the other?

We want to be able to think clearly and exactly how behavior, feeling, perception, space, and time are interlocked. We cannot understand them if we simply assert that they are each just there, as if they were things which first just lie there, and then relate.

In the classical positional model, space is three parameters, and time is one more. If you first fix your gaze at any one point in empty Euclidean space, what you see changes if you move your gaze to the left or right, or up or down, or further forward or back. But if you hold your position and wait a while, what you see right there in that one spot will also change. It will change in time.

Without holding a spot constant one would not notice time separately at all. (See Gendlin 1984.) Only by fixing the gaze at one spot can we find a change that happens only in time. Then one can turn about and say that the other changes—and change in general—happen in time. But all this concerns positional space and time.

The space and time of the old model are very limited. They cannot be accepted as an ultimate frame of reality. They are very abstract positional relations of comparison imposed by someone. Who? Obviously a perceiver, and not one who perceives-in-behavior, but rather a perceiver who only perceives and does only comparing, a spectator who has only an external relation to what is perceived. But "external" is something we cannot derive until VII—in fact later in VII, VII-B. In order not to assume that this kind of perception and its space and time are "basic" we need an alternative. Otherwise, even if it is our general position to reject all "basic" models and all assertions, the old model remains basic after all, since we cannot help but assume it in everything we actually think (although we might reject it all in general).

To think more deeply than positional relations is not just a general question. Nearly every specific parameter in physics involves the old model of time and space. For example, velocity is distance per unit time. The structure of localization is soon also revealed inside most concepts even when they don't mention it explicitly. Social science concepts and "common sense" concepts render "things" in space and time.

But what does the perceiving and holding at one spot? What or who compares and notices the change so as to generate the four abstract dimensions of change? Obviously something that has memory and continuity. The moving images in the spectated frame cannot be primary and ultimate at all.

The point is not to give up science and computers; the point is to think further. In VII we will become able to generate positional space and time and thereby also to grasp their limitations and how we can formulate assertions that go beyond them.

As human beings, of course we begin with human experience.

From ourselves we develop concepts about what is less than human, and supposedly earlier. But perception need not be our "basic" model-instance—especially not just perception cut off from behavior and the body, mere positions that are external to each other. (What are positions? They *are* pure externality.)

In our model there is as yet no distinction between an "external" environment and "internal" experience. We will derive that distinction in VII-B.

Our own bodies generate a kind of space and time, and from this we can say that all life process does so. There is always already the implying which occurring carries forward.

We have now built the concepts of a doubled implying and a doubled bodily-and-behavioral occurring which generates a doubled space and a doubled time. The doubled body-process generates itself with the sentient having of the occurring.

In our model the inherent tie between space and time lies in behavioral implying. There is not yet even a distinction between space and time in the physically focaled behavior possibilities. Let me show this exactly:

Say someone throws a snowball at you, and it is coming on. Now you are living (feeling and perceiving) the future "time" (the snowball hitting you) and you are living in the space between it and you, trying to move out of the way and also duck which is hard to do, perhaps also trying to catch it, jump, run, drop to the ground, crawl, retaliate—many more which make up the "space" and "time," the context *in which* all this happens.

The relation between what we call "space" and "time" is internal to the very way behavior forms and occurs into an implying. Within behavior we can now separate the spatial (not just here) from the temporal (not just now), but we have found them together in behavioral implying.

From behavior can we set "had time" up as something that is separately had? But if not, if we leave had space and time together, then what we called "had space" is not just space, either. Of course, implying and behavior space already involved time. "Behavior space" was already "*had space and time.*"

The cat stands before the door, calling. She wants to go out, and lives in the behavior of going out the door and beyond. I say she *has* space and time in a way a tree or an amoeba do not. Her bodily implying includes the doubled implying of running out the door, and if the door remains closed, this doubled implying remains "the same" and occurs in slightly changed *versions* as she run-readies and meows in front of the door.

In this way our concepts link body, behavior, feeling, perception, and had space-and-time in any single behavior sequence.

(c-3) Two open cycle sectors

For some years it seemed to me that the staggered way the open cycle is both ahead and behind the body's implying might require two sectors of body structure. The implying is part of occurring and is changed by that very occurring. In carrying forward the implying is, is changed, and is also the changed. Since implying is both ahead and behind, I thought that two body-sectors might be needed.

This went further when I thought that the body *actually* gives itself the response it implies. For instance:

I am driving the car and I step on the brake. The car has a burst of speed (I have unintentionally stepped on the gas pedal instead. The gas pedal is softer, so I stepped on it hard.) In such a case I notice that I have already sensed the car slowing down, even though it did not do so. When the feedback is not what my body implied, I notice that *there are two different feedbacks*: the one my body gives itself, and the one that comes with the environmental interaction.

This leads me to ask the question: are there two open cycle sectors just alike, so that either can be the one called ahead, or the one called behind? Then the body can *have* the behavior sequence's next (although it cannot move the body to that next without the cooperation of the actual en [b-en]—if that is lacking, the behavior sequence stops). The carrying forward would happen staggeredly in both.

This seemed a theoretically uncomfortable duplication. I don't like duplications of terms; usually they indicate an error. Moreover, behavior would *not* be going on between the two open cycles; it would have to happen between each and the whole body in its actual en. *There would be no direct connection between the two sectors.*

I told my results to my colleague Ward Halstead, and he said, "Oh yes, stereo." This was a way of saying that a whole space can be had, felt and sensed, if there are two. It isn't exactly the same point, but it is related.

I realized that the model had *derived the bilateral symmetry of the bodies* of most animals. This includes the two brain halves, but it is an error to deal with the brain as if it functioned alone, rather than as a part of whole-body functions.

Our model also seems to derive and explain the puzzling fact that the brain-halves need not be directly connected. Their function goes through both sides of the whole body, and only so can it move the body.

In humans one side is usually differentiated by certain language functions, but research suggests that differences between the two sides are more complicated than the popular understanding (e.g., Gazzaniga 2005). Let us postpone the development of language until VII.

(d) Pyramiding

We have already said that when a sequence would be focally implied, something new might happen as the actual en happens into the eveving. Then the new sequence is and remains part of the eveving, and part of the behavior space. If the same circumstances recur, the new sequence will form freshly again, and the old sequence might never form. But if there is a small change in the body or the environment so that the new sequence cannot form, then the old sequence will, if it can.

If a still newer sequence develops, it is the new-new one, and the previous "new" sequence becomes the old-new one. When many sequences form in this way, I say that the new ones are "*pyramided*" over the old ones.

Most current sequences of a person's behavior space are pyramided. The old sequence always remains implicit. Of course "it" ("the old sequence") is not quite the same as before the new formation, since the new sequence (and much else that happened meanwhile) is now implicit in the contexts that "the old sequence" is now a string of. In dreams and with hypnosis and drugs, the usual behavior space is narrowed so that it does not implicitly contain as much as it would in the waking state. We find that very old ("primitive") sequences form then, and implicitly contain some (a variable amount) of the usual context of implicit sequences. In those states we can observe the familiar experiences still forming, and we can notice how many are implicit and focaled in ordinary experiences. (See the theory section in Gendlin 2004b.)

The occurring of a sequence is always a fresh formation; in that sense any sequence is new, and implicitly contains much of what has happened since the last time the observer saw it.

A great many sequences are pyramided under the usual repertoire of every animal. They might not have formed in a great many generations. (A certain bird from the Atlantic Ocean has no mating dance. A similar species from the Pacific still does it. If a Pacific bird is presented to an Atlantic one, it will do a mating dance that species hasn't done in thousands of years.)

The behavior space is inherited along with the body-structure. (I say more about inherited behavior in section k of the appendix.) The individual organism never actually sequences most of the implicit behaviors that are pyramided over. But the common behaviors are also formed in a pyramided way, over each other.

(e) Object formation: objects fall out

Objects form pyramidedly. Let me first discuss object formation and then show the pyramided aspect.

Let us say the cat is running after a bird, tracking the bird. By running the cat keeps the bird steady in front. The steady bird is kept "the same" *by* the tracking behavior. The object is kept "the same" by *the changes* of the behavior sequence. I say that the steady object "*falls out*" as "the same object" which the sequence makes.

A behavior-object (it is always also a perceptual object) is made by the behavior sequence.

A behavior-object falls out against the background of the changing behavior spaces. The cat keeps the bird steady by rapidly changing the rest of the scene. Everything else swiftly buzzes by, as the cat runs.

But the cat feels the space standing still! If the earth moved, the cat would stop. Although the space is going by and bopping up and down, the running sequence keeps the behavior space "the same" by carrying it forward. The "same space" is the behavior space of the bird and the ground moving-by. If the cat stops, the bird escapes and the behavior space has changed. So the running keeps not only the cat and bird steady; the rapid changes of the running also maintain the "same" behavior space, the food-chasing space.

In a behavior sequence each bit is a changed *version* of "the same" behavior context. I also say that each bit of the sequence "*reconstitutes*" the context. The whole behavior space is needed for the object to fall out.

In III the body never *has* an object present to it. The object is implied only when missing. If it recurs, the process resumes and the object is no longer implied. Now we have derived an object that remains. It is kept steady by the sequence, and it falls out from the sequence.

Since the body implies the sequences and they keep objects steady, it follows that *the bodily eveving now implies the objects by* implying the sequences.

So behavior space consists of objects, but only insofar as it consists of implicit behavior sequences. If many other sequences and their objects were not implicit in any behavior-context, the cat would not avoid the boulders while chasing the bird.[8]

Our III object could only be absent, but the VI object can be present, and it can also be absent. This is because the open cycle may include the implicit sequence even when its focal object is absent. *The "slot" of an object may exist in behavior space even when the object is absent. Then it can be perceived as absent.*

Let us go another step: since the "slot" of an object may remain, the object is perceived as present in the slot in which it could be absent. The food can now be perceived as present, absent, present again, or half eaten.

A behavior space in which many objects have fallen out is an advanced stage found only in higher animals. Behavior space does not first consist of objects.

Can we say **both** that an object "falls out *from* a sequence" and also that it carries the sequence forward? Yes, but more precisely it is the open cycle that does the carrying forward. But since the open cycle consists of implicit sequences and their objects, the objects do carry the sequences forward. But we need to remember that an object only comes along with the whole sequence of contexts, i.e., the steady scene. What carries forward is not just one aspect, but the whole scene, the series of open cycles. (Open cycle = scene = behavior space = context of implicit sequences.) An object is always implicitly the whole scene, the whole context, the whole mesh of other sequences.

For example, the bird seems separate from the power wire on which it sits, and from everything else in the scene. But the scene and the other objects are implicit in the separate bird. A bird that would stick to the power line would be a different object, not a real bird. Every object, that seems at first quite self-contained, *is* really the mesh of *how it falls out*, and only because those remain implicit, does it stay "the same" in different scenes. So it always implies the many sequences from which it has its itness.

Take something that usually moves, but does not move right now. Suppose the bird perches. The cat also stops, lies in wait. The observer sees nothing happening, but the cat's muscles are tight; it is readying to jump, gauging the distance and the moment. The cat is doing a lot. *Jump-readying is a complex behavior.*[9]

The cat's readying and the not-changing of the perched bird are further sequences that form in the context that implies the moving bird.

A further example: suppose we have a photograph of a bull. That bull stands still. Now, let's make a motion picture, many photographs of the bull in slightly different stills. The bull moves. Now suppose we want the bull to stand still *in the motion picture.* Then picture after picture must go by with the bull in the same position. To have the bull stand still you don't stop the film. Many almost unchanged slides make it stand still. For us the perched bird falls out from a sequence of versions of the behavior context in which its motions are implicit.

As the cat quietly crouches, consider the complexity of its behavior. Each bird movement is followed with pupils, with muscle-tightening, with directioning. The non-flying bird falls out from a sequence in which its slightest move feeds back to precision the cat's jump-readying. The perched bird sequence and its scene implicitly focal a great many not-occurring leaps of the cat.

Objects involve other implicit sequences in their very formation.

Appendix to VI

The following sections of VI contain indispensable concepts of behavior. I place them in an appendix because the reader can go on to VII, and look these concepts up later when they are cited and employed.

It can be wearying to read about one new concept after another without seeing them used. Therefore I send the reader ahead.

(f) Resting perception, impact perception, and perceiving behind one's back

(f-1) Resting perception
Once the open cycle is eveved as part of the body-process, the body can *feel* itself at rest in the mesh of the sequences which are reiteratingly implied. I call this kind of sequence "*resting perception.*"

(f-2) Impact perception
Therefore a change in the environment may be perceived and felt even without behavior. I call this kind of sequence "*impact perception.*"

Like the cat's jump-readying, these kinds of perception and feeling are special kinds of behavior sequences.

(f-3) Perception behind one's back

Merleau-Ponty pointed out that we perceive and feel the space behind us even without hearing or seeing anything directly. You can check this directly. With our concepts we can now derive this fact:

Say the animal saw or smelled a predator a while ago, and is now running away. It has not yet run far enough that it can relax. The predator is now being perceived—not in the usual sense but certainly in our sense. The predator is part of each bit of the open cycle as the animal runs. The animal is putting distance between itself and the predator who is behind it somewhere. The motivation to get away is being carried forward by each tree going by. What is perceived is not just the trees, but the behavior context being carried forward by the moving trees.

They are perceived as putting distance between the animal and the predator behind it.

Obviously the felt and perceived behavior space includes much that is not the "perception" of the five senses. Rather, the body perceives and feels the behavior space—one sequence that carries the mutually implicit sequences forward. Implicit are, for example, behaviors of turning back, of stopping and resting, and of going sideways. These would bring the predator. The animal runs forward in a space consisting of the many sequences that are implicitly part of forming (eveing) this behavior. The ongoing behavior consists of versions of the perceived and felt behavior space, of course behind it as well as in front.

I discuss this further in section (m) below.

We have derived the wider perception which is part of carrying forward the behavior space that is implied by the body.

(g) Relevanting

Can an object bring about a sequence that was not already focally implied? For example, must the cat have focally implied tree-climbing before it found the tree? Or can the climbing sequence occur because the cat encounters a tree?

We can say that if the tree-climbing sequence forms, the tree "was relevant," but we can also say that the tree helped to make its relevance. "Relevance" is, in a way, another word for eveing. The en happens into the eveing. So, yes. By occurring, the tree enters the eveing so that climbing it may become focally implied.

Let us make a verb of it: the tree can actively "***relevant***" the sequence. (This was already evident in IV.) If the behavior sequence ensues, the relevanting was itself the first bit of the behavior.

An object may relevant a sequence with another object. The cat sees an open door and runs through it after a bird, paying the door no heed. But the door is part of the behavior space of the bird, like the boulder that the cat runs around.

(h) Juncturing

Each bit of a behavior sequence relevants the next bit. Therefore it can be difficult for another behavior sequence to become relevant while this one is going on. Some en-aspect might relevant a sequence if it occurs before another sequence relevants. If it occurs during the other sequence, it might not. Also, if the sequence goes to a consummation, this may change the body so much that the other en-aspect would no longer relevant its sequence.

This gives behavior a certain stability, and organization. An object may be able to relevant a sequence at one juncture, but not at another. Behavior is organized by "***juncturing***."

By behaving, the animal changes its behavior space. Other behaviors become implicit and can be relevanted. This is not only a change from externals. The behavior space is constituted by the body in interaction with en. By behaving, the animal changes its body and its behavior space.

(i) Compression

"Compression" is a concept we will need later when we come to language and human action. The concept develops first from animal behavior.

Studies of animals show that behavior has a tendency to become simplified, ritualized, more compressed higher up on the scale of evolution. For example, in an earlier species there is a complex mating ceremony. The female swims away from her prospective mate, and toward the other males, then she turns and swims back to him, then out again toward the others. She does this six or seven times. In a later species the female keeps her neck turned toward her mate and she swims out toward the others—just once! What was an elaborate sequence earlier is now performed by a single short "ritualized" behavior. Our model will enable us to derive the first theory with which one can think about this:

As more and more sequences develop, there is a greater change when a sequence becomes focally implied. When behavior first formed, the first bit brought only a small change. Now it is a great change when the first bit focally relevants the sequence. Of course, the whole sequence still makes more change, but the first bit—the mere relevanting—may now be a great change, certainly much more than the first bit brought at the stage when the sequence first formed.

At this developed stage it might seem that the sequence has already happened as soon as it becomes focally implied, but that is not so. For example, I am not at the door just by moving toward it. Nevertheless, the whole situation may be drastically changed if I just begin to move to the door.

It need not be the first bit. In our example with the ducks, the great change is made at the moment when she swims out and turns back. That moment soon brings the change which required many sequences when the behavior first formed.

Or the compressed bit might be the last, so that consummation is reached more quickly. For example, a fight between male monkeys ends when one of them turns his back at last. But in some social species, each monkey turns his back whenever he sees one who is higher in the hierarchy. Then there is no fight. The consummation is reached directly. The turn is a compression of the whole sequence. But the fight is still implicit, and occurs if a monkey does not turn in hierarchical order.

Whenever a bit of behavior changes the eveving very greatly, the change may be sufficient so that something else can relevant. Then the rest of the sequence may no longer occur.[10]

In elaborate behavior, space compression makes for rapid carrying forward with swift transitions across. After a few bits of a sequence another sequence may become focally implied.

Compression is a kind of pyramiding. The whole sequence is still implicit, but the new compressed one occurs instead.

Konrad Lorenz tells about a duck which he led up several flights of stairs every day after some experiments. Once there was a loud noise in the street while they were on the second floor landing. The duck ran into a room there and looked out the window, then quieted down and went on up the rest of the stairs. From then on each day when they reached the landing, the duck made a little loop toward the room and then went on up. But one day many months later, the duck failed to make the loop. After a few steps up, she turned, went back down and all the way into the room to the window. Then she went on up the stairs.

The example shows that the whole sequence remained implicit in the little compressed loop. When the "new" loop sequence did not occur, the whole old sequence became focally implied and occurred.

(j) "Breaking back" to a more primitive level

This is another term that we will need in VII.

Higher animals develop more and more behavior and more and more objects that can relevant behavior. If the cat is not hungry, not sexually engaged, not tracking something or escaping, she may go about, sniffing something here, turning to listen to a noise, meandering over there, looking into a hole, sitting a while. Various objects relevant sequences that are interrupted by other objects which relevant other sequences.

Suddenly a mouse appears and the cat is on the other side of the room before we know what happened. Nor is she easily interrupted in this pursuit until it is over. Animal psychologists call this sudden behavior a "fixed action pattern" (FAP) because it goes off in a very regular and uninterruptible way.

A FAP seems to be a throwback to a more primitive level of development. The behavior space seems not to include all those sequences with passably interesting objects. Actually they are still there, as we can see from the fact that the cat skillfully avoids those objects despite her speed and the uninterruptible quality of her tracking. So the FAP is not simply primitive. Some of the later objects are implicit in the behavior context which the FAP carries forward, but most of them are not. In midst of a FAP most later-developed objects will not relevant a different sequence. During a FAP the eveving and focaling omits a great deal which it otherwise includes.

I call the narrowed eveving of a FAP *"breaking back," a return to an earlier manner with fewer objects and a more whole-bodied formation*. We will need the concept to understand how human emotions differ from the holistic bodily feeling of eveving the whole context.

(k) Behavioral body-development

We saw earlier that changes in body structure continue and are speeded up by the development of behavior. I call such change "VI-into-V." These are often large and rapid changes. (For example, in one generation bees in a hive may be born with a changed body structure in response to changed behavioral circumstances.) Earlier stages do not remain the same. Later stages develop the earlier ones further.

Some behaviors develop new consummations and thereby also new stoppages in the body-process. Animals develop many bodily motivations that did not exist before behavior formed. Behavior is a detour, a string of *versions* of a stoppage of a body-process, but it may create and carry forward new or changed stoppages.

The current gap between physiology and psychology is not a gap between the body and behavior. It is rather the gap between the current *vocabularies and concepts* of the two fields. If one doesn't develop concepts for the bodily development of sentience, both sides become mysterious. Then the body seems to be a machine, and the behavioral terms have to come from a new and false beginning that floats without the body. Then our concepts of body and behavior never acquire the inherent internal connections.[11]

If we have succeeded in thinking of body-process and behavior within one paradigm, we can show how the bodily structure of each species is just what is needed for its behavior. This is not quite so mysterious if behavior *is* a certain kind of carrying forward and change of the body.

The other side of the same relationship is the current puzzle of inherited behavior. If the body is inherited, so is its implicit behavior, of course.

In evolution the body and behavior develop together. This seems mysterious only if one splits between matter and process, between body and functioning.

Would you think the lungs inherited, but breathing learned? Would you think the heart inherited but the pumping not? And why would legs be inherited but not walking? I ask students: "How do tiny children learn to walk? They answer "From watching the adults." Then I ask: how do they learn to crawl?

For a long time the behaviorists insisted that the animals must learn their complex behaviors. When animals were raised in a cage in a lab, they thought the animals must have learned while they were carried in the womb. But what is learning? Without some equipment, no thing can learn. Something is always inherited when there is learning. You can't teach a tree to catch mice.

There is a continuum from innate to learned in various combinations. A kitten must "learn" the complex way of jumping on a mouse. The mother demonstrates—once—and it is learned. It is inherited but requires a bit of learning. Stimulating certain brain cells elicits the behavior also without mother. But don't say it is the brain. A brain cannot jump on mice. The whole body is restructured as behavior develops; the whole body is inherited along with its behaviors.

(I) Habit

It has long been a puzzle why repetition seems to build habits. Mere repetition does not explain it. The answer is that the development of habit is a certain kind of *bodily* change.

The "repetition" occurs in different circumstances. Each time it carries forward a somewhat different behavior context. Each time the behavior becomes implicit in many different sequences in which it was not implicit before.

We have seen that the visible form of two behaviors may seem the same, yet many different behaviors may be implicit in it. A behavior becomes a habit when it has become implicit in a great many other behavior sequences, and they in it (in the context of which it is a string). The more sequences involve it implicitly, the more difficult it is for a new sequence to pyramid over it and occur instead. When it is implicit in many sequences, it never disappears completely.

A new behavior can become a habit if it leads to a new consummation, or to an old one more quickly. This is why a "reward" can build a habit. Sometimes one time is enough to build a habit. On the other hand, without a "reward" (some kind of consummation) no habit may form, even with a great many repetitions in various contexts.

Does habit-formation contradict my assertion that occurrence is always a fresh formation? Our new concepts show that it does not. A habit *forms freshly* each time, as with any other sequence. It is freshly relevanted and focaled.

When the same thing happens again under the same conditions, we can call it "recurrent causation": the same thing forms again in the same way it formed in the first place.

(m) Kination (imagination and felt sense)

In the old model one begins with experience already broken up into different kinds. One assumes that "basic" reality consists of just one way in which we have already diagramed, distinguished, and remade anything. (In VII we will understand ourselves in such remaking.)

If one could not trace how something was received (for example, by light waves or sound waves impinging on a sense organ from the object), then it had to be called "imagination." Imagination was always mysterious, the experience of objects—without objects.

It seemed that imagination must be something like a memory of what was once present, old experiences, perhaps creatively rearranged.

Freud and Jung discovered that imagination and dreams are much wider than individual experience. They discovered the "unconscious" of the human race, the "collective unconscious" which can create images from primitive times when culture was first created. These seem similar the world over and can be elicited from most anyone by certain chemicals, hypnosis, or sleep.

With the old model everything is explained by tracing some units back to an earlier time, to show that what seems new is only a rearrangement. It seemed easy to explain dreams and imagination as a *re*play or *re*arrangement of old experiences. The real problem is to understand how experience happens in the first place.

It has long been recognized that even when something does impinge, the body must still also **produce** the experience. The object may be next to a stone, but that is not sufficient to let the stone experience it. Some equipment is necessary to produce experience—whatever "experience" is. Most of what happens in imagining and reproducing an experience has to happen also when we first experience anything.

Kant said that imagination is involved not only in replay but just as much in first experiencing. He wrote in *Critique of Pure Reason* of the "productive imagination" which comes before the "re-productive" one. He said that this capacity lies "deeply hidden" in us, and that we would scarcely ever observe it. But he saw that actually ongoing experience happens **in** (with the participation of) the imagination.

In building our model we have now arrived at a similar place. The animal moves in its own homegrown environment, the open cycle which has become behavior space, the mutually implicit sequences.

One big difference is that the open cycle is implied by the whole body. The whole body **is** an interaction with the environment. In traditional Western philosophy the whole body was ignored. Experience had to be built out of receptions by the five sense-organs. In order to think of those as the source of experience, one had to jump from colors and smells to the experience of objects, things, and situations. One was not supposed to notice that even the simplest situation cannot be thought of as bits of color and smell.

In (f) above we took up how a situation (a behavior context) includes objects perceived and felt behind the body as much as in front. Behavior space includes the predator behind the escaping animal. Behavior space does not consist of bits of color and smell, but of the bodily implied behaviors and their objects.

In the earlier example, we said that the animal's running carries forward a felt and perceived space of many possible behaviors. The running and the passing trees carry forward its bodily escape-motivation. Of course, it feels and perceives the trees behind it. The animal feels that if it were to back up at a slant, it would hit the tree, and it feels this quite without first looking. If the animal were to back up, it would reverse their passing. If it were to take a rest, the trees would stop passing, but the pursuing predator would come closer. If the animal were to hide behind one of those trees, the predator might pass by, but might not. The animal's body (the "collective unconscious" of pyramided-over sequences of its species) "knows" whether this kind of predator will smell it if it hides, and whether the predator can climb trees better than it can. That is all already part of the context from which the passing trees fall out as objects in the behavior space in which it runs.

If we now say that behavior space is "imagination," the word would come to mean what is actually present in body-environment interaction. I think this is true in some sense of human imagination as well, but only in VII can we examine the whole question. Here we can be sure that "imagination" is not off from body-en interaction, as if it could be simply false. With animals we have derived this *interactionally real* imagination. When we come to humans it will be *this* imagination which we will want to develop further.

"Imagination" might be misleading if "images" are thought of only as visual, or only of the five senses. The word "kinesthetic" (from kinesis, motion) is still too poor if one thinks of motion as just a change of location in empty space. Later we will see that pure motion involves a prior behavior space and, of course, the whole body. I coin the word "kination" to use where "imagination" usually comes.

"*Kination*" is the doubled, bodily implied behavior space. For example, the cat meows before the door; she "imagines" running outside. The door is in behavior space along with what is on both sides of the door. The behavior space consists of many behaviors the cat does out there and what it does now in here. There is no great division between the door it sees, and the outdoors it does not see. The bodily implied kination is always vastly wider than what can be photographed at the moment.

There is no break between physicalist sensing and kination.

Kination = behavior eveving = open cycle carrying forward = feeling (the evev-evev changes) = perception (the open cycle versioning).

We can say that behavior happens *in kination* if we remember that kination is doubled ongoing body-en interaction. Kination is not an autistic inner space.

These concepts are the first of their kind; they are not likely to be perfect or the best. By using them, better ones will develop.

Culture, Symbol, and Language

VII-A. Symbolic Process

(a) Bodylooks

At last we are ready to derive symboling. By "derive" of course, I mean build concepts that will let us think clearly about what it is to be a symbol, how something can be "of" in the way a symbol is. We will see that much of the foregoing has been necessary.

To think clearly, one needs concepts that share an internal structure, that develop together, so to speak. What each is, and what the others are, constitute a single structure so that one can grasp what each does in relation to the others.

It won't do just to add one thing to another. We don't enable clear thought and we don't penetrate into experiences, if we just announce: "Humans have a power to symbolize." Everyone already knows that.

In developing the symbol power, as it seems, from animal behavior and body-process, I am not trying to do a natural history. I think, quite in the opposite order, that those who study actual developments of this sort will be aided by the concepts developed here. Why? Because these concepts stem from out of what symboling is.

Why then have we needed to reformulate body-process and behavior? Because only by developing those concepts more clearly, and more in accord with what symboling is, can we hope to think about it. The body and behavior are once and for all involved in what symboling is, and we cannot think *about symboling* in the poor concepts now in use about the body and also about behavior, perception, feeling, space and time. That will now become clear.

Let me now lead to symboling by discussing briefly that kind of animal behavior which is most like it, namely "animal gestures" and "animal rituals." That will let us see shortly exactly what symboling adds to the animals, and what it does not. We cannot just say "language" is added. We need to understand the kind of experiencing which language involves.

The higher animals are and do most everything that humans are and do. For example, Jane Goodall reports that a chimpanzee mother of an infant that has polio carefully arranges his limp arms and legs (Good-all 2000, 215). When an adult male chimpanzee was wounded, his small brother sat carefully pushing the lips of a gaping wound together.

The symboling kind of experience is not necessary for differentiated communication. The sound-patterns of bird calls have recently been analyzed. One male bird sang something like 150 different calls per day. When his mate was taken away he sang just one call, all that day. Next when she was restored, he sang his 150 calls again.

Animals groom each other and pick fleas even when there are no fleas, just to keep each other company. We know this from our dogs, cats, and horses. When my cat is especially pleased about sitting next to me, he "brushes the fur" on my hand, although he can sense that there is no fur there. This kind of communication happens among them and with us.

What is the kind of experiencing that language involves, which the animals do not have? Let me call it "aboutness."

For example, Mary lives alone with her cat. When Mary takes her suitcase off the shelf, her cat becomes sad. The cat knows it means Mary is going on a trip soon, and will leave the cat alone for some days. But if Mary is only storing some things in the suitcase, there is no way to tell this to the cat except by putting the actual suitcase back on the shelf.

In animal experiencing there is nothing which is only an "about," rather than being the behavior which is actually is. Animals don't respond to pictures as mere pictures. One cannot shift to a behavior context without actually being in it.

However, there are animal behaviors which come very close to such a shift. They are called "animal gestures" or "animal rituals." Certain special behaviors, often quite small in themselves, can bring about a major shift.

Sexual intercourse, fighting, nest-building, and other important behavior sequences can be initiated by certain postures and sounds on the part of another animal. When a male cat sees another, its tail gets thick and it hisses and growls. This either causes flight or fight-readying on the part of the other cat. The behaviors, postures, and sounds of each cat carry forward the other. In a mating dance one bird may display certain feathers, the design and color of which carry forward the other animal's intercourse-readying, which in turn affects the first, and so on into intercourse. One monkey's raising an arm to hit may carry forward the other's fight-readying, and fighting. In the fighting, when one monkey is ready for flight he turns his back and this stops the fighting sequence.

Among animals who live together in the same territory there is a social hierarchy. Each monkey turns his back when he sees those above him in the order, and receives this submissive gesture from all those below him. This animal ritual, so-called, *takes the place of* the fighting sequence. Only the last bit of fighting sequence occurs, and obviates the fighting. However, if the lower monkey fails to turn his back, then fighting does occur. The fighting sequence is implicit, even though it rarely occurs.

In these ways the higher animals, and especially the social ones, have a functional role for *some special way their bodies look or sound*, which drastically shifts the behavior context. That is why they are called "gestures" or "rituals." These small changes in body looks, moves, and sounds come very close to being something like symbols inasmuch as their small occurrence drastically shifts the behavior context, which is to say that they "mean" so much more than they are. Nevertheless they are just behaviors and do not constitute an "aboutness." The growl, the turning to run, the beginning to hit, are part of behavior sequences.

An animal "gesture" can make quite a major difference. The shift in the body that is involved in getting ready to fight, for example, is a major bodily shift. There is nothing slight or subtle about the changes in circulation, muscles, posture, and other bodily aspects in such a major shift. The whole behavior space is suddenly shifted by such a gesture, and this is also a major bodily (evev) shift.

Some very small single movements or ways the body can look or sound can now make very big differences, for instance between fighting and not fighting.

(b) The dance

Let us suppose that two monkeys meet, but neither turns its back, and yet the fighting sequence doesn't form (either because it cannot, for some reason—say there is a river between them—or because something new *does* form).

Let us imagine, instead of either fighting or back-turning, that the initial "threat gesture" repeats, only slightly differently. The "threat gesture" is the relevanting first bit of the fighting sequence. That bit is also a major bodily shift, fight-readying. (As usual in our schematic, if a first bit has happened, the implying of the whole sequence is altered. If the rest of the sequence doesn't occur, it is still implied. So it begins to happen again, if it can begin. Hence the first bit keeps recurring, always in an altered way.)

The "threat gesture" had a large-body-shifting effect. If this "gesture," this way the body looks and sounds and moves its arm, is now somewhat different, the effect on the other monkey will also be different. That will alter that monkey's bodylook, sound, and movement somewhat. This, in turn, will carry the first monkey forward somewhat differently, and so on.

We get a sequence of slightly different *versions* of the same "gesture." I call this *a dance*. (It is a new kind of versioning sequence.)

The effect of one monkey on the other, each time, is a version of the major shift in the body (evev and its behavior context) which such "gestures" already have in animal behavior. A change in such a "gesture" would have a changed effect. Each monkey changes this shift in the other's body. Instead of one shift, we get first that shift and then a whole string of versions of how that shift is. A somewhat different bodylook and sound on the body of each makes for a somewhat different body-evev in the other, and hence a different bodylook and sound.

This elaboration of the "gesture" into a whole string is *a pause* in the usual behavior. The behavior context is not cfed. Instead of fighting, or back-turning, this string of versions keeps the behavior context the same.

In this new sequence each bodylook is a version of the same behavior context. The behavior context is not changed as it would be in behavior. For instance, fighting is focally implied, but fighting is not occurring. It continues to be implied. The behavior context continues to be the one that implies fighting. The new sequence is not behavior; it does not change the behavior context as a behavior sequence would. The new sequence is a string of versions of the (otherwise) unchanged behavior context.

The new sequence is a string of renditions of the behavior context in terms of how-the-body-looks-in-that-behavior-context. The new sequence is a string of bodylook renditions of the same behavior context.

Just as behavior was a detour within body-process, so now this dance is a detour within behavior; it pauses (is a string of versions of) the same body-process stoppage and the same behavior context.

(c) Representation

In this sequence there is a new kind of carrying forward, a new relation: the bodylook (let me use that word to include sound and movement) of the other is a bodylook rendition of how this one's body just was.

A new use of the word "recognize" fits here. (Schematically, this is a re-re-recognition, since we used the word twice already; we used "recognize" in III, and "re-recognize" in VI.) The body recognizes the other's look as how it itself just was. But this recognition is made *by* the sequence, and is a relationship within the sequence. The bodily expression now cfs. This recognition is expression (without quotation marks, not too early now).

We are not assuming that a body would know or sense what it looks like, and see the likeness on another body. Just the opposite. Animals exhibit looks and sounds that we humans recognize, but which are not recognized among the animals. In our new sequence the *other's* bodylook first carries the body forward. Thereby a given way the body is comes to imply such a sequence.

Before the new sequence forms, most of the characteristic body-looks and sounds have no function. Only some few specific bodylooks are "animal gestures," but even these do not form a kind of sequence of their own. They merely relevant behavior. Only now is there a sequence of bodylooks.

The bodylooks are whatever the body looks like in the given behavior context, only now there is a string of versions of this.

The human observer could have said, before the sequence ever formed, that the way the animal looks is expressive and characteristic of that behavior context. But now, the bodylook in that behavior context carries the animals themselves into a sequence.

The behavior context is thus rendered or represented in terms of bodylooks. We can say that the bodylooks are *symbols* of being in that behavior context. They are not "conventional symbols" arbitrarily using just this look or sound or movement to mark just this behavior context. Rather, there is an inherent organismic bodily relationship between the bodylooks and the behavior context they render. They are (versions of) how that species' body happens to look and sound and move *in that behavior context.*

Bodylooks are a new kind of environment that renders the bodily evev, carries it forward into the next bodily way of being with *its* bodylook. In this sequence each bodylook implies the next. More exactly: *each bodylook is the look of a bodily evev which implies the next bodylook.* When that next bodylook occurs on the other's body, it occurs into this implying. But this implying is generated by the sequence. At first the sequence is cfed by the variations of the relevanting shift. Once it occurs, the sequence *finds itself* with this new relationship. Each bodylook is how the other's body *just was.* Only the sequence gives the bodily evev an implying of bodylooks.

There is now a way of feeling, having, sequencing, an unchanged behavior context. It can be had without being cfed. Before, there were only the behavior context changes as perception (open cycle) and as feeling (body-changes). Now there is a new kind of perception, the bodylook sequence (how the body looks in that behavior context), and a new string of body-changes (feeling). There is a new kind of environment and a new kind of rendering.

But in ordinary behavior the body feels the behavior context. It perceives how it moved. Is this not a feeling *of,* and a perception *of* its behavior? Only in a "too early" sense of "of." Behavior is felt only in-behaving itself.

Now, for the first time we can use the word "of" or "about." The dance is *about* the fight-implying behavior context. The dance is not a fighting, nor a fight-readying, nor a fight-ending. It is not among the behavior sequences that make up the context, but about it.

A time-span is made during which the fight-context is sequenced about, rather than in.

Here emerges empathy, representation, likeness, universality, symbol, meaning, picture, and a good deal more. Let us take these up slowly.

The human aspects we are concerned about develop very much further, of course. This rudimentary schematic sequence gives us grounds for conceptualizing the later developments.

Empathy is often talked about as if I naturally somehow know what my own body looks like when I feel a certain way. Then, when I see someone else looking that way, I assume that they feel as I do, when I look that way. This view fails to wonder how I can know what my body looks like, considering that I rarely see my own body from the outside. Since G. H. Mead, many others have also reversed this order. First others respond to how I look, and only thereby does my body feeling come to imply a look.

Empathy comes first, that is to say: first there is a bodily shift made by how *another* body looks. My body thereby comes to imply another's looks, and only then does my body imply its own looks. (We will have to examine this lone implying further. Right now only the sequence with another is implied.)

This sequence first generates the likeness between the other's body and my own. Our bodies are alike, but this fact appears to the developed human en#1 observer. That observer could always have said that the species' members have bodies that look alike. But only now, for the first time, are we making concepts with which to understand how the human observer can notice, have, sense, *likeness.* Representation is born. But we have not yet gone far with this. We have only shown how a bodylook can come to be *had* in a sequence of its own, rather than a relevanting behavior.

A *likeness*, a picture, a pattern, something that is here *and* there, is a universal, a kind. But we will have to understand this much more clearly and further.

Looks as looks are now implied and carry forward. They are *had*, sequenced. A look, we might say, is no concrete thing. What is it, after all? These two bodies are of the same kind, have the same kind of look, they look *like* that . . . when they are in that behavior context.

(d) Doubling

On the one hand, our new sequence is a rendering of the behavior context, which is thereby had, felt, sequenced (continues to imply the next behavior that isn't happening). In this respect the new sequence is *about* the behavior context.

On the other hand, the new sequence is itself a special kind of behaving, a kind of moving around, or raising an arm or other limbs, and throat muscles.

Each bit *is* a kind of behaving and also *represents* (renders in bodylook) a behavior context.

Taking it as itself, behavior, the sequence requires the same open cycle feedback as any behavior sequence. For example, the dance would stop at the edge of a cliff, or move around a boulder.

Every bit of our new sequence is doubled—it is two kinds of carrying forward: the VI type and our new bodylook VII type. I call this *doubling*.

On its behavior side our new sequence is a special case. First of all it seems rather simple—just certain movements, gestures, and sounds. Compared to complex behavior (e.g., nesting, tracking, etc.), gesture sequences can be very simple: just turning the body, or moving the arm, or a face muscle.

But the seeming simplicity must not fool us. These movements are *doubled*, they version (they reconstitute, are the having of) the behavior context in each bit. The sequence is both a simple movement and versions of the major bodily shift which the "animal gesture" was (the relevanting of some behavior sequence). What is rendered is here, going on *in the body*, being shifted, even if we observers don't see the behavior context and the behavior sequences being implied. We see only the (sometimes simple) movements.

Behavior goes on in behavior space, a "filled" (we said) space consisting of all the implied behavior sequences. The simple gesture movements go on in *another space*, bodylook space, or gesture space or *simple movement space*. But this space is doubled. It is the doubled space of simple movements. The behavior context is not being changed as it would be in behaving. Rather, it is being versioned, rendered, sequenced, had, felt, while staying "the same." (Of course, this is also a major bodily change sequence, but not as behavior would cf the behavior context away into another behavior context.) We have generated a *symbolic space*, that is to say a double space, the space of movements that symbolize. The behavior context is versioned. Behavior is not going on. The movements do not, as movements, alter the implied behavior possibilities, the implicit behaviors, and the focally implied next behavior. *Therefore* these movements move in an *empty space*.

Pure movement exists now for the first time in our scheme, in what for the first time is an *empty space*, that is to say *a space of pure movements*. But we won't forget that this space of these sequences is doubled, it is also bodily the sequence of versions of the behavior context, the full space.

While the change made by the new kind of sequence isn't behavior, it is a bodily change. (*Later* we will remember this, when we understand that an initiation ritual, for example, really does *physically* change people into adults in a bodily way.) (This dance is not yet a ritual. See section a.) Similarly, healing rituals. Rituals (which we haven't yet defined) are not merely signs of something. For us, so far, a symbol sequence is bodily changes (a string of *versions of* the major kind of change which occurs when a behavior sequence is suddenly relevanted by an "animal gesture").

Our human being moves in a new simple movement space (three dimensions, just space and ground and the other's simple motions) *as well as* in the behavior-context in which the one turn was a fight-obviating gesture. The gesture-sequence occurs both *in* a simple movement-space and *in* the complex behavior context which it versions. The simple three-dimensional movement space derives from here. The monkey always turned in complex behavior space, not in the simple movement space which people can have, and in which they observe the monkey. The simple movement space (and thus most of the ways people have thought about behavior) is a human product, a result of the doubling sequence.

But this simple movement space is symbolic: simple movements version the behavior context. The sequence is a set of bodyshifts (feeling), which are versions of how the body is in that behavior context. This feeling, sequencing, and versioning is *a new way* of changing the "same" behavior context in all its complexity. A little motion of this kind is a string of versions of the powerful shift we noted, that an animal gesture makes.

This space is symbolic: a move of the arm *is* a feeling-versioning sequence of a whole behavior context and all its implicit sequences.

Raising the arm with the fist relevants fighting. The versioning sequence alters how fighting is implied. It alters the behavior context in a way behavior cannot do.

Think of yourself sitting in a meeting. It comes to a vote. By the simple raising of your arm you vote and perhaps alter your whole situation. Humans live very largely in terms of symbolic sequences. By signing your name in a certain spot you may alter your whole situation. These premature examples only show here that a behavior context can be altered by simple movements that are not physically related to it. Our dance sequence is the first kind of such a sequence. It does not yet provide any of these capacities. It forms only in the behavior context of which it is a versioning, and we don't yet know how it could form at any other place or time. It changes the behavior context in a new way, but we don't know what difference that makes; for example, if the dance versioned the fight-implying behavior context, we don't know how the fighting would be different. (It would still be implied; the behavior context is "the same" after the dance is over). But the new sequence has the doubled character; it is both its own kind of behaving and moving, and also each bit is a version of a behavior context that is not being behaved in. It is *about*.

How did we achieve this? It was with bodily expressive looks and sounds and moves, which *we* see in the animals, but most of which have no function among them. We took this as a new kind of rendering. What the complex body in a given behavior context looks like gives humans a new way to feel and have how they are in the behavior context.

(e) Expression

In VI, I defined "expression" in a too early way, along with "re-recognizing." Expression proper is at home here in VII. How the body is, in a given behavior context is expressed by the bodylooks and sounds and moves.

There is an inherent tie between body-in-behavior-context and bodylooks. For a given species the body looks just as it happens to look, and sounds as it does, in the given behavior context. This is not a system made up by anyone. (How symbols develop beyond this expressive relation we will see in VII-B.) Here it is important, in order to understand the relation between symbols and the body, how there is a symbolic relation in the body's own nature.

Expression always involves being carried forward. We cannot call something "expression" from an external point of view only. Beautiful ice patterns are expressive to us, who are carried forward by patterns, but not to the ice. The animals express quite a lot, but except for special behaviors, these carry only us forward. The animals do not express, therefore, to each other. What does carry them forward is that they behave with each other. Or you might say that for them behaving and expressing are not yet differentiated into two different levels.

We must therefore understand exactly how expressive patterns of bodylook come to carry us forward. Then we will be able to also look at other patterns, not only those that derived from bodylooks.

(f) The new kind of cf

The new sequence can be called a gesture sequence in the true sense (whereas animal "gesture" is in quotation marks, not really a gesture). The new sequence can also be called symboling, behavior-context-versioning. I called the first such sequence that ever developed a dance sequence.

Once such a sequence is implied, a body-evev implies the other's look and sound and moves, which, if it occurs on the other body, carries this one forward.

Each evev of the sequence also, of course, still implies the next behavior which is not happening.

The body goes through a string of versions of "the same" behavior context. Behavior and behavior context don't have such a string. It is a cfing rendition of the behavior context as versioned—not as before.

What can this mean? The body is already in VI sentient and conscious of how it behaves. But now this behavior context is each time repeated in a slightly different version of a bodylook. The behavior context's occurring is already sentient, felt, and now this new sequence is a string of such felt behavior context versions. These consist of bodylooks, not of the behavior context. The body, in this sequence, has feeling and perception of what it already feels and perceives, namely, its being in the behavior context. Oho! Our schematic has formed some concepts that can let us think about *selfconsciousness*!

Sentience in ordinary behavior is of course conscious. Feeling and perception are conscious. In behaving the body is conscious of the changes in its environment and in itself that are the behaving. The behavior context (the way behavior space is, just then) is bodily implied, and as carried forward it is felt.

And now there is a sequence about what is felt, a new string of body changes and environmental changes (the en is now the bodylooks) in which one sequences, has, feels . . . what one feels, namely, one's being in that behavior context.

Now to be very exact: it isn't right to say that the new sequence lets one feel about what one felt before. Exactly, the behavior context that one feels is not the one from before, but the one that is being versioned now. It is not *like* looking back and perceiving and feeling what was, but more exactly *the new sequence* is doubled. The new sequence reconstitutes "the same" behavior context, as a result of versioning, and not as remembered or looked back to.

What we are self-conscious *of* is not what was before but a new creation of the self-conscious sequence. "The same" behavior context across the new sequence is of course related to the behavior context before versioning, but it isn't some mysterious reflecting, like a mirror, on what was already there. It is a new product.

I would be unhappy if you take away from this only that through bodylooks a sequence can be about a behavior context. It is really about something quite new, "the same behavior context" that results from the symboling sequence itself. Symboling creates a new world, as is well known and will become clearly thinkable here. Right here this is only a technical difference; we don't as yet see how this versioned "same" context is profoundly different. But later when we do see, we will need to remember this technical point. What is really versioned is the versioned context that results from the versioning sequence.

Self-consciousness is not at all consciousness of literally what was there before, although we could not think about it without seeing the more exact relation in which versions of what was there make a new sequence from which a new "the same" falls out. What falls out? A pattern of bodylook . . . doubled with a (not directly perceived) behavior context. What is felt is doubled. The pattern is of the same behavior context.

The body is conscious *of* the versions *of* the behavior context. (There are two "of" relations.) It feels (over a time-span) the feel of being in that behavior context without cfing it (as behavior would). What could only be a bit in a feeling-change sequence in-behaving, is now "the same" over a string of versions. So there is a feel of the feeling in that context, which could not happen before. Only a sequence of body-changes can be felt, and in behavior such a bit was not felt except as it was cfed away into a different one.

In this schematic so far we have developed three kinds of occurring into the implying which just was: body-process; behavior; and now gesturing. In behavior the open cycle occurs and cfs by its version of what the body just was as b-en, how the body just changed or behaved. Gesturing is a pause in behaving. The bodylooks are a new kind of environmental rendering. When they occur they cf the body into feeling the behavior context it feels. Through this sequence and its bodylooks it feels itself feeling the behavior context.

The first animals who found themselves suddenly human in a versioning sequence must have had an exciting time of it, being self-conscious! Suddenly, in so moving each other, in so dancing, they were aware of being aware.

Of course this is only a thin scheme. So far we have only the beginnings of VII, and also in general concepts are just a scheme. I am not saying that this is all self-consciousness is. I am concerned with developing some concepts that can grasp some important aspects of how humans experience and think.

Here we have just become able to be exact about how symbols enable self-awareness. As cfing renditions they are the means, "the perceptions" of the sequence. Conversely, we can also say exactly how one can be aware of a symbol only in self-awareness.

Patterns carry forward a self-conscious process. Patterns cannot have an impact on us *as patterns* except by being about (something other than pattern), and they can do this only by carrying us forward, in a double way (both with this pattern, and also as a versioning of something). We feel ourselves feeling what it is about, and thus we feel ourselves feeling.

It will be clear here that self-consciousness is not, at least not to begin with, a consciousness of a self, as if the self were what we are conscious about. Rather, we are conscious of being conscious of whatever it is about.

There are special further developments in which we can perhaps employ the word "self" in a more usual way, but it will turn out to be very important to see that there is self-consciousness and a sense of self without there being an entity, a content, separate from other contents, that is said to be the self.

All this is too early for our rudimentary scheme, and yet it must be said here, because the concepts that will clarify and explicate the more complex developments *in a new way*, are being fashioned right here *in this new way*.

Of course, since we respond to patterns, we see them everywhere, and we explain much with them. But that is a question we must ask: why do patterns work as explanatory? Why can we predict nature by means of patterns? We will answer that question in VII-B. Here we are conceptualizing a way to think about how patterns carry our bodies forward and are also *about*. And we have seen the doubled carrying forward that this involves.

Later derivatives might look like a floating symbol related to some denotation out there that it is about. We have to grasp first how a symbol, here a pattern, comes to have a power to be about, and to have this power for our bodies.

We will become even more exact in the next section.

So far our humans are human and self-conscious only in an interaction between at least two of them. The capacity to supply one's own bodylook cfing comes later.

(g) Pictures

The bodylook version is a kind of picture of the behavior context. Let me now try to say what a picture really is, and why a picture can only occur in VII.

Animals don't respond to pictures of something. The cat will either treat the picture of a cat as a piece of cardboard to sit on or to shove with its paw, or else, if the cat does recognize the pictured cat, it will respond to it as to a real present cat. (There may or may not be some very few exceptions in chimpanzees and then only with human training. I don't insist that the human/animal division is a sharp line; it might be a gradation.) To respond to a picture as a picture is to live an aboutness. A picture is *of* something that need not be present. To respond to a picture is different than to behave at the object pictured as if it were present.

When humans gesture, they do it in the versioned behavior context. It need not be physically present (but it is present in the new VII sense of being versioned). Humans can bring a behavior context about by versioning—they don't need it to be present literally. Since we have our bodies with us, we can make the sounds, moves, and looks anytime and thereby put ourselves into that behavior context. It is the bodylooks that do the cfing (and not the physical behavior context being versioned).

But can't we find animal behaviors done with the bodylook?

The ethologist studying animals finds that when one bird spreads its wings and displays a certain red feather the other animal goes into the mating dance. This could happen anytime the ethologist spreads the other animal's wings or even displays a picture of such a wing with the red feather on it. Nevertheless, the dancing animal is not expressing *about* the sexual intercourse context but is behaving in one, and it is bodily getting ready to engage in intercourse. Even if the ethologist shows only a picture, the animal is not responding to a picture. There is no such level of responding, and of course the red feathers are not normally displayed except in a behavior context leading to sexual intercourse. Thus the fact is artificial (observed by us in the sense of en#1) that the mating dance could be done at any time and in the absence of the sexual behavior context.

Traditional philosophy constructed human reality out of rational structuring and bits of sensation. This meant that since animals don't have rational structure (which was conceived of as floating forms imposed), they had to be mere machines. We find it hard to imagine how those philosophers reconciled this basic view of reality with their experience of animals. But, today, existential and phenomenological philosophy does nearly the same. There are two basic kinds of beings, humans with their possibility-sketching, and things which are mere results. I call it a "city philosophy," nothing but people and stones. But neither human reason nor human life-projecting meets Being for the first time. The human is embedded in nature (and not at all a separate alienated pole, though we may think of ourselves that way). Reason and language are embedded in behavior and the body.

How animals are thought about is only a sign of truth or error, much as any other blatant error would lead one to reconsider.

Here it is clear that for animals there are the two levels of body-process and behavior sequences, but not yet the "aboutness" level. Although the aboutness level radically remakes the world, nevertheless there is an important way in which the higher animals have much of what we have but without the distinction. I have already shown that aboutness is not at all adding a mere reflecting, as though animals felt, but were not aware of feeling. One cannot feel except as a doubled feeling of.

For example, animals have empathy but it isn't on a separate "about" level. The animal will sense your mood and relate to you in it (but not about it).

The same answer needs to be given about particulars and universals in animals. (We will change the meaning of those terms drastically, anyway, in VIII.) Animals could be said to treat everything as universals, every tree the same way. Or one can say that animals don't respond to a class as such, but always only to this, here. The distinction doesn't exist yet. The animal mother's bodily changes, which she feels when she runs to her young (or wants to), are not all that different from ours.

So it would be wrong to say flatly that a cat cannot feel about something that is absent. It is true that the male cat will either get angry (ready to fight), right now, if there is another male cat here, or the fight-readying will subside. The cat cannot sit at home and nurse its anger, as we can, by reconstituting a situation symbolically, and feeling in it.

But a day later, coming to the same spot where that other cat was, our cat will sniff and search. It *behaves* this looking for that cat, it is not separately talking *about* that cat. And neither we nor cats can gesture to our cat about that other cat.

Again here, shall we say that the cat relates only to a present cat, looked for now, or to the cat of yesterday who isn't here? It is an inapplicable distinction, there are not different levels.

Similarly, the fight-inducing "animal gesture" is not "about," it is behaving.

(h) Seens and heards

Behavior space now includes some sequences with pauses (dance, gesturing) in them.

When an object relevants such a sequence, and the other humans aren't there to form it with, the gestural pause is focally implied and cannot occur. The implied gestural sequence would function implicitly in whatever does occur.

Say the first bit occurs, and then the sequence is still mostly implied, and if it cannot form, the first bit might occur again somewhat differently.

A new gestural sequence forms with the object, and pauses the behavior with it. It might be much or little, opening parts or something further.

VII-B will be more exact about this development. I must first let these developments develop so that they will form a cluster of concepts. As we then sharpen these, they will, in VII-B, enable us to be more exact about this development.

These gestures might be perhaps some grunts, or moves of the arm, or both, or some bit of dance. The object has occurred into this gesture-implying, and in the sequence that forms, the object is also perceived differently. Now it falls out not only from the behavior, but also from the gesturing (the bodylook-bodylook carrying forward). What sort of object falls out from a double sequence? What of the object carries forward a bodylook sequence? The object carries forward by its look, its sound, and its simple movement if it has any.

For the first time an object has a look, a sound, or just a movement, that is to say the humans have an object's look, sound, or movement.

The gestural sequence is doubled, so the object is still the behavior object, but in this sequence it carries forward by its look. I call such a doubled object a *seen* (for short, since it includes heard, moved, etc.).

The sequence thus has both the human's own looks, sounds and moves, and the object's, for its perceptual side.

Gestures are patterns. Such a look or sound is also a pattern. We shall say much more about patterns soon.

I don't know if this swiftly happens with all objects, or if at first such a seen sequence would form only with a special object. If the latter, our monkey who is human so far only during the dance would find this object very precious. The object would have the power to turn our monkey intermittently human again. It would certainly be a highly prized object.

There is now self-consciousness of the object, even when alone.

The object's look is symbolic. The object's look cfs in symbolic space, like the dancer. The look is a pattern in empty space.

One can now see an object as that kind of object (belonging to that behavior context) without behaving.

The object can be seen, sequenced, felt, for what it is in behaving, without behaving. (This includes: without behavior-readying which, for us, is also behaving.) The object is seen *as* that kind. (More about kinds shortly.)

(i) Action

As these seen-sequences (they are seen + gesturing sequences) multiply, behavior space now has many sequences that have seen-gesture pauses in them. Whether actually sequenced or not, they are implicit and carried forward indirectly in behavior. The self-consciousness-pauses are implicit along with the sequences they are in. As behavior carries forward, it implicitly carries them forward (it carries forward the evevs that include them). Such behavior is *implicitly self-conscious*. I call it *action*. Behavior contexts with such pauses are *situations*.

Most action will include some occurring versioning sequences. Most action will thus be paused at times and at these times it is explicitly self-conscious; at other times implicitly so.

(j) Universals (kinds)

(j-1) Separate senses

A seen is a pattern. It is not the food (say the object is food) but its look and sound. One cannot feed on a look or a sound. At first a seen does not resume behavior and is not sequenced in behavior, only gesturing. The seen is (for example) the configuration *of* the food. A seen is *of*. It is *about*. It is a versioning. A seen is a new kind of object, a kind.

The separation of the different senses (vision, hearing, smell) arises here. It is a symbolic product. Behaviorally the separation does not exist. No animal behaves with a visualness, or a sounding. Behavior is always with the bird or the cat. Only the human observer who can already separate and respond to visuals and sounds *as such* can notice that the bird reacts to *the outline shape* of the cat's head, or that the cat responds to the *sound* of a bird. The bird reacts to a cat, and the cat to a bird.

For example, ethologists find that the male of a certain species of small fish fights when it sees the red dot on the side of another male. The ethologist suspends a little white piece of cardboard with a red dot on it from a toothpick, and when the fish sees this it immediately begins fighting behavior. Doesn't this show that the fish do respond to a configuration of just color? But it is the ethologist who has discovered a just color configuration. For the fish it is another fish, not a red circle. (See later, on how scientific patterns are valid in nature.)

Only humans can hear "a sound" or see something that is only visual. To be only visual it must be a picture; even if it is the present object's look, or sound, it is taken as look, or sound. Of course something purely visual or auditory doesn't exist! A disjunction is made between, say the piece of cardboard which does exist, and the look of a person or a tree which is pictured.

The purely visual, or the sound, the smell—these are symbolic products, that is to say, they are possible only after, and because of, a having, sequencing, in a way that is not behaving—just as we don't behave with the mere look of a tree. We don't climb the look of a tree. Of course, once there is the having of a look, then the tree we climb also has the tree-look. We have developed concepts for the kind of sequence that is the having of a look, something purely visual. Only thereby does it become possible to divide the senses, and consider sounds as separate from sights and from smells, because only thereby are there sounds, sights, and smells.[1]

(j-2) Kinds

A visual, or a sounding (a seen)—these are universals. They are the sound *of* . . . or the look *of* . . . We also say this is what the object looks or sounds *like.* Or we say it has the look of *a* tree, or the sound of *a* bird, or *a* rifle.

Bodylooks and objects' seens are both symbolic *of* behavior contexts (and contexts are a mesh of mutually implying sequences, one of them focal).

The bodylook is how the human body looks in that *kind* of behavior context.

But we have not yet shown how a kind, or a likeness, might be sequenced and had as such. We won't be able to do that until VII-B. The seen is a looklike, but it doesn't enable the human to think (have, feel, sequence) the class of objects that look like that. The seen, the pattern, is a kind of universal, but for now we have only shown that a pattern can carry forward, that the humans can see and hear patterns. I will explain this difference exactly now.

(j-3) Three universals

A "universal" is something that "applies" in many "instances." To understand what a universal is we must also ask what an instance is.

We have agreed not to assume a reality that is neatly cut into classifications so that particulars are already grouped under class-definitions called "universals." Indeed, when we understand the derivation of all this, we will also think about it very differently indeed.

We are cutting deeper into the grounds of thinking.

How are events or things made in such a way that they fit "under" universals? What makes something an "instance"?

The history of philosophy from Plato on has much discussion of this question. Particulars "participate" in universals, Plato said, with a good deal of discussion of what that relation is. Particulars "imitate" universal forms, he also said. Aristotle, who established this schema, also viewed the highest cause as one that is "imitated" (see, e.g., *Ethics* 7.13, 1153b31–32). Kant viewed it as a question of grouping together or unifying. He only gave a formal account of how objects are made with reason's unifying, which is then also the way objects can be grouped. We want to grasp what kinds are, together with what instances of kinds are.

I call the kind of universals to which we are accustomed "third universals," or simply "thirds." Two more basic kinds must be understood, or we can't grasp what is involved in these usual ones.

The usual universal, for example a word (also a more technically structured concept), is used *as such*, and with its use some particular situation is thereby changed, or some particular object is reached. It seems that the universal could occur alone, without applying to a particular, though this would be very odd. (For instance, why would one say a word just alone? To illustrate a point in philosophy? To define the word? There is always a particular context as well as the universal.)

At any rate, the usual universals can actually occur, they can be had, sequenced *as such* (together with the particular). Such universals can *also function implicitly,* for instance when we act with a particular object, knowing it for the kind of thing it is, without thinking or saying that kind as such.

The two more primitive "universals" I want to discuss do not happen as such, as universals. When they actually occur, they don't function as universals. They function as universals *only implicitly.*

A new bodylook versioning or "new expression" (the dance sequence) is a "first universal." It forms in a behavior context. But then it functions *implicitly* in the formation of many seen sequences (gestures during action, and patterns of objects that carry forward). A whole cluster of such "second sequences" forms, in all of which the "first sequence" *applies.* Of course this is an odd (a too early) use of the word "applying." I call it "original applying."

But why call the new expression dance sequence a universal at all? I do so because it is the first step on the way to the usual universals. It is a pattern sequence and it is *the same sequence functioning in many different instances.*

We are now able to think just about this aspect of universals and particulars, how there is an *internal* relation between many different instances, and also between each of these and some same single sequence.

But this is so only because that single sequence has functioned *in the formation* of the many instances.

The sequence can of course also occur itself, and has. But when it occurs, it does not, as yet, function as what is similar in these different instances.

The many instances are different from each other. Each object has its own different pattern and gestures made with it. *We* could sort out the recurringly same objects, and separate them from the different ones. To do that we would use our capacity to sequence similarities as such, third universals.

The dance functions implicitly in the formation of the many different patterns of objects. The similarity of a given group (of instances that we would call "the same") is not the dance. It is a sequence *we* can have. We don't yet understand how we observers are able to do that, and now we are getting close to the point where we will be able to understand it. So we are not now blindly going to assume universals as commonalities *externally imposed* by observers on particulars. Instead, we want to grasp the *internal* relation among particulars that make them all instances, and their internal relation to the universal of which they are instances.

To understand this, we must grasp how these instances are made by, and with, the universal. We have done that. We have seen how a new formation can carry forward in a new way, the implying for an expression sequence that cannot, just then, occur. The expression sequence functions implicitly in the formation of the instance.

We thus have a "first" kind of universal, one which functions implicitly, and "*applies*" as it functions in the formation of what now occurs.

We saw there that we must not assume already-cut formed likenesses that determine how the past functions in the present. If that were so, the present could only be a rearrangement of the past, and the past could not have occurred at all (except as rearranging its past, and so on). We saw that a past is something that functions implicitly in a new way, in the occurring of a present. That is how past experience functions as it "applies." The applying is newly made.

We see the creation of instances in this kind of applying. The dance sequence functions implicitly to help form a kind of instance of itself as applying. All past experience does this, but the dance sequence is a pattern sequence. So a pattern sequence has newly applied to generate patterns of objects, and further gestures. These have in them the implicit functioning of the dance sequence patterns.

I call seens "second universals." They are still not the ones we are used to. Those will be called "thirds."

Instances and universals must be made together, or at least grasped together.

Our likenesses here are developing in an odd order—we have (to think of it in the old way) instances of a commonality that hasn't yet itself developed. Universals used to be thought of as commonalities. By the time we develop these, you will see that commonality is a too-poor way of thinking of them. Here now the seens are like the dance sequences, but there is as yet no way to sequence their likeness as such. They are not literally alike, but different formations from the same implied bodylook sequence. Their commonality has never formed as such, and wouldn't be the dance sequence exactly, even if we knew how likeness-as-such could be sequenced and had.

Without forming as a likeness as such, the patterns of objects and gestures are made as instances of an originally applying "first universal."

This is an instance of what, in Gendlin 1997a, I called "the reversal of the usual order" (which is really backwards). Metaphors do not depend on preexisting likeness; rather, a metaphor creates a new likeness. In metaphors such a likeness is a new third. Even so, we can be more exact about this formation now.

The metaphor creates the likeness with something else (the old literal meaning of the words) which functions in the new formation in this new and different context.

People want to think that a likeness, a third, is already in existence, so that one merely compares externally and notices the similarity without changing anything.

Instead, we see that something can function in the formation of something else, and thereby an *internal* relationship can come to be, between the new formation and what functions in it.

We also see here that a likeness need not first occur in many places, in order to be externally noticed, and become a likeness. Any pattern is always already a look-like, a sound-like, a configuration, a pattern— something that has already come loose from the particular behavior-object. A pattern is already a picture, quite without anyone's external comparing as yet. It need not yet be a commonality; it is enough if it occurs once. A pattern is always *a pattern of . . .*

So far we have grasped this "of" (as the having of versions of a behavior-context via the sequence of bodylooks, how the body looks in that context).

We have also grasped how such patterns then function implicitly in the formation of the patterns of objects and gestures. In seen-formation, the same bodylook patterns which belong to one context now function implicitly in many other contexts. The patterns are all variations of how the body looks in the one context, so the patterns are no longer expressive in these other contexts.

All patterns are likenesses. And yet, the kind of likeness we think of, the commonality as such, has not yet formed. *Even without it,* the many contexts and their patterns are internally related to each other, and to the "first" expression sequence.

The groundwork is now laid for the kind of sequence that would carry forward a whole kind, a whole class, and would be the having of the likeness as such, if only we knew how such a sequence would actually form.

Our scheme lets us think clearly, for the first time, about this major question.

In order that particular objects and situations be grouped "under" some rubric of comparison or likeness, the objects must be re-created so, they must be patterned. It cannot be that they are a lot of separate objects with traits, which are then grouped by someone from outside, who comes with grouping-forms. That mysterious person, and that application, must be understood.

Objects don't remain the same, as if they are merely being compared and classified, unbeknownst to themselves, as if they were simply fenced in, or cross-indexed by floating ghostly abstractions. It has seemed so, because people put those universals first, which are really third. Before they can emerge, a kind of universal must be *created* with which the patterned things are re-recreated.

Kant saw that there must be an inherent reason why our forms apply to objects necessarily. He saw that the universal forms must have gone into the very making of the objects, and in this requirement he has to be right. But he simply insisted the commonalities, the grouping-forms (the thirds) into the objects. Since he knew what he was doing, he realized that this meant objects that exist only for an externally imposing comparer and grouper, the observer. He attributed the forms to "the human mind" and let it go at that. (The "mysterious depths of the human imagination.")

We are concerned with grasping this more deeply. The commonalities of judgments (all mortals, all cats, etc.) are to be distinguished from the "first" and "second" kinds of universals. Before likeness is had *as such*, pattern or likeness can be in two more basic ways, as body-expression and the way objects look, once humans are carried forward by such bodylook expression.

Kant created the world *de novo* out of an encounter between reason-forms and sense bits. That is a kind of creation myth in which the mature philosopher's mind meets sense bits and they create the world together.

We do not need to say that the tree is made with grouping-forms, even though *we* already have these when we begin to philosophize. We see that patterns are an elaborate development, not simply assumed unifiers like paper clips or fence-enclosures. A pattern is symbolic, it is a way of versioning and having (feeling, sequencing) a complex situation (behavior context) by a simple movement. The behavior objects now carry forward human simple-movement sequences in empty space. The objects are remade, so that they have their own doubling patterns.

The object comes into human pattern space. More exactly: it *is* fallen out from many sequences and these have now acquired pattern-sequences as pauses in them. The object carries these forward as it can— with what thereby comes to be as *its* pattern or likeness. Given human bodylook pattern sequences carrying forward, the object then has its own pattern (which is not at all arbitrary. It is the look of that object, once patterns can cf).

(j-4) The pre-formed implicit (type a)

There is not yet a way of sequencing likenesses as "such." But these likenesses are already formed, only not as such. (Many more will form too, of course.) They are implicit. Something can be implicit in two ways: implicit *type a* will refer to what is already formed but never as yet sequenced. I call it pre-formed, or "type a."

Implicit *type b* will mean already sequenced.

A type-a-implicit sequence functions implicitly in certain ways, even though as yet it has never formed. Let us use a concrete example.

In flying into the wind, a bird perceives the wind but not "*the sound of*" the wind. Sounds, sights, temperature, have not been separated. The wind is the fallen-out in each of the mutually implicit behavior sequences.

When seens develop, the human can hear *the sound of* the wind, separately, as a sound-pattern. Sitting somewhere out of the wind, the mere sound of the wind can be heard. That human can also look up and see the sheer patterns of clouds. The tree now has a look quite apart from behaving with the tree at all.

In the formation of the wind-sound, cloud-pattern, and tree-look the human bodylooks functioned implicitly. Into the implicit functioning of human moaning and singing occurs the wind, and now carries forward with *its* sound. Into the simple movement space of human bodylook expression the tree comes and has its look of spreading and reaching. Clouds now have patterns.

But it is *not* the case that these humans as yet sequence (have, feel) the likeness between human moaning and the wind, or human reaching and the tree. Yet the patterns of wind and tree were made with the implicit functioning of the human patterns.

Later on there will be a sequence of having the likeness. Then the wind can sound like someone moaning, and the clouds can look like people. Right now the wind sounds like the wind, and the clouds have cloud patterns.

Another way to put it: the human moan occurs in one action context (situation), and the wind-sound occurs in a different action context. There is as yet no such context as "sequencing human moaning but in the wind-context" or "seeing human figures, but in the clouds." For this to be had, there must be a way to be in one context while really in another. We must exactly see this basic human capacity to do that, and we have not yet done so.

The *implicit* functioning of the dance in the generating of the seens has made the likeness, *we* can say. But is the likeness already there? No, it isn't there, it is a *type-a* implicit.

(k) Action and gesturing

So far, action and gesturing are distinct. Each goes on with the sequences of the other functioning implicitly. This means that any elaboration of one affects the other.

A new dance (a first universal or "first sequence"), when it then functions implicitly, makes for a whole gamut of new or altered seens and gesture-pauses in action. When a new dance again versions some behavior context, the above developments are part of the behavior context (action context). The new dance versions all that, and is therefore influenced by the developments of action.

In the next section we will see that action is influenced by more than only gestural pauses, and also in VII-B this distinction will change.

But even here we see a mutual influence.

A new dance is a new first universal. The many developments from it are a whole cluster of "second sequences" (or changes in sequences that were extant). Then the development would cease until a new first sequence provided a new type of pattern dimension for a new gamut of developments.

Let us leave this overly simple, until we can work with it and develop more concepts. Then we will return to make it much more exact.

This mutual relation, in a very different way, can still be seen today. Does art provide new dimensions of seeing and hearing, which then enable us to develop a host of ordinary things along new designs? Certainly yes. Does art mirror the already extant things, our machine age for example, and our ways of living? Also certainly yes. Art still versions what is, and yet also thereby generates *new expression patterns*. Later we will see how that is different from this rudimentary stage.

A layering develops, many tiers of new first dance, cluster of changes, and again new first dance. This layering removes the patterning more and more from recognizable human expressions as they would naturally be part of an original bodily expression. I will explain this better later.

(l) Slotted rituals

Although animal behavior sequences form freshly (they are not taken from a repertoire), an observer could notice that certain gestures form in certain junctures. Similarly, a dance, and also the gestural pauses in the midst of action, often form at certain junctures. Although they are pauses and don't cf action-contexts, the action doesn't proceed until after they form. I call such gesture sequences "slotted."

Such a gesture sequence enables the action to proceed. (It is a detour in behavior, just as behavior was a detour in body-process.) Slotted gestural sequences and dances are *rituals*.

Not all gestural pauses are slotted; some form only once, or differently each time.

The dances function in generating a whole gamut of cultural forms. We can think with some clarity now about how a ritual generates a cultural context (as has often been said).

We also call "ritual" those pauses before or in the midst of action, without which action no longer proceeds. These are seemingly unnecessary elaborations without which one does not eat, have sexual intercourse, or sleep, etc. These are not, as they might be today, just extras. They enable a physical change, a bodily change without which the rest of the action is not focally implied and would not form.

We see here how, at least at this early stage, an initiation ritual, for example, changes one bodily into an adult, and without it that would not happen in the same way.

Even we today might have our appetite spoiled if certain cultural forms are not observed first, and then we could not eat, or at least not equally well.

We are working through with a mesh of sequences, ways of being carried forward, implied *by the body*. We can think about this implicitly functioning mesh.

On the other hand, those who see ritual not as creative of culture, but as mirroring the kinship structure and the modes of hunting, and so on, are right too, as each new dance is a string of versions of the action contexts. But we recall that these versions are bodily moves, only symbols of the action contexts. Nevertheless bodies who perform certain actions would then also dance and bodily express differently. The relation is through the body, not a borrowing of forms or patterns directly.

Rituals as first dances can be understood as generative or, when they recur, as re-generative of cultural forms.

Are these rituals "spontaneous" or "very mechanical" and routined? Both. The ambiguity comes from our use of the word "spontaneous," which means both "without deliberation directly from the body" and also "unforced." In this double meaning lies hidden one modern longing for action that will be as full-bodied (fully cfing) and another modern longing for individual novelty and creativity. Indeed, it is going to be one of our questions, just what a "new expression," a "new first sequence" for us today would be. For reasons that will appear in VII-B, it can no longer be a dance or a work of art that re-creates the whole cultural mesh.

The rituals we are discussing were majorly cfing and full-bodied, compared to current cultural action. But *we* would think them very rigid, if we observed them. They must have happened mostly just so—not because one obeyed rules, but because they formed, by recurrent causation, in the same way, though quite freshly. Both action and gesture would strike us as highly fixed, even though great elaboration has developed, compared to animal behavior.

The capacity to stop and *deliberately* do something else than always forms has not yet developed. The pauses in action, and the capacity to have (feel, sequence) action-contexts, are one ingredient of the capacity to act deliberately. But these pauses still form freshly; they cannot yet be called in, or *used*, as it were, to think and decide to do something else.

At what point in these developments language begins and just what it adds, we will see in VII-B. Right now we cannot say.

So far we have kept action and gesturing distinct, the latter being pauses in the former. But it is obvious that action cannot remain unaffected by the fact that every action-object also implies seen sequences.

(m) Making and images

Animals make things, nests, beehives, spider webs, etc. But humans make by rearranging the patterns of things.

The highest apes can barely put one stick into the hollowed-out end of another stick, to reach a banana. They are not carried forward by the patterns of things. (There is a gradation here too, but no *separate* pattern sequencing.)

We don't want just to announce that humans can do that, we want to understand it.

We can already think of the human way to pause behavior, to have (feel, sequence) the action-context by gesturing.

We can also think clearly how objects come to cf our pattern-implying and so become themselves patterned.

We understood how pure visuals, pure sounds and movement *patterns come loose*, so to speak, from the behavior objects, and can be sequenced and had.

The patterns can form sequences which the behavior-objects could not (and the action-objects cannot either). The tree-pattern is sequenced in many ways that the tree is not.

But we will not simply say that humans can *imagine* the object looking very different from how it now is in front of them. That is what we wish to understand.

We formulated (in VI) the concept of "kination," realizing clearly there that behavior space is wider than what appears in a physicalist sense before the animal. It includes the space behind, since it is the body's implying of the mutually implicit behavior sequences. Turning back and backing up are among such sequences, along with what else might be behaved after that. This derived a kind of imagination for us which we called "kination." We thus transcended the traditional split between perception and imagination. There is no great difference whether something is presently impinging on sense organs or not, if it is in the behavior-possibilities-space.

Once pattern-cfing objects are part of action, the sufficiently long stick is focally implied, if the available sticks are too short. A stick (that is to say, anything with that pattern) is focally implied, if something were too far to reach. The focally implied pattern functions in whatever else one perceives. One looks up into a tree and sees one's stick there, one pulls it down and tears off the leaves and extra branches.

At first, such making develops slowly, since only few patterns have formed. As more form, making accelerates.

So we have a second definition of imagining, in addition to kination (the senses were not yet distinguishable in kination). Rather, in addition, we have the capacity to cf and focally imply patterns, that is to say visual configurations, sound configurations, movement patterns.

The patterns of things and of human movements are of course related. The thing carries forward implicit human sequences, and does so with its own pattern. It has a visual, auditory, or movement pattern only as it does so.

Thus we can gesture a stick, either by moving as if we had one in our hands, or by extending our hands and implying the shape of a stick. Imaging in this sense is pattern-cfing. Patterns are never real, anyway, as if they were just there, physically, alone. Seens are inherently images in this sense.

(n) Fresh formation of sequences and tools

Making is a kind of gestural pause in action. One is not reaching for the bananas while making a stick. Or if the stick is for walking, one is not walking while making it. Making requires pausing action, that is to say versioning action. One must of course have (feel, sequence-here version) the action-context or one would not know why one wanted a stick, any more.

So far as we have come, it is true that after the bananas are reached, the stick would lose its meaning. We don't yet have "third" sequences by which the general useful category of sticks would be had (felt, sequenced). So far a tool is meaningful only in an action context in which it is focally implied. Was there actually such a stage?

Some years after these concepts developed, I learned that for millions of years people made hunting tools and left them at the hunting sites. Only very much later are tools found at home sites, that is to say they were brought home and saved. This is certainly corroborative of these concepts.

(o) Schematic terms: meshed; implicit functioning; held; reconstituted

(o-1) Meshed

We need a term to hold, for us, that a sequence does not lose its individuality when it functions implicitly. It can still recur as itself, despite functioning in the mesh of mutually implying sequences. I call it *"meshed."*

A sequence is a string of contexts. Each context is a mesh of mutually implicit sequences. We also spoke of them as possible sequences, behavior-possibilities and now gesture-possibilities.

With further developments the contexts of our sequence now include new implicit sequences. When the sequence recurs, it isn't quite the same. New sequences have become implicit in ours, and ours in them.

Another way to say this: by functioning implicitly in the formation of new sequences, the sequence is itself changed. *What it functions implicitly in, comes to be implicit in it.* Or we can say, every new way it can "apply" (function in) comes to be implicit in it.

Such a mesh is pyramided (see VI) and layered, as we just saw. One might think that the sequence can never recur as it was, since its contexts are now different. A sequence *is* a string of contexts, hence if these contexts now include new sequences, then even if the sequence might look the same to an observer, it is a string of newly enriched contexts, not the string of the old ones.

How then, can the sequence ever again occur as it was before the newer sequences became part of the contexts?

We see, first, that it is ambiguous to speak of "the sequence" having changed, and now having something further more implicit in its contexts. We say ambiguously that "it" now has implicit in it the new way it is functioned. This is not literally the same sequence. When "it" recurs, really a new sequence occurs that has never yet formed.

A mesh of mutually implying sequences is pyramided (see VI) and layered as we just saw. It is not on one layer or level or plane only. New sequences develop so that they become focally implied instead of the previous, but if the new one cannot occur, the previous one still can. (See VI.)

A meshed sequence is always still *literally* implicit, as it originally was, as well as in its new form.

An actually occurring sequence is freshly formed. ("Use" of standard sequences as in a repertoire doesn't develop till VII-B. Even then there is always a fresh bodily eveving.) The bodily eveving determines what occurs, or rather, is the occurring.

Under certain circumstances this bodily implying can still be that of the original sequence. Such circumstances are quite special, but a "meshed" sequence is always in a pyramided-upon way still there, in its original form, *as well as* in the present, fully eveved mesh.

The term "meshed" is about "both . . . and." "It" is *both* further developed, altered, as new developments occur, as it functions implicitly in eveving, *and also* still itself a behavior possibility in its original form, if what has developed since cannot occur.

Drugs, hypnosis, sleep stimulus–deprivation, and other conditions are such that much of the usual whole eveving cannot occur.

Very primitive sequences that usually never occur for humans, still can, and so can what happened on one's fifth birthday. (Of course the body is different than it was then, but the sequence as it originally was is still there, given that now it can occur only via special conditions that make it impossible for the whole mesh to be bodily lived. Hence these conditions are largely bodily changes.)

By participating in further eveving, therefore, a sequence both is and is not changed.

We must allow this concept to function and apply for us for a while, so that we can later define it more clearly, when it will have acquired applications.

(o-2) Implicit functioning

To function is to occur—but the sequences that "function implicitly" do not occur; rather, just this one occurring sequence does. There are two ways of phrasing which together make this problem:

In one way of phrasing (which I will continue to use) we say inaccurately that "the sequence functions implicitly." A more exact phrasing would be: "a sequence functions implicitly only insofar as it succeeds in participating to shape what occurs." If the sequence functioned in every respect, then it would be occurring. The eveving going on now would be the eveving of its first bit, and the next, and so on. But "it" doesn't function as itself; a different eveving is now going on, and only insofar as our sequence participates in that is it functioning now.

This is how we made the concept of "eveving" in IV. It is what we get when we don't assume fixed parts that determine what happens by keeping their own nature fixed (so that the result is determined by them all). Instead, eveving is a new making of parts as well as "relations," so that if we trace an old part into eveving, we would say that "it" functions only as determined by the new event, and not as fully determined by its previous character as the part it was. So, when "it," the part, functions implicitly, then really not all of it does, but only what is determined to participate by the new eveving.

Further, we saw many times since then that there is novelty in this "insofar as it participates in the new event." The new event is really new, or can be. It is always fresh, so far as we have developed concepts, and we have as yet no concepts for a "use" of a repertoire of anything. The observer may see an event that is just like a previous one, but the event is fresh to itself. (We don't yet know how to think about the observer's capacity to sequence [have] a similarity as such. We could, of course, employ our own capacity to do this, to think, and then later come to grasp how we do that. But our model fundamentally avoids assuming that everything comes in preexisting already-cut and fixed parts.)

The effect of a sequence functioning implicitly need not be something that was already part of the sequence (for example, thrashing in V). Nor will it be totally unrelated to that sequence. (For example, in V thrashing happens when walking in water is attempted. The movements are wider and different than in walking.)

So we cannot divide in the sequence between the "insofar as it functions now" and the "insofar as it does not." To try to divide the sequence is to assume that it can function only as how it itself was, and its effect now must have been *part* of it. And it needn't have been!

The contexts (or bodily evevs and environmental cfings) of the occurring sequence do occur. And yet also, a context is a mesh of *implicitly functioning* sequences. If we were to say that these do simply not occur, then the occurring sequence wouldn't either. A context is the occurring body-event and en, but these imply many sequences and each *is* a specific eveving of all these sequences.

So the implicitly functioning sequences do occur insofar as they participate in the shaping of this occurring one.

Any of the other sequences (now implicit) would also be a string of contexts that would carry this (now occurring) one forward, but they would carry it forward differently.

As the ongoing sequence carries the context forward, all the implicit ones are still implicit, now somewhat differently.

If another sequence had occurred instead, it too would have changed how all these sequences are implicit, but would have done so differently.

Thus the way the implicit sequence functions is not directly part of it. The ongoing sequence changes the context of the implicit one, but it doesn't change it as the implicit one itself would have done, had it occurred. If we wanted to compare the difference, we could not do it in terms of the implicit sequence alone. We cannot get at its implicit functioning by making divisions within it.

How a sequence functions implicitly is not a way that it can function as itself.

It helps to reiterate that a sequence is a forming. A sequence consists of a string of evevs, as we conceived of it. So the sequence itself is the forming that it is, and therefore, if it were the only forming that is happening, then it would be occurring itself. If the sequence functions implicitly, it means that the events are formed not just by it, the eveving is more, and therefore how the sequence functions implicitly is not just up to it.

Again, this shows that we cannot divide *in the sequence* what does, and what does not, participate in the new eveving, because how the sequence functions is made in the new eveving and may not have been in any sense in the sequence before.

It is *the first law of explication* that an explication has *more or different parts* than what occurred when what is now explicated "was" implicit. In typical cases of "explication" there are *more* parts. If you are asked to explicate a sentence you have written, you understand that you are asked for several more sentences. In this way "your point" will now be explicit in terms of more meaning units than it was in the one sentence (see "comprehension" in Gendlin 1997a). Here I have said "more or different" parts, because for us "explication" has a wider meaning and application.

We saw in IV that something is schematized *by* schematizing. The implicitly functioning sequence is itself changed by so functioning. Its shaping effect is not, as we just saw, part of itself. Something new happens to the sequence when it functions implicitly. New roles for past experience are made in present process. Insofar as it now functions, it now occurs. When it recurs as itself, it may be quite different. At any rate it will have implicit in it the sequence in which it just now functions implicitly. The now occurring sequence will then be part of the context.

(o-3) Held

Since a sequence does not function implicitly simply as itself, there is a distinction to be made. As we saw, it is not a division within the sequence.

Let me call "insofar as" the sequence does *not* function implicitly by saying that in that regard it is *"held."*

Let us now push the question a step further. If a sequence functions implicitly, are the sequences implicit in it also now functioning implicitly? And those implicit in the implicit ones, and so on?

The question needs to be stated more exactly so that we can see if we have already answered it.

We have already seen that the sequence functions implicitly only *insofar* as it actually participates in the eveing, that is to say in the shaping, in the formation of the occurring sequence. So our question, more exactly, is: insofar as the implicit one functions, do all those implicit in it too, and in turn those that are implicit in the implicit ones in it?

The question comes down to this "insofar." Does it include also the "insofar" of the sequences implicit in the implicit one, and so on? The answer is yes, one "insofar" (one eveing—that of the occurring sequence) determines also the function of the sequences implicit in the implicit one. But, if the implicit sequence were itself to occur, then how those implicit in it would function would be different.

Thus the sequences are not implicit as fixed parts would be. Of course, this is what we have said all along. Each sequence is a different eveing. The many sequences are all implicit in each other, but "they" are not the same, when they function in different eveings.

If we said earlier that all sequences are mutually implicit and each is a string of the context, made up of all of them, we need now to introduce the concept of "held." All implicit sequences are in some respects "held" and in some functioning implicitly. What this actually means is not the same from one sequence to the next. Otherwise they would all be the same and everything would always function, and in the same way.

If the implicit sequence we discussed were to occur, it would make a new distinction between "held" and functioning implicitly. (*Its* eveing would do that, rather than that of the sequence occurring now.)

Thus it is eveing which makes the distinction in each case, and this is another way to define "eveing."

The following will show this point in more steps and in more detail.

Let me begin with assumptions that the old model would lead us to make, and then correct them.

One might be inclined to think that what is implicit in an implicit sequence is itself functioning implicitly. If the implicit sequence actually occurred, nothing new would be implicit in it which wasn't implicitly functioning already (when the sequence was implicit). Then, by explicating, nothing new would become implicit. However much one explicated, still only that would be implicit which was implicit in the first place.

Of course, one would say, one gets to understand one's point better by explicating it more and more, but nothing further would come to function implicitly, as one did so.

We are finding, on the contrary, that as one explicates, new aspects come to function implicitly, which did not, before (when the now-occurring sequence was only functioning implicitly).

In the above assumption one treats "what functions implicitly" as fixed pieces which somehow are thought to move from darkness into the light. (All along we have said that implying is not like that. The implicit is not of the same sort as the explicit, only hidden—or only "not yet.")

We must also remember that bodily formation (and all sequences are that) is not made up of sequences. It implies sequences, and more exactly, implies itself being carried forward *in some way.* So we cannot do what the old model would lead to. We cannot think of bodily eveing as if it consisted of fixed parts, namely, the sequences themselves. Rather, a new formation always forms, even if it looks familiar to an observer. The body generates sequences; it is not sequences, not explicitly structured parts.

If everything that would be implicit if a sequence occurred were already functioning implicitly when the sequence functions implicitly, then all sequences would really be the same. It would mean nothing that something was explicit, and something else implicit; that would be an illusory distinction.

For us, occurring and implicit are one event. This occurring sequence is different events than if another were occurring. Since the sequence is an eveing of the others, it is a different eveing than they would be. The context, which implies them all, actually occurs, but it is this sequence's eveing, and the next bit is this sequence's focal implying, carried forward. It is not how the other sequence would change the context. What is eveed and occurs as this sequence is what determines exactly which other sequences function implicitly and how.

If one of the now implicit sequences actually occurred, its eveing (its contexts) would be actually occurring, and how other sequences actually function implicitly would be different.

Let this be our *second law of explication*:[2] to explicate what functioned implicitly allows something else to function implicitly, which might not have been implicit before.

This might have been "held" before. Or it might be new.

As I said in Gendlin 1964, if what now functions implicitly in a person is responded to, and made to occur as a carried forward process, then other aspects which were not even implicit are thereby reconstituted and become implicit.

The distinction between "held" and "functioning implicitly" is neither within the sequence (which we already showed), nor between those sequences that do, and those that do not, now function implicitly. To so view it is to assume fixed parts lasting through change, again. How a sequence functions (really, what it is) is determined differently in each eveing. We have also several times showed how new sequences can come to be implicitly before they ever occur (type-a implicit).

What is "held" does *not* participate in shaping occurrence, and is not changed by occurrence (except in the twisted sense that its absence might, by an observer, be thought to influence the occurrence).

All this has important consequences for understanding and rethinking "the unconscious."

It is vital that we don't read the old model into our new terms. If we did that, we wouldn't really have new terms, just new words. The implicit, and explication, have never been clearly thought about, just because concepts were all modeled on the explicit formed, only, so that the implicit had always to be construed as if it were of the same sort as the explicit, only hidden. It is therefore very important to allow our concepts to develop clear and sharp internal structure, as they have just been doing.

(o-4) Reconstituting

This term will help us further understand what is usually called "imagination," but I cannot turn to that until near the end of this section.

We have already used this term. A sequence "reconstitutes" the context which it versions. Each bit of the sequence is a version of the context (an eveving), and the sequence as a whole is a way of having (feeling, sequencing) the context. I say the sequence reconstitutes the context.

We can now see more exactly that *the context actually occurs.* The sequence *is* the string of contexts which reconstitute the-context-as-had. When an object falls out, this doesn't mean that the object occurs and the contexts are only implicit—they also occur. For example, when the cat tracks the bird (as in VI), this bird stands steady as the scene moves rapidly by (as the cat runs to keep the bird steady). The whizzing-by scenes *do also occur*, or the bird would not fall out from them.

This becomes confusing, because we also say that a context is a mesh of *implicitly* functioning sequences.

We have just straightened this confusion out, since we found that insofar as a sequence actually functions implicitly, it does occur. Implying and occurring are one real event, together.

What made us think the implicitly functioning sequences didn't occur? It was because we didn't have the term "held" and the distinction between it and "implicitly functioning." If we talk of "implicit sequences," then there are ways in which they occur, and ways in which not. And we have now distinguished these. "Implicitly functioning" is thus much more specific than just "implicit."

The "reconstituted" context can be said to "fall out" from the sequence as truly as the object does. The cat runs in a scene that is perceived as steady and even unmoving, despite the fact that it whizzes by and bops up and down! (Kant already remarked on this difference between subjective and objective perception.) The "reconstituted" scene is the steady one, the "kept-same" one, in which the cat runs after the bird.

Each bit, each version of the context consists of implicit sequences which, if any occurred, would change the context their way. Instead, it is being changed in this sequence's way. Either way, contexts occur, they are not *merely* implicit.

We always fundamentally meant that anything "implicit" functions importantly, and is an important real aspect of an occurring event. It is the notion of "held" that is new.

If the contexts are changed as a sequence changes them, by cfing, I call this simply "carried forward." But when an implicit sequence's contexts are changed, not as it would, but as the occurring sequence changes them, I say the implicit sequence is being *"indirectly carried forward."* I need this term since the implicitly functioning sequence is now being changed in this occurring. How it can happen, at each point in the occurring sequence, differs. The context in which it would occur is being carried forward and reconstituted by this sequence.

Our second law (about reconstituting) is now shown. The sequence which does occur, does also change what functions implicitly. We already saw that, and see it now in terms of the context which the occurring sequence reconstitutes.

What is "held" does not function, does not occur, and is not indirectly carried forward. It remains the same. If in another sequence something new is explicit, something new also functions implicitly. Therefore what was held in the previous sequence may now function implicitly.

directly carried forward	implicitly carried forward indirectly carried forward	not carried forward
the occurring sequence, the string of contexts or evevs constituting the occurring sequence	the implicitly functioning sequences which constitute the contexts or evevs of the occurring sequence are cfed by the occurring sequence	"held": how the implicitly functioning sequence is not functioning; whatever is not in the occurring evev
versioned behavior context or action context, as in dance and seens		

The eveving, the occurring, makes the distinction between what occurs and what does not.

Occurring is not just one among a system of separate possibilities. Occurring changes what the old model would use as determinative. What the sequences themselves are and can be is altered, added to, by occurring.

When we say that some old sequence functions implicitly and is thereby altered, is it the old or the altered sequence which functions implicitly? It is the altered one. Evev is already how the differences have made differences to how they make differences (IV).

An occurring sequence changes the other sequences as possibilities (and they have not yet themselves occurred in that changed way).

In participating in the formation of seens and action-objects, the dance sequences are altered. Conversely, a new "first" dance alters all or many of the sequences implicit in the action context it versions. When these implicit sequences (gestural pauses and actions) occur, it will be differently. But this difference occurring, too, will further alter the next dance.

The change is not all finished by the dance. As the changed sequences themselves occur, their different evevs make a further change.

(This is an important principle we will need later: the actual occurring of a type-a implicit sequence makes *further* change.)

Not only are the bodily evevs changed, but also the implied (open cycle) environment too, and how it can carry forward. The new dance implicitly alters the looks and sounds of objects and of the people gesturing at the objects. What new sounds and moves they will make, and what patterns they will hear and see, is changed in the dance in a type-a implicit way.

Behavior space (action space) is not just bodily implied, but the eveving of the environmental occurring, which occurs into that implying. Eveving is just that.

Let us now see how this helps us with "imagination." The puzzle of it seems to be how the body can create an environment that is physically absent. We have already seen that the body always does so in more developed behavior space (end of chapter VI). Many possible sequences, which are implied by the body and en that now occur, are moves backwards or behind the animal, for example. There are objects in its behavior space which it doesn't see, but would see, if it turned, or went a certain way. These are occurring in its space.

Our term "reconstituted" says exactly in what way behavior space or action space *occurs*, and in what way the implicit sequences do, and do not, literally occur.

The whole space is *directly* carried forward. The behavior possibilities from it that are implicit, are indirectly carried forward and thereby altered. The animal behaves (the occurring sequence is) in the reconstituted space. (That space occurs, it is not implicit.) It would not be behavior space if it did not consist of implicit behavior-possibilities, but these actually occur as this sequence's evevs and environments. (From the start, implying is an aspect of real events, as is occurring.)

With symboling there is an added question: are the reconstituted behavior contexts actually occurring, or only the patterns and bodylooks? Although one may literally see only the seen patterns or dance moves, the behavior-context that they version is reconstituted, and does occur. Let me show that exactly.

The doubled symboling sequence keeps a behavior context "the same," by versioning how the body is (and looks and moves) in that behavior context. The symbol sequence reconstitutes that behavior context (the body's being in it). The behavior context occurs; each doubled bit is a version of it.

Therefore we must *not* say that in a symboling sequence the behavior context is implicit. It is occurring. It is reconstituted (and had, felt, sequenced) by the symboling. One lives in that situation, when one symbols it.

If this were not so, if the versioned behavior context were implicit, it would be the same as all the other contexts that are mutually implicit. One could not know which context is being symbolized (versioned). For instance, in making something (VII-A-m) a pattern versions the present action context. Of course one is in that actually occurring context. We would not feel (cf. have) the symbolized context, the one we are in, if symboling didn't reconstitute it, as occurring in each versioning bit.

We have not yet reached the stage at which humans can live in a situation that is not physically present. (Although even higher animals live in a space that far exceeds what is physically present, it is always the present one.) In VII-B we will see how that stage develops, and we will remember that the reconstituted context is not dependent only on what is physically and literally impinging.

If there were ever a reason that one would come up with gestures that reconstitute an absent situation, if we knew how such gestures would ever form, then we would also know how humans can be in situations that (by the old model) we call "imagined." We will say "live in" the next hunt, and not only in the home-going context in which they actually are, when they decide to take the tools home. But we will see that this is not a small change. Most of what we still miss in our new humans develops along with it.

Again, for us the stakes are not in the correct natural history. On the contrary, our concepts will help further discoveries of that. The stakes for us are to grasp what exactly is involved in these human capacities, and just exactly how the various aspects are inherently connected in each other. All we can say is that the new sequence would be pertinent (see V) to the stoppage.

VII-B. Protolanguage

(a) Internal space

VII-space is inherently internal/external. VII-sequences set up this distinction.

The gestures version the behavior context, but they are simple movements. The behavior context is "the same"; each of the bodylooks is a version of *how the body looks in that behavior context*. Each gesture reconstitutes the behavior context. But what is perceived is the gesture. The gestures are "external," the behavior context is the string of evevs, it is felt. *The gestures are not behaviors among the behavior context's possibilities.* The gesture doesn't change how the behaviors are possible. The gestures do not go on in the "filled space" of the behavior possibilities. *Rather, the simple movements make a new, seemingly "empty" space.*

The change in the evevs (which are versions of the same behavior context) is *only* felt; nothing changes in the behavior context. *This change is "internal." The space of the simple movements is "external,"* and different from the kept-same behavior space.

There is now a sharp difference between the external movement in "empty" space, and the movement as a version of the complex filled behavior context, which is sequenced only "inwardly."

One sees only the simple movements, not what they version and carry forward in the body. What each body sees on the other (is carried forward by, on the other) is one thing (bodylook, movement), and what is felt, had, and sequenced in the body is another (the evevs = behavior contexts or action contexts). Thereby there is an internal and an external.

We have always had an internal and an external, but only now do we have concepts with which to think about that distinction. As usual, I am not so much concerned with the natural history of the origin of the distinction, as with making concepts to think clearly about it. No doubt someday there will be better concepts. But it is startling to realize that there have been no concepts at all about that until now. This has made for much philosophical nonsense, very poor theory in the study of people, and difficulties with an unthinkable observer in physics.[3]

The simple movements of gesturing let one sequence, version, have, feel, the behavior context without changing it. Gestures don't change a behavior context, at least not in the way a behavior would change it (one sequence being a change in how all the others are physically possible). Some move in the dance may change how one of these behaviors might be done, but this is now accidental. The dance carries forward by body-looks and not by changing the behavior context.

Versioning is change, of course, but different in kind, than behavior.

We must keep in mind that to feel or sense or perceive generates time, it is always a sequence. When we say we feel "something," we say this on the model of a thing, "something." But to feel is a change-sequence. Behavior's evevs are felt as they are carried forward. In versioning again there is a string of changing evevs, but now they are all of them *of* "the same" behavior context. That context *is* changed in each version of the string, only not as behavior would change it.

There is thus a hidden aspect to the simple movements; we feel not only the bodylook–carrying forward we see, but also the behavior-context versioning, the change of which we feel and don't actually see.

The external of simple movements and patterns, and *the internal* of action-context-versioning, are generated together, of course. *One* sequence of this doubled kind makes that distinction.

External and internal are now both clear during gesturing—one does and sees the simple movements in an external space of mere movements. The internal is the felt; it is how the movements are of, and pause the action-context of, mutually implicit sequences (as well as being the feeling of these movements themselves).

But when gesturing stops and there is again action, what then is internal and what is external?

At a certain (still to be defined) point (I call it the FLIP), the actions come to be in the external space. But until then, the external/ internal occurs only in gesturing (and functions implicitly in action).

The new inner and outer spaces are both necessarily symbolic. The outer is pattern-space. Objects come into pattern-space. The inner is the string of versions of the action context while one perceives only the simple movements.

The ("internal") feeling is *of* the bodylooks *and of* the versioned action context. The bodylooks are symbols. (One has a sense *of* the symbol itself *and* also *of* its meaning, so this duality is correct.) The same *perception* (perception bit, or opfucy bit)—the "external"—*is* the simple movement *and is of* the action context (it carries forward the one evev which implies the behaviors or actions and also implies the gesture sequence that versions this action context).

This clarifies the difference between two uses of "of." The feeling (bodily carrying forward) is said to be "of." As we just showed, feeling is both of the symbol and of what the symbol stands for (what it versions, and reconstitutes). The symbol, the perceived gesture, is, and is of what it versions and reconstitutes.

(b) The FLIP

But at what exact point does this new internal/external space become *the* space in which action and gesturing go on?[4] Until the end of VII-A everything still happened in behavior space. The behavior contexts were elaborated, each with its gestures, but the gestures were only pauses during action. Gestures and action went on in action-contexts. These related to each other as the behavior contexts did (a given sequence changes how the others could happen), in behavior space.

Gesturing is double, and hence the movements are external in empty space, and this reconstituted action-context here, now, is had and felt, even while one looks at the gestures. While gesturing occurs, there is this duality. But when it ceases and action resumes, one is in behavior space again, and has been there all along.

It is not the gestures that make relationships between different situations, it is still the actions.

It is not in empty space that different physical settings are located, but still in behavior space.

After the FLIP, the contexts are no longer the physical settings, but the inter-human gestural contexts. Their connections are not those of behavior space, not how a physical action changes the context for other actions. Rather, their connections are how a given gesturing between people changes *their* situation, the one they have with each other. Many physical settings might be involved—for instance they might argue over who owns a given tree. They might contend about this in the garden, in front of the tree, or at home, sitting in the wooden longhouse, leaning against the wall. The tree is in their situation whether they are physically present where it is, or not.

After the FLIP everything is located in the gestural external empty space, and the gestural interaction supersedes and defines what each situation is.

Before we can see exactly at what stage this FLIP occurs, let us become exact first about what is involved. There are a number of other developments that we must also grasp, exactly. These are each pieces required for a theory of language, necessary although not sufficient. After we have them each clear, we may try to see in what relation to each other they can develop.

Does it require the FLIP (indeed, is it the same question) to gesture about the tree in the longhouse at home?

The gestures can of course be made anywhere; they don't require the actual tree. The gestures are not *among* the behavior space mesh. A gesture does not change how behaviors are physically possible thereafter.[5] But although *we* see the gestures could be made at home, why would someone make them, so to speak, in the "wrong context"? How would the people ever discover that they can form there, why would they want to? How would they be relevanted? So it seems that this must wait until contexts are interactively determined, and not physically, i.e., until the FLIP.

We would like to see more exactly how interaction contexts develop, and in what way they are implicit in each other. Another way to say the same thing: we want to see how an interaction (a gesture sequence) changes how other interactions can or cannot now occur.

It is important to notice that our theory stands before this hurdle, so to speak. *We* might imagine, for instance, that someone would just discover that the gestures belonging to another context can be made in a different one, but our theory resists that. Why would they form? What would relevant them?[6] Paleontology bears us out: there was really a long time when tools were made freshly at each new hunt site, and left there. Once the hunt-context was no more, the tools lost their significance. There was no way to save anything: it was always fresh formation, as in our theory. The patterns in making the tools were only pauses in the behavior of hunting. These might have been very elaborate, but they were *in* behavior space, not yet in one interaction space. The patterns lost their capacity to carry forward when they were not in the action-context they paused, even if those patterns were already there, on the objects. Nor were such patterns formed out of their physical contexts. And then—all this did happen, and the people acted *in* their gesturally defined interaction-context, and no longer in behavior space. That is the FLIP.

Action comes to be in terms of the people with each other, even when they deal with objects, even when others are absent. The tree is that person's tree even when that person is absent. If chopping down that person's tree is action, it is, now, not because of the change in possible behaviors with a felled tree as against a standing one. Rather, it is action because the relation with the other person is changed by cutting down that person's tree. And it is one action if that person asked for it, and another quite different action if that person wanted to prevent it.

To understand the FLIP we need a new distinction. *The behavior distinction between gesturing and action has now been superseded, because the gestural sequences have become determinative of what action is,* rather than the physical actions with objects. *We need a new term for the latter: let us call it "doing."* Doing is visible activity with objects; from observing a doing we cannot know whether it is action or not (whether it changes the inter-action context or not), nor can we know just what the action is (just how it changes the context).

Let us call the contexts *interaction contexts* (iacxt).

We defined "action" as a carrying-forward change in the action con-text. "Versioning" was only a string of versions that kept the action con-text "the same." Let me keep this distinction but let it be functional. It no longer coincides with whether a sequence is physically a doing with objects (or with others as physical objects) or whether it is gestural. In either case it might be action, or it might be only versioning. What was a two-way distinction has become a four-way distinction.

What looks like physical behavior can be either action or only "doing." What looks like gestures can be either action or only versioning.

Let me keep the term "action," as before, to refer to a carrying forward of the context, now the interaction context. On the other hand, "versioning" (as before) refers to a string of keeping the context (now interaction context) the same.

New criteria from VII, symbolic criteria, now determine whether a sequence is action, or only a versioning or only a doing. For example, if I don't sign the check, the whole thing wasn't action. If I say "I quit" when the boss isn't listening, it wasn't an action. Also, if I say "I quit" to my boss in a certain context and tone of voice, again it wasn't an action, but only an expression of dismay, a versioning of the interaction context but not a carrying forward of it.

The buyer on the Chicago Grain Exchange raises a finger and has thereby bought a hundred carloads of grain. Many different seemingly more active behaviors would have been mere doings, not actions. The buyer cannot obtain the carloads by going to the railroad siding, where they actually stand. Jumping onto the cars, feeling the grain in one car, shouting at the workers there, loudly claiming ownership, all those would *only* be doings.

I call them "VII-criteria," the ways we determine what is action and what is not. They derive from the gestural interaction contexts them-selves.

There is thus a new distinction between sequences that *function* as actions, and those that do not. This cannot be seen; it must be had as part of the interaction context.

The grain buyer's gesture is an action when performed on the floor of the Grain Exchange while bidding is going on. But if you are not famil-iar with that context, you might not even see it. The people shouting and milling around the floor would be much more noticeable, but both the doings and the gestures in this milling around are not actions. I am saving the action/versioning distinction, but it is now determined by VII-criteria. *Both are interactions* and go on *in* interaction contexts.

An example of versioning might be a long discussion that leads to no change. Another example is the expressive gestures of our people on the Grain Exchange floor. (Of course, versioning too changes the interaction context, but not in the same way as action.)

People live and act in situations (which now means: in interaction contexts). Situations are not the physically external facts, but the context of interactions with others, which also determines how these facts are defined. (A locked door is one thing if I am hiding from someone, but if I am trying to get out, quite something else.)

In terms of the internal/external distinction, action is now always partly internal, that is to say it involves interaction-context-change which one doesn't see because it lies in the gesturing between people, which is now also action. But this aspect of the context-change is internal not just to one person but to others, of course. It would be wrong to say that people now live in internal space as if situations were private, as if one had them alone and spatially inside. People live with others who are external to them and can be located outside of them in external space. But interaction contexts are not arrangements in this external space either.

This has made them difficult to study with the kind of concepts current until now, the kind that are modeled on things in external space.

Both external and internal are results of (are formed together with) versioning or symbolic interaction between people. The external space becomes overarching when the interaction-context becomes overarching, and doing goes on *in* it.

(c) The order

Let us now look at some of the steps of development that would lead to the FLIP. We will try to be exact about the formations and understand exactly what is involved in each. This should let us say in just what order they develop, what is already involved along with each, and what forms later.

(1) In the *first dance* the *whole bodylook* of each carries the other forward. There is no sequence without the other.

(2) The individual alone gestures at objects and also perceives the object's look. (We called this "seen-formation.") Let me also call this "*lone carrying forward.*"

Let us say several individuals are in the forest, a few hundred yards apart. A bird flies over, and they each alone gesture at it, and see its look.

(3) If they are now together again, when one of them gestures at an object, the others watching that individual are *also carried forward* by that

individual's gestures. (They know what that individual is gesturing.) Let me call this "*also carrying forward.*"

In the above three steps the people are in the actual physical context, the object is present. To carry forward the garden at home at night requires a carrying forward by patterns *rather than whole bodylook.* The whole body at home does not look like the whole body does in the garden.

Seen-formation is already no longer a whole bodylook carrying forward. The object does not return the human bodylook. Its own pattern, its own look, forms (with human bodylook carrying forward implicitly functioning). *The gesturing at the object is not a bodylookbodylook sequence.*

When others are *also carried forward,* they are looking at the individual. But their being carried forward is not in a bodylookbodylook sequence with that individual. That individual need not look at them, and is not feeding back to their bodylooks. The gesture sequence forms between individual and object. The individual is carried forward thereby, and the others *also. They are carried forward by the gestures themselves,* not the whole bodylook, and they are carried forward by just watching, not by having their own body effect make a rendition on the other body in turn.

Something quite fundamental happens at the second step (in seen-formation). (In section VII-B-e the exact way seens form will become clear.) Patterns carry forward, that are only part of the body, and they carry forward not between two bodies but between body and pattern. Since bodylook as a whole is already a pattern, let me call these new ones "*patterns themselves.*"

It is therefore true, as G. H. Mead said, that our lone carrying forward develops in a prior context of interactional carrying forward (of response to each other), but there is a third type of carrying forward with each other, which is different and develops only after lone carrying forward.[7]

I do not call these patterns as *such* because "such" means third universals. Also, it is not clear at what stage of the development of seens, the FLIP occurs.

Let us say they all look away from each other and at the object. They are then each "alone" and their interaction with each other is implicit. *Thus the scheme comes out the same way whether they are at first physically present or not, and "alone" refers to the sequence: person-object, rather than person-person body-look.* And the person-object sequence must happen before the new level is reached, and happens only in an implicitly interaction-including context.

Each such pattern sequence carries forward the other people also and for the same reason it formed in the first place, for each of them. (We called it also carrying forward.) Now they are each carried forward by their own gestures themselves, and by the same gestures of others.

The carrying forward is complete on the side of each person: they each alone know their own gestures, without anyone's feedback, and also know the gestures themselves, which the others may make.

The other's being also carried forward is implicit in any such sequence. (When actual others are also carried forward, that is of course a different sequence than lone carrying forward with only an implicit sequence of others being carried forward.)

Subsequent interactions between the people directly have the lone-carrying-forward sequences implicit. New interactions develop between the people in the context that includes the lone-carrying-forward sequences. And when they are again alone (or directed at the objects with others looking on), new lone-carrying-forward sequences develop, as more interaction sequences are now implicit. The development goes back and forth. Each type is implicit in the other.

Interaction after the third step is quite different than at the first. *Each now knows (is carried forward by) what the other does*, and they are also each carried forward by what they themselves do. *They each have the other's being carried forward as part of the context.* They each know that the others know that they know.

It is not only that lone-carrying-forward sequences are implicit. The interaction is a new and different one. Its events have developed with lone carrying-forward and are much more elaborate and different.

Interactions as we know them are all of the kind after lone carrying-forward. What our interactions are, involves our carrying forward ourselves as well as the others, and involves their carrying forward themselves as well as us, all of that actually in every bit of the ongoing interaction sequence.

Now that patterns themselves carry forward (the pattern of the object, and of the gesture at the object), such patterns carry forward even if separate from the rest of their physical context. A pattern carries forward even if the rest of the body is not as it would usually be. The pattern of an object carries forward even if the object is not otherwise present. One can "recognize" a picture. The look-of-a-rabbit carries forward even without the rest of what a rabbit is. The gestures a person makes at a rabbit carry forward even if no rabbit were present (though we still haven't figured out how one would ever form such gestures if there were no rabbit). But also, ordinary actions like chasing a rabbit would occur in pattern space. One could do only just some part of the chasing moves and these would be recognized (would carry forward) even if there was no rabbit expected or present (though we don't know why one would do that).

Thus longhouse carrying forward (at home) about the garden depends on the carrying forward by patterns-themselves.

We must go several steps further before we can think about language. We cannot yet fully understand what has developed so far.

However, we can already be clear here about the inherent interrelation between the formation and power of patterns-themselves (symbols) and the other developments above. They develop together. But we are not saying that they develop together because we found them so in natural history, or because that would be convenient. We understand each of these developments from inside, and thereby we see how they are inherently related. Lone carrying forward is by patterns themselves (since there is no other human body to respond to). Also carrying-forward, and hence at-home carrying-forward, require lone carrying-forward, so that interaction now includes lone carrying forward. They are carried forward by their own gestures, as well as those of the other.

(d) Absent context in this present context

Let us now see further how interaction contexts develop that are mutually implicit in each other.

How would it come about that the people would gesture an absent context (for instance, the garden) while in a different physical context (for instance, the longhouse at home at night)? *Why would anyone do the "wrong" gesture in the "wrong" context?*

Patterns themselves carry forward no matter where they are made. These gestures (to put it schematically) reconstitute the context they version. The gesture is a string of versions of that context, hence people would have-feel-sequence it. They can live in the "absent" situation.

But it sounds now as if, when they gesture the tree at home, they experience themselves in the garden: would they no longer know if they are in the garden or at home?

They obviously must be *different sequences*, to version the garden in the garden, and to do it at home. The same gesture would be a different sequence, and so it would not be *the same* gesture in the garden sequence and in the longhouse. Of course, at home the whole body doesn't look as if working in the garden, but one could use the same patterns themselves in the garden too. Even then these cannot be the same, at least not as the whole sequence. We have to see exactly how they are different.

The people can interact in the garden about a rabbit that is present in the garden, as well as about one that isn't present while they are in the garden, as well as about a rabbit that isn't present because they are at home in the longhouse—but *is* present in the garden, as well as about a rabbit that is absent in the absent garden while they are at home.

All these have to be different sequences. The patterns that version a present rabbit (seens) function in the formation of the other sequences. Exactly how?

We must not jump ahead as if there were language, the same phrases used—so far as we have gone each sequence forms freshly (by recurrent causation in the same routines but freshly).

Versioning the garden at home is a different interaction context, than versioning the garden in the garden. The patterns that form will not be the same, although the patterns from one will function implicitly in the new formation in the other.

We have to keep it clear that we are thinking about the original *formation* of various patterns themselves. Later, with language, there will be *the same* patterns, *used* in various contexts. Right now we are at a certain stage of the development of such patterns. There is not yet a stock of them, usably extant, nor do we yet understand "use." They are forming, freshly. *The sequence will not be the same in different contexts, we have not yet developed such "same" sequences that can occur in various contexts.* The interaction context is the garden-in-longhouse context.[8]

Carrying forward by patterns themselves doesn't mean the patterns are the same in different contexts. *Different patterns form in (or as) different interaction contexts.*

When I call the garden and the longhouse two contexts, I am thinking physically before the FLIP. Their trees could come up in their interaction at home after the FLIP, since then it would be one context, their interaction context. Until the FLIP, however, the contexts are still those of behavior space, and related through behavior changing other behavior possibilities. At this stage we see the interaction contexts *forming.* The interaction sequences do each function in the formation of new ones, but they are still separated; each is a pause in a behavior context.

Since they function in the formation of each other, the interactions from other behavior contexts *are* implicit in the gestures which pause this one. If these implicit gestures occurred, they would reconstitute the other behavior contexts. But, as we saw (VII-A-o), what is implicitly functioning is not all of what we term an implicit sequence, but only what participates now in the occurring one.

More exactly: a reconstituted context occurs. The behavior context which a given set of gestures version *is* occurring, had, and felt. That is the context they know they are in, as they gesture. But the other contexts are not occurring, except insofar as the given context *is* what the others could take off from. As we saw exactly (in VI), these are the other behaviors which make up this space, in the form in which they could occur from this spot. But why cannot the other gestures occur from this context? That is exactly like saying, "Why is there not yet *one* space formed by all gesture sequences mutually implicit in each other?" That is exactly what is now *forming*, and we don't yet know at what stage it will have developed sufficiently, nor just how it takes over in the FLIP.

We have gotten four clarifications:

(1) The sequence will be different as the whole body is different, at home, and in the garden. The patterns themselves, which form freshly still, will not be the same (though each will function implicitly in the formation of the other, as they elaborate).

(2) There is not yet language, not the *use* of a stock of *the same* patterns-as-such. Patterns themselves now carry forward, but they form freshly and differently in different contexts.

(3) We should therefore not say "the same sequence" happens in different contexts; it will be a different sequence. The notion of the same sequence in two contexts assumes language, whereas we want to see how such a sequence can develop. It has not yet. Also, it is always a different context. If they versioned the garden-context at home, they would experience themselves in the garden and lose track of being home. No, they version the garden-at-home context, not the garden context.[9]

(4) The FLIP is not yet. Interaction contexts are developing, but each is still only within its behavior context, as a pause. Gesture sequences do function in the formation of new ones, and are implicit in them, therefore. Such an implicit sequence would, if it occurred, reconstitute the behavior context it versions. But the contexts have not formed a unity, a space of their own yet. That would be the FLIP, exactly.

(e) Crossing of clusters, and so-called conventional symbols; exactly why they are no longer iconic of the body in each situation, and how they are nevertheless organic rather than arbitrary: the internal relations of protolinguistic symbols

Let us now examine much more closely the formation of these gestures and symbolings we have been discussing, to see some further, necessary ingredients of language-formation. The symbols we are discussing are not yet language, but its preconditions.

It is well known that at some stage in the development of language there had to be a shift from direct bodily expression to signs of a kind that are not directly expressive. When signs still look and sound as the body would in the signified situation (usually called "expressive"), I will call that "onomatopoeic" or "iconic." (I want to hold the term "expression" to the technical meaning we have given it.) But little clear thought has been possible on just when, why, and how signs change, and indeed how signs could possibly develop, that are not themselves like what they mean.

When one calls such signs "conventional," the word alludes to a meeting of people, convened for the purpose of adopting some kind of agreement which is then called a "convention." Of course, everyone knows that this is not how language signs came about. The word "conventional" means non-iconic or not onomatopoeic. But how can signs like that form, if there is no inherent relation between the sign and what it means?

The difficulty has been that signs have been thought about as if they were units (just as everything else, in the old model, is studied in units). Viewed that way, one tends to think that signs are related as direct expressions to the situation in which they are used, or else there is no inherent relation at all. But inherent relations can be much more complex, as we will see.

Then also, language confronts its students as an extremely complex *system*. If it is broken into units whose arrangements make meaning, then implicit rules, the syntactical system of language, appears unnecessarily complex and puzzling. The intricate system is first cut away, as if language sounds fell from heaven like separate hailstones, and then that system returns as a puzzle. But the system suggests that the units formed as a system, that is to say they formed in and with their complex internal relations.

But how can we think from bodily onomatopoeic expression to sounds that are not iconic, and yet intricately and systematically related to the contexts in which they form? We can and we now will.

We have seen a little of that already, in a general way. The patterns of objects, and gestures with them, formed, we said, with bodily expressive (dance) sequences functioning in their formation. This already meant that many gesture sequences formed in many action contexts, which were not onomatopoeic for those action contexts (but only in the one action context in which the dance appeared). All other action contexts now have that one dance implicit. Their elaborations look and sound like that dance, and not as the body would look or sound in the given action.

Recalling this more exactly: the first dance versions some action context. That context (behavior space as it is just then) consists of many other behavior-possibilities, although just then it is this occurring action which carries forward, not the others. All these other sequences, if they occur, will have the present one implicit in their contexts. But the present sequence now has the dance-pause. That dance is therefore implicit in all the other behaviors. That doesn't mean the dance will occur in them, but rather, what of it can occur, will.

What I call a whole *"cluster"* of pattern elaborations (gestures, and patterns of objects) will form, each differently, but each with the dance functioning in the formation.[10]

All this has been said before. I say it here to show that already such a first cluster is no longer onomatopoeic, except for the first dance itself.

Let us say all of this cluster is finished actually occurring (a whole cluster of "second sequences"). A new "first" dance now arises in some action context. (That action context already has some derivatives from the first "first" dance.) Again, a whole new cluster of derivatives from this new dance is now pre-formed, and will form, since all those action sequences are implicit in the danced one, and it is now implicit in them. In each of these actions, when they occur, the change from the new dance will cross with the previous change, and something new will arise. The gesturing from the very first "first" dance is now further altered by those from the new one. *I call this interaction of the whole first cluster with the second, "crossing."*

For instance, let us say that earlier there was a dance that versioned fighting. The whole cluster of behavior contexts was elaborated by gestures derivative from (similar to) the fight-versioning dance. Then a dance that versioned hunting developed. Now the whole system of contexts is elaborated by the derivatives from the hunting dance, forming in a crossed way with the extant fighting-dance-derived patterns. A further new dance, versioning sexual intercourse, would now provide new gestures, functioning implicitly, *so that the gestures in all the action contexts would form as crossed products from the extant gestures and these new ones.*

The whole crossed system would look more like the body does in the three danced contexts than in any of the others.

We can now *show exactly* how patterns develop which are *not* "onomatopoeic" or whole-body expressive! When there was only one first dance, the patterns in all the action contexts are derivatives from only the *one* dance. *Thus they are already expressive only of that one danced context, yet the derivatives form in all the contexts.* The one dance has provided a pattern dimension. With the next new dance, the whole cluster is crossed with another, so the resulting gesture sequences are even further away from what the whole body is like in each action context.

For example, suppose a certain hand-motion forms as a first dance.[11] All or many of the extant sequences making up that context now form with some hand-motion (as well as perhaps other alterations due to interaffecting, in the crossing). These will be many, many different hand-motions, "like" each other in being derivative from this new hand-sequence, but otherwise different in various ways.

The original hand-motion that versioned the action context of the dance was a sequence of variations of some hand-motion or hand-posture which really occurs in that action context. The hand-motion sequence would be "onomatopoeic" for that context, but obviously the derivative hand-motions will not be onomatopoeic for the many other action contexts in which, by crossing, they form.

The "likeness" I just mentioned cannot yet be sequenced or seen or heard, at this stage. *We* were saying the above. An important point must be noticed here: *two gestures may seem very much alike, only slightly different, yet they may version and reconstitute very different action contexts.* To an external en#1 observer the likeness can seem striking, the difference minimal. But when one such gesture forms, both for a person doing it and another perceiving it, it forms as a versioning of an action context. The other action context which has a look-similar gesture is quite far from their minds, or rather, their bodies as they are now. This is so also for us. If the contexts of *similar-sounding* words occurred to us as we speak or hear at all, we could not talk or think.

Language theory has never had a way of understanding how such minimal differences in *similar* sounds reconstitute different contexts.

Symbolic communication thus becomes separate from expressive communication by whole bodylook and sound and movement. The patterns, after a few crossings of clusters, look much more like each other than like the body in the given action context.

In all the derivative sequences that are crossed, it is no longer whole body carrying forward. And yet another new "first dance" can form, that is again whole body carrying forward.[12] As we will see later, this cannot continue indefinitely.

I call it a "first sequence" if it functions like a new dance. I call all the many thereby changed sequences making up the cluster "second sequences." Seens are second sequences, as are makings and all the pattern sequences of pausing in action. Each new first sequence gives a new cluster which crosses with the already crossed earlier clusters.

Each second sequence, when it occurs in its new way, becomes implicit that way in the already formed ones, and in the subsequently forming ones.

The relation between one second sequence and another is like that of one behavior sequence and another, except that we are now speaking of doubled sequences. Therefore the formation of each sequence alters both how actions are done and their gestural aspect. Are these two levels quite clear to us?

The behavior contexts are implicit in each other in how one behavior or action changes how the others are possible. If you chop the tree down, you can't then climb it. If you climb it and it's chopped down while you're on it, you can't climb down. This is the relation of the actions within one cluster. When gestures form, they relate to each other via how the action-contexts they version relate to each other.

But there are also other inherent relations, not only those of the behavior sequences to each other.

The gestures arise from how the body looks and moves in a given context. The body implies the behavior space—all the sequences. The body implies just this sequence by eveing them all into just this focal implying. So the behavior sequences are related not only externally (if you chop the tree down, you can't climb it), but also in the body.[13] Therefore how the body looks is related inherently to this behavior context, and also constitutes always an eveed relation between all the contexts.

The different ways the body looks in different contexts are related to each other in both the above ways.

As one context is versioned (each bit of a gesturing sequence reconstitutes the same behavior context slightly differently), a whole new set of bodily organic relations arises, as each bit versions the context which, after all, consists of all the sequences. So the gestures (the symbols) in a given context are inherently related internally within the body to other contexts with their gestures.

Crossing is a bodily meshing, as every body-event is an eveing.

While the gesture is now no longer how the body looks in this given behavior, it is a crossed product of how the body is in this behavior, and how it is in the danced behavior context, from which the gestures derive. Whatever does form, forms from the body in this given context, crossed with the implicit dance sequence. So it is not a matter of arbitrarily sticking derived patterns and gestures into the given context. It forms organically and the crossing happens in the formation of body-events.

This applies both to the body's sound, looks, and motions, as well as to the patterns of objects. Both are their own patterns, but they form in the eveing that includes the implying of the dance sequence patterns.[14]

The patterns are therefore inherently related to what they "mean" (what they version and reconstitute, what they let one have and feel and sequence and "keep the same").

Gesture and meaning form as one event. The having (sequencing, feeling, "keeping same") is a string of slightly different versions—which have not been before. The word "same" is in quotation marks; to version a behavior context (and thus have and feel it) is to create a whole new set of versions. (It is the versioned context, that is felt and had, not the original one, of course.) Again this shows that between gesture and what is reconstituted the relation is not arbitrary, but organic.

The same is the case with the relation of different gesture sequences to each other. They are related not only as their contexts were already related in behavior space, but also through the formation and crossing just described.

But since the contexts are versioned, and thus vastly re-created, and this happens in gesturing, the relations among the gesture-formations also give the contexts a new kind of relation between them. And these new relations are not just added on, but are inherently part of how these contexts are re-created (or, if you like, elaborated).

Directly iconic onomatopoeia is now very far away, but it is through non-arbitrary bodily and environmental formations that a cluster of often-crossed derivatives of pattern sequences elaborates action.

The system of interrelated gesture sequences in different contexts has thereby a very deep bodily underpinning of inter-crossed relations. It far exceeds in complexity any mere spatial positioning of unit sounds or moves. It is symbolic not by one-to-one label relations to objects or situations or actions. The system beneath language has in fact the character of bodily organization, the system we also described formally as the meta-structure. I will say much more about it in VIII. Obviously, it far exceeds the kind of relations set out in the usual logics.

The body functions here, in these formations, so that it isn't possible to reduce the formation to arrangements of preexisting units. Between behavior and how the body looks in it, the nature of the body is involved. Again, between the gestures in a given crossed cluster, and the next crossing, again bodily formation is involved. And it is not just a physical outwardly moving and sounding body, but one that implies the behavior sequences and behavior space.

If I call these elaborated contexts "interaction contexts," then I speak after the FLIP. I have been speaking about their formation, and not yet their taking over, as the space in which action occurs. Here we don't yet see how this happens, only how the interaction contexts form as inherently related to each other and to their gestures, as the gestures are related also to each other. The body event and the bodily implying during gesturing reconstitutes (is an occurring, a feeling, having, and carrying forward of) the elaborated behavior context as well, of course, so that the relations I have been setting forth are all one system. It is a new system of how the gesturally (interactionally) elaborated action sequences are implicit in each other.

Filling in what we have said schematically, what can it mean to say that the gestures elaborate and also newly connect different action contexts? It means that the interactions between people (which at first merely seem "about" action contexts) come to be the more important inter-relations between the contexts. The symboling sequences between the people are not now so much about action; rather, action comes to be about the relations between the people. That is the meaning of that FLIP which we have not yet derived, although the system of interrelated interaction contexts has formed before us.

What has been presented are essentials for an understanding of the formation of language and culture. Of course, these essential parameters would not need to be couched in the terms of our schematic, but they cannot be done without. They can be translated into other terms if someone will devise other, hopefully ever better, terms.

Among the tasks of this work are: to reconceptualize *the body* so that we could understand how focusing is possible, how we can feel complex situations, how the body can come up with an answer to a complex human living question we cannot figure out, how body and cognition are not just split apart. That obviously requires a different conception of the body than physiology currently offers. I think I have shown why (IV) both what physiology says, and the *kinds* of concepts it uses, cannot conceptualize these aspects of the body we know and have.

Another task, quite similar, is to form *concepts for the preconceptual.* (This is the same point without attributing it to the body.) We want to be able to think about what a felt sense or an "experiential sense" is, before we have explicated. Even before that it has already an incredibly fine structure. Without our scheme, that is about all one can say: experience is not indeterminate, it is very finely ordered but not like concepts (a helpless statement I have made so often). "Not arbitrary but not conceptually determined." Not this, not that. Here we are deriving the way to think about what it is. We are formulating how language develops in a bodily way, and the sort of "system" its internal relations are. Language is not something grafted on to the body. Speech forms directly from the body. Its inherent order is vastly more than arrangements of its audible units.

Further, we need to be able to think how the human individual is actually part of an interactional system, and how the basic "psychic contents" are really process aspects of interaction.

(When we have enough concepts we will then be able to go on in those, to see if we can state how we did it: how were we able to think about what is before thought?)

Culture has to be conceived as a system of *situations*, that is to say interaction contexts, or an implicit mesh of possible interactions. Culture is what one does (and says) in different situations—but of course, a situation is inherently itself made up as a system of interrelated possible acts and their consequences, how the situation is thereby changed.

Action goes on *in* a situation, and thereby changes a situation. Conversely, a situation *is* the need (the focal implying) for some action. If one does not act to carry the situation forward, one has "not met the situation." There is always much mere doing, which fails to meet a situation.

Different cultures cannot be said to have different ways of meeting "the same" situations, because the latter are not the same, of course. As yet we have said nothing about how cultural variety enters. What we have seen is that the rudiments of language and of culture form together, but a crucial development has yet to come before there is language. So far we have had only freshly formed (not "used") sequences.

The formation of the archetypes of human culture (if we call them that) is before language as such.

(f) Language formation: two kinds of crossing

(f-1) The mediate carrying forward, what language use is

When language is *used* each word and phrase carries forward *its own* universal context (as it seems) regardless of what context it is used in. The words have *their own* meaning, so that we can say what that is, quite apart from the particular situation, now, in which the words are used.

To define how a word is used, we would tell a situation and also what the use of the word does to the situation. For instance, "democracy" has to do with large groups living together, with government, with dividing things up, and then in that context "democracy" refers to a certain way of doing that, namely . . . Or, another example, "voluntarily" comes up in situations where some act could have been done on one's own, or one might have been forced, and, in that context, "voluntarily" is used when we want to mark the situation as one in which it was done on one's own. Every word or phrase, if used, changes the situation a certain predetermined way. The word "means" both the situation (the context) *and* just how the use of the word changes that context (how the use of the word carries the situation forward).

Both of these are the word's *own* context, it has *its own* carrying forward of *its own* context.

By means of the word's *own* carrying forward we also do something in this particular situation, now, if we use the word now.

The structure of *uses* involves an indirectness; it is "mediate." We carry forward this present situation, now, *by means of* the word's carrying forward *its own.*

(f-2) Collecting context(s), the formation of kinds

How does the word or phrase acquire its own context? This is the question of how universals form—the kind I call "thirds." (For "first" and "seconds," see VII-A.)

We have seen that patterns are versionings—each bit of a pattern sequence is a version of a behavior-context that is "kept-same," so that the string of versions enables us to have and feel and sequence the "same" behavior context over time. I also say that the versioning-sequence (the gesture sequence) *reconstitutes* the behavior context. It occurs, it is felt, had, lived in, bodily. We saw this as the way symbols enable us to live and feel (sequence over time) the behavior context.

The way the body moves and sounds in that behavior context is what does this versioning. First it is the *whole* bodylook (including sound and movement), then what we called "patterns themselves" carry forward. The phrase in quotes means that some *specific visual or sound-pattern* does the carrying forward, not the effect of the whole bodylook of one person on another.

If we wanted to assume kinds and categories from the start (as *we* can do), we would say that the pattern stems from how the body looks in that *kind* of behavior context. We, with our capacity for universals, would observe that the body always looks that *kind* of way in that *kind* of context.

We could then say (by assuming kinds to begin with) that we grasp how kinds form: the pattern, after all, reconstitutes not just this context now, but also each of the other contexts (of that kind). We could ask: "Which context does the pattern reconstitute and enable one to feel? This one, or yesterday's or one long ago, or another long ago?" The answer would have to be all of them, at once. (Of course, we don't want to assume that everything is already organized in kinds; we want to derive that, and understand what is involved. But let that wait for a moment.)

I say that a word or phrase reconstitutes its context(s). This way of writing the plural "s" marks how, in one sense there are many contexts reconstituted, while in some other sense it is all one universal kind of context.

We see that patterns have inherently this kind of relation to particulars: they reconstitute all of them. But of course, we don't assume that someone has gone in advance and has organized and grouped contexts into kind-piles; we want to understand, not assume, that. So we don't say the pattern reconstitutes all of that kind.

We therefore first turn the above around and say: it is *by reconstituting* that the pattern creates a kind or a category. (We must still see how.)

Let us say that the pattern-sequence reconstitutes whatever it reconstitutes, and then let us see what that would be. It isn't just only this behavior context now, because it reconstitutes via how the body is in this context, and that is also how the body is in other contexts of that kind—but there are not yet kinds. It follows that the reconstituting will make a kind-relation *by* reconstituting—it will enable the person to feel (have, sequence) the context(s), now. Thereby a kind is forming.

As this happens again and again, what is reconstituted is different each time, but is the context(s) each time. Every new one is versioned in the present now, by being reconstituted as the context(s). The fresh one is of course newly part of this collecting, and affects just how or what the others, as reconstituted now, are.

They are all *crossed* with this one. What is reconstituted now is a crossed product of this one and the (somewhat new) way in which all the others are now reconstituted along with this one.

All the above is an instance of how *metaphor* was dealt with in Gendlin 1997a. We do not assume antecedently existing "similarities" or "commonalities," but see them forming *by* the crossing of the present context with another or others.

The kinds are a result—along with the words and phrases that reconstitute them.

We have just seen the formation of kinds, but not yet their use. On the contrary, we see clearly that in each situation there is a fresh formation of a versioning, and it only happens to reconstitute the context(s), rather than only this one. The present context is thereby elaborated; we can even say that it is thereby kind*ed*. What it is involves the others that are reconstituted with it. But there is not yet the use of a stable extant stock. These are still fresh sound-formations. The context(s) and the reconstituting sounds are made together.

(f-3) Lateral crossing and collective crossing

Traditionally, it was thought that the different details of all these situations drop out, leaving a commonality, an abstraction, just what the different situations have in common. I will show that this is an error, a very bad error. The collected context(s) is all the richness and complexity of each context *crossed* with every new one. In crossing the details don't drop out, they are part of the eveving that a bodily event is. I will say more about that in a separate discussion in the Appendix to f at the end of VII-B.

Let me contrast the crossing we have had, with this new collecting-crossing.

We saw earlier how a new pattern dimension (from a new dance) has a whole cluster implicit (type-a implicit, pre-formed), namely all the behavior sequences that make up the behavior space—how they will each be elaborated or modified by this new pattern dimension. In each or most behavior sequences some new elaborations will form, which have the new pattern-dimensions from the dance implicit in their formation.

We next said that when that has all happened, and a further new dance gives again a new pattern dimension, the new implicit cluster will cross with the extant cluster. Later a still newer pattern dimension will again cross with the already-crossed cluster, and so on.

I call that kind of crossing "lateral crossing." It is based on the way the behaviors in behavior space form a mutually implicit cluster.

Our new kind of crossing is not like that. Collecting crosses contexts of a kind, rather than the behavior-space cluster.

For example, running relates in behavior space to many *other* behaviors. If the animal runs, it cannot drink, and if it drinks it cannot run. Every behavior implicitly involves a mesh of *other* behaviors that are different.

In contrast, running *as a kind* would collect all the instances of running. An animal's running does not bring with it all the other instances of running. Running does not collect.

(Past experience functions, as described in IV. Past times of running may function in the present running. But past experience does not function along kinds, only—as is so often wrongly assumed. The kind structure must not be assumed as a basic reality given in advance. We want to understand it.)

(f-4) Word-formation

Let us see these two kinds of crossing:

Say a sound, kinnickinnick from a dance, now functions in the formation of many different sounds in many different contexts. This type of sound now functions in the formation of many different sounds that have the "k" or "kin" sound.

Although the "kin" sound is derived from how the body is in some one behavior context, this now crosses (as we saw in the last section) with how the body is in every other behavior context (that was implicit in the first one). And that is called "lateral crossing."

As "kin" is used in one context, and "kind" in another, and "ken" in still another, these sounds each reconstitute and thus create their kinds. Each collects its context(s). "King" comes to collect context(s), and so does "child."

These collected context(s) are not as our universals in logic; "kind" reconstitutes not only all of the members of the clan, but also how one acts toward a member of the clan differently than toward an outsider.[15] The sound "ken" reconstitutes the context(s) of familiarity. The collected context(s) are not a logically pure fenced-in multiplicity of exact particulars, like stamped-out pennies that differ only in particularity. On the contrary, it would be an endless job to state logically what a word collects, and reconstitutes.

Each time it forms, it also adds to the collected context(s) a fresh complex context, in which it can form (since it did).

We see clearly that the details of each context are not at all dropped out in favor of abstract bones. On the contrary, the details are retained and crossed with the collected context(s). The universal forms as the crossed product of these contexts.

(f-5) Short units

We can derive from the above, that there is a strong tendency toward the shortest units, as a result of the collecting of context(s).

Let me first think about this in the wrong old way that assumes similarity in advance, and then rethink it more correctly.

Say two long sequences form in two different contexts. Some parts of these two are the same, the rest differs. The part that is the same in both would collect the two context(s) and would exist as an independent unit. Thus the units would get shorter and shorter, until syllables would have *their own* meaning, i.e., their own collected context(s) which they carry forward.

Instead, we say that it is by collecting that a "part" comes to form as a part. It is by collecting that there is first a sameness. (Collecting, we said, involves reconstituting a context which is the crossed product, what can form, with the many reconstituted contexts at once.)

So we need not assume in advance that the longer sequences already come as a string of parts. Nor need we assume that certain sounds exist as "similar" or "the same." It is only when the sound finds itself reconstituting the collected context(s) that "it" becomes a sound-part in its own right, something that can recur as itself, something that can *be* both its other occurrences and this occurrence; in short, something that can be *such*.

Collective crossing thus makes for the shortest units. As soon as some incomplete sequence reconstitutes collected context(s) it becomes an "it," becomes an independent entity, "a" part, and it falls out as such. It does so because it now has carried forward *its own* collected context(s). It reconstitutes its collected context(s)—that is to say, its carrying forward in them—even without the rest of the sequence.[16]

We see this as soon as we look for it: most longer words in a language are combinations of syllabic words that can mean independently. Original word-formation appears to have broken sound sequences down to syllabic units. The first words were all the way down to syllabic units. Then, when word-formation in the sense of the creation of language was over, new words were (and are still) formed by combination or metaphor—which is not the original creation of language.

We will inquire shortly what this critical point is at which language-creation ceases, and all further new formations must use only certain combines of what is extant. It is obvious that many *sounds* which would be just as useful as those in a language are always possible, but this is not how new words are formed once the original creation of language ceases. This cessation happened long before all obvious new possible syllables were exhausted. This shows also that the formation of word-units was anything but an arbitrary use of possible syllables, but rather a very specific process that must have been involved, which could go no further at some point.[17]

(f-6) The context of a word; collected contexts and interaction contexts

When fallen out—because it reconstitutes its own context(s)—a word-unit retains its relations to other contexts and to other word-units. We can see this exactly, if we consider:

A context consists of many other implicit sequences not now occurring. The occurring sequence carries the context forward in its way, whereas the implicit sequences in the context would carry it forward in other ways. Therefore a sequence is always also implicit relations to other sequences.

We saw earlier that the gestural sequences make new relations both among the contexts they version, and among the patterns themselves. Until the FLIP, the gestures still occur as pauses in the sequences of behavior space. After the FLIP, even actions go on in the mutually implying interaction sequences as the overarching (internal/external) space.

Every word-unit is therefore implicitly a very large system of mutually implicit sequences, as well as being its own occurring, its own carrying forward of its own context(s). These mutually implicit sequences are gestural and of course reconstitute action-contexts. Both the sounds, and also the contexts, mutually imply each other, and are implicit as the context that the word-unit reconstitutes.

The word therefore forms only in certain interaction-contexts, and only in certain relations to other words, only in certain places in a sequence.

It is important to realize that for us today, also, words form in a bodily way. The right words *must come* to us. (If they don't, there is little we can do about it, except wait, and in a bodily way, sense what our situation is, and what we sensed that we were about to try to say.) It is our bodily being in the situation we are in, that lets the right words come. If the reader would stop for a moment, and self-observe, it will be immediately clear. The words of speech and thought "just come." How do they come? We do not sift through many wrong words, as if going through a file. We don't "select" words from among many other words. The right words, or close to the right words, "just come." What precedes this coming? Sometimes a bodily sense of the situation. But often there is no separately attended to sense of this kind. Being in the situation lets the words come.

The system of interrelated words and the system of interrelated situations and interactions is, in some basic way, a single system. And, in another basic way, there are two interrelated systems: the system of words and the system of our living in situations.

The basic link between the two, in schematic terms, is the way patterns reconstitute (we feel, have, sequence over time) situations without changing them as action would. A pattern is a pattern of . . . , and lets us version a situation without acting in it. After the FLIP, however, such gestural sequences become the main action (interaction), and new marks come to determine the difference between changing a situation and merely doing or merely talking about. The basic division is no longer between gesturing and action.

After the FLIP, therefore, the two systems are no longer distinguished by the differences between gesturing and acting. Rather, it is now the difference between the words' own collective context(s) on the one hand, and the particular present situation they mediately carry forward now.

The situations thereby, as we said, become kind*ed*, so that every situation is not only this one, but also *a* situation of a given kind.

The difference remains, therefore. Words are *used*—because they always carry forward their context(s), and only mediately do they carry forward this context now. Interactions are not used—one uses words *in* interactions. Of course, the very same speech-act is both. Let me show this more exactly:

You say to your friend, "I'm tired. Let's stop working for a while."

You are using existing words. But the interaction is fresh, you are tired now. Could we try to say that the interaction is also used? In our culture it is an appropriate move (we might try to argue) to say that one is tired. It will usually obtain a rest period or an approved cessation of work. In another culture one might have to *use* a different excuse. But there is a difference here! Your friend will resent it if this is indeed a move you are *using*, whereas no resentment is involved in *using* words. We see that, indeed, one can use interactional moves, but it is a special case. The normal case is that interactions do not form as existing moves that are used.

The speech-act as words is a use, but as interaction it is fresh.

There are two systems of contexts here, the mutually implicit situations which I will call the *interaction life context*, and the mutually implicit collected context(s) of each word, which as the language system I will call the collected life interaction contexts (coliacxt). The words thus always carry forward *their own* life contexts, and we use them to carry forward this present fresh one in which we live.

Notice that the culture as a system is the collected life interaction contcxt—it is the same single system formed along with language-formation as kinds of situations. We saw earlier how interaction-contexts and language form together.

The interaction contexts we live in are particular, although of course the collected life interaction context is always implicit in our situations.

Let us not forget that before language, even before humans, behavior space is very complex. Gestures and patterns version and elaborate this vastly. By no means is it the case that all this disappears, as though we were left only with the relatively few kind relations, as abstractions. Kind relations version and reconstitute situation(s), *with* all their details and complexity. Thus vastly more occurs than is kinded. Also, in the kinded situations, and in the collected contexts, vastly more occurs than only what is kinded in them.

It is also clear that vast crossed complexity occurs in the collected context(s) as such; words can have much more cultural meaning than an individual grasps, and usually they do. *It is not at all* the case that the collected(s) are poorer. The universal is not only *commonalities*.[18] Nor are individuals merely mental—they are bodies that imply the collected life interaction context.

The fresh situations we live can certainly exceed the collected life interaction context, since we live fresh formations. But it must be kept clear that the collected life interaction context also vastly exceeds what we can reflect upon. (We have not yet discussed the kind of sequences in which we reflect upon what we are living interactionally.)

(f-7) Syntax

Before a shorter unit fell out, something like that unit was an event in the longer sequence. Like any event in a sequence, it implied the rest of the sequence.

As short units carry forward context(s) of their own, that is now quite a different sequence. But each unit still implies the rest of the sequence (now the new one).

The use of any word changes what other words can now be used. We have seen this in terms of the interrelation of situations (contexts), and also in terms of the interrelation of words. But the use of any word also changes what other words could occur to complete what used to be a single gesture sequence.

In the previous example, you say to your friend, "I'm tired. Let's stop working." You couldn't have said "I'm round," because the word "round" belongs to a different context. But you also couldn't have said "I'm tired. Let's." This is because the word "Let's" implies that another word will come.

Every word is also implicitly the system of all the words that could come next, and sometimes also words in further spots down the line.

You could finish the sentence with "Let's" if you follow it with some gesture or indication, for example, you could point at the door. This shows that it is an interaction unit, not necessarily a word, that must come. But words imply these slots for other words also where there is no meaning content that can substitute for it. For example, word order. You cannot say "I tired am," even though the meaning would be clear. You cannot say "I'm tiredness."

It has been noted that the syntactical structure of language is far more complex than seems warranted by the requirements of meaning. It is also an odd kind of structure difficult to reduce to explicit rules. It is in fact the kind of structure the body has and makes. It shows the bodily origin of the character of bodily behavior sequences, and their relation to each other.

Syntax has the complexity and mutual interrelatedness characteristic of the body. We can *feel* the need for a certain word, not only from the situation we are in, but also from the words we have used up to the given point. The word is implied focally, even if it doesn't come, much as exhaling is implied when we hold our breath, or eating when hungry.

Therefore there is no mystery how people speak without knowing the "rules" of syntax, any more than how people manage to sit down in a chair without falling, even though they know neither anatomy nor physics. The "rules" we explicate are a very late product, and they are never quite successful—if we had only the "rules" as stated we would not speak very well, and we could not do all that we do with language. If we had only the rules of sitting we would fall down. But these "rules" do show something of the nature of one aspect of the possibilities space, one aspect of the collected life interaction context a word brings with it, and reconstitutes for us in a bodily way we can feel.

It is right to say, in a way, that the structure of syntax is inborn, as is also much of behavior and of interaction.[19] One could explicate many structural aspects of behavior and of interaction. The relation between learning and inborn must be taken up—every sequence is both, and in a variety of ways. Of course it isn't syntax alone, as such, that is inherited. The body is inherited. We have seen that the living body is a functional and interaction system. Its ongoing interacting with the environment is inherited, including how it builds cells, mating dances, gestural bodylook interaction, and the basic human interaction contexts. Along with all this there is also syntax.

Of course, it seems mysterious how syntax could be "built into" the kind of body physiology conceptualizes. But that is equally true of all functional implying, of all behavior and human interaction. The animal organism has been conceived of too simply and mechanically. There is then no bridge from physiological concepts to behavior ones. How can the squirrel's innate nut-burying be "built in" the body is another mystery like syntax. But the gap is not at all between body and behavior and symboling. It is between the kind of concepts currently used in physiology, and the kind we need in the study of animal behavior and symbolic interaction. Therefore we have reconceptualized body-process (I–V).

True, physiology books usually assert that the body is functional and interactional. But the detailed concepts are all along the lines of the old unit model, so that there is no way to think about any specific bodily processes in functional terms. Although still general, we have taken many steps into making new specific concepts for body-process, with which we can think about the body character of behavior and now symboling.

Of course, what is inborn is not "the rules" that linguists formulate. It is the body which is inherited—but not only the physical body, also its functioning. Indeed, the physical body itself is a kind of product of its functioning, of life process. We inherit not only the lungs, but how we breathe, and not just the stomach but how it digests and what food it can take. This applies also to what must also be learned. Nothing can be learned unless *by* some organism, which already has the sort of structure which makes it possible to learn that.

Some of the structure of the human brain is related to language, and much else in the human body as well, I would add. The development of language and culture is the development of humanness, of how the human *body* differs from other living bodies. It is not only a question of the brain but of the whole body in which the brain functions, the whole system of action and interaction which this body implies.

No doubt, there can be many other different concepts, and others will develop better ones. But let us be glad to have at least one set, and the questions and derivations that set gives us. It lets us enter territory not charted until now, or, to shift metaphors, how body and language (and much else we discussed) relate allows us to think one whole level deeper, under most of what has been said on these topics till now.

(f-8) Language use; novel situations

We saw earlier that we are always at a specific "spot" in the collected life interaction context, depending of course on how we are in our interactional life context (in which the collected life interaction context is implicit). There is therefore a set of speech-acts focally implied by the situation. Or, we can say more exactly, that certain further interactions are focally implied (that is what a situation is, it has to be "met," that is to say, it requires or implies certain further actions). Only some of these focally implied next interactions are speech-acts.

When circumstances are routine, the next interaction is also routine. But even when a situation is novel, when we don't know exactly what to say or do, there is nevertheless a very finely exact implying of the next interaction. Only, the next interaction is new, it has never happened before.

Is it surprising that something which has never happened could be focally implied? Not at all! That has been so in this schematic from the start. In changed circumstances either the body dies or something new happens (see IV, V, VI). A body event *is* an eveving; it always also *is* the implying of a next (and a whole) sequence.

But we also said throughout, that even when the observer seems to know exactly what next event is focally implied, we say the implying is never equivalent to a structured sequence. It is rather an implying for *some* way of carrying forward, not necessarily for the way familiar to the observer.

We have been able to think about development and novelty more clearly in this way. A new sequence may happen instead of the one that usually happens at this focal implying. The new one is then pyramided on the old one. The old one will recur if the new one cannot. Every sequence is a new one, from its own viewpoint. The new sequence is the new-new (the old one was also a new one).

Now, however, these syllabic word-units (and combinations) have developed, which are their own carrying forward of their own context(s). As always, the formation of the actual speech sequences is fresh and new. But it is a formation that consists of new arrangements of extant units that carry forward on their own. I must explain this more exactly.

The formation of these words in this sentence now is the interaction which, as we said, forms freshly.

The reason linguists form "rules" is because language-use is creative. The regularity is not what is said. That shows a great creative variety. There is a regularity in how these creative sentences all must be structured. The notion of "rules" deals with this kind of regularity in the formation of irregular creative variety within certain regularities.

These rules are not just about order and combination. As we saw, each word implies what other words can come next, also in terms of meaning contexts, not only in terms of sequence order.

One is always at a given spot in one's interactional life context, and hence a given spot of the collected life context. If exact words and sentences are not extant, nevertheless one's being in the interaction life context implies in a definite way.

It is now this implying which *re-evevs* the extant words (and the vast system of implicit sequences, which each word is).

Language use, in our schematic terms, is this *re-eveving*.

One might call every renewed eveving "re-eveving," but I use the term here because words constitute a repertoire. "Repertoire" is another word indicating use and re-eveving: each piece in the repertoire is its own eveving, already. To use them, one does a fresh eveving.

The next section will make this clear.

(f-9) Discursive use versus art; re-eveving versus re-recognition

When a painter borrows a motif, for example, a raggedy dead tree like those Ruysdael freshly created, could we say the motif is "used" like words are used? The answer is no, but exactly why not? After all, it is well known that such a tree adds a desolate, and at the same time dramatic effect. When that effect is wanted, the painter might "use" such a tree. We could think of a painting put together almost completely out of well-known elements, and some very bad paintings are made like that.

A painted tree is a visual pattern. The quality of its lines and colors affect us. A melody affects us through the quality of the sound-pattern. In contrast, a word does *not* affect us through the quality of its sound-pattern. We must *recognize* (the "re" is like the "re" in "re-evev") the word, and so we must recognize the sound-pattern that the word is. But the recognition then has an effect that is independent of the quality of that sound-pattern as sound. Except for the few words that are onomatopoeic, the sound effect doesn't matter.

When the painter uses a Ruysdael tree, it is still the quality of the visual pattern that affects us. For example, if instead of the tree a little plaque were painted in, saying "dramatic desolate tree," the effect would not occur. The tree also has to work together visually in terms of line and color patterns with the rest of the painting. A word, in contrast, must work with other words not in terms of sound quality, but in terms of the system of other words and sequences which the word implies. It doesn't matter about the sounds, except in poetry—which is again a type of art.

Each artwork is a fresh new whole, *not* made up of units each of which is its own whole. This is a second difference. Does it relate to the fact that art still has its effect in terms of sound and visual quality? Yes.

Both speech and art build a fresh whole, and of both one can say that the effect of each part is different in context than separately. But the units of speech are, so to speak, self-enclosed. Each unit must first have *its own* effect, and only then do these effects build to a whole that modifies each. If words were still carrying forward by sound-quality, each subsequent one would merge into the effect being accumulated. A sound just after another has a *completely* different effect than if it came after a different one. The only reason words are independent of this merger is because their effects are in terms of meaning, not sound. But meaning is precisely not the sound-effect. It is no longer the sound-quality but the "*re*-recognition." In terms of my schematic use of that word it would be the re-re-recognition, since I used that word in a too early sense twice already. Here, however, it is used in a different way, precisely not as a recognition by the body of its own "expressive" production. That relation still obtains in the total effect of one's speech: one responds to the meaning one has expressed, and if that is not what one was about to convey, then the sequence stops. So our technical sense of re-re-recognizing applies to the achieved meaning. It does not apply to the independent meaning of each word or phrase. The terms I have chosen for that new relation are "re-eveving" and "repertoire."

The word-unit is, in a self-enclosed way, *its own* eveving and carrying forward of its own context(s), and that independent eveving is then re-eveved in the speech-act.

(f-10) New expression

Art creates new visual and sound and movement patterns. These then function in most other action and interaction. For example, even today, new art influences how we can perceive. How we see nature and design furniture and arrange our rooms is affected by visual art, and what sounds music first lets us perceive influence what sounds nice to us, and what doesn't. Conversely, of course, art creates new patterns by versioning aspects of our world that have not been pattern-versioned before. For example, industrial machinery and noises are versioned in music, and in painting, whereupon the patterns themselves then are also used in new factory design. (I wish the newer music would also influence ordinary noise-production but it hasn't, so far as I know.)

When patterns first emerged for humans, they were not art. They were culture-forming and human-making. Then as now the patterns versioned ordinary contexts (versioned = sequenced, let us feel, have, spend time having). Then as now these patterns are symbolic of our living contexts, because they version. Although just patterns, they are also a bodily feeling and having of the life-contexts they reconstitute. But there is a big difference: now such patterns are art, that is to say, a separated and different context, not life but art. But it isn't art that has changed—in art a new pattern still does what it always did: it versions our living in a new way, and it also elaborates and re-creates our living. What has changed is that now there is language, and our living situations (our interaction contexts) are structured with language.

There is therefore (with the exception of VIII, to come) no way, now, for visual or sound or movement patterns to act like a "first dance," and to regenerate the whole culture. This effect is now minor (although very precious).

When language developed, there was also a split between language and art. This split is because of the self-enclosed (I also call them "discursive") units of language, in contrast with the new visual and sound expression that a new work of art always is.

But exactly at what point did art get split off so that a culture-regenerating new expression could no longer happen as in a "first dance"? That is the same point at which short, independently functioning units of language developed.

(f-11) Fresh sentences

Having seen more exactly what discursive units are, we can finish discussing the fresh formation in language use.

We said that as interaction, the speech-acts are fresh formations. As a use of words, they are a re-eveving, since each word and phrase is its own eveving already.

The "rules" have to be understood as the re-eveving, the ways that one can fit together units each of which is a huge system of implicit sequences, that is to say, possible further steps.

Whereas until now a whole sequence was likely to go through uninterruptedly (as we said in VI under relevanting) before a new sequence would form, now there is a new eveving between each unit and the next. That is another way to define "re-eveving."

What seems like a system of rules added on to units, in order to combine them, is really inherent in each unit. Each is many implicit sequences. To combine units is to re-evev the evevings that each is.

In doing this a new kind of novelty is possible, not any longer new sound-patterns. The new kind of novelty is combinations, which stay and become units in their own right, as well as metaphors (see Gendlin 1997a) wherein a same unit acquires a radically new context(s). This is done from the crossing of the two (the old and the new use of the word) in the metaphor. There are other ways new words and phrases come to be, but always out of the static stock of ancient syllable word-units.

Even the routine use of words as usual is creative, however. The exact sentences we say might never have been said before. The interaction life context (the way all our situations, mutually implicit in each other, are) is now a certain way. But our situations are speech-structured. The interaction contexts developed, and continue to develop, along with language. The distinctions that structure one situation differently than another, which make this a learning situation and that a friendly discussion, for example, are not two separate systems: the situations, and the language use in them. Without language there would be no way at all to have so many distinctly different kinds of situations. It is only because of the fineness of language that our situations are so varied and finely structured. Or, say it in reverse: the formation of language is also the formation of finely distinguished situations. The situations are distinguished not only by what one says in them, of course, but by how one interacts. But so much of the latter is spoken interaction, that the rest cannot stand alone.

People have seen these things separately, and thus unclearly. Culture has been studied in terms of odd rituals and beliefs. But, of course, culture is the way one behaves in different situations, just what these situations are. It is how one says good-bye and what else one does before leaving, when one gets up to go, and the kind of meetings one might have, the roles of the kinds of people that exist, just when one feels insulted and just when one is content to go along, when and how one fights or argues, and about what. In short, culture is a patterning of situations, and this patterning is very considerably (certainly not wholly) linguistic. It would ignore the most important interactions of life to say that it was all linguistic—but even the very physical and spiritual interactions that are seemingly before and beyond words are implicitly very rich in the distinctions and experiences that involve or have involved words as part of what happens.

Language must be understood as part of the system of culturally structured situations, which also means human roles and identities, and also means living, interacting.

Only so can we then easily think how it is that even when we are in a quite new situation and do not know what to do or say, there is an implying not only of what we next need to do, but (as part of that) what we need to say.

(It is a further distinction, in VII, that some saying *is* interacting, while some is only about. There is a strong tendency for the about-saying itself to become interaction in its own right. You are only confiding in this person, talking about your relation to another person. Still, you are thereby also living your relating to this new confidante. In this new relation what you talk about also changes. It is itself an interaction now.)

At any point in our living, words are implied, both as further carrying this situation forward, and also as being "only" about it, helping to have, feel, sequence, and sense it, without changing it (in the way interacting with the people concerned would change it).

Language is always implicit, not at all as a new addition. When we explicate in words some private feeling that seems utterly autistic and only our own, words are nevertheless already implicit in it, because they are implicit in our very living, our bodies, our interactions. Putting words to a feeling is never the first time words and that feeling have met.

Ever since V, we have seen novelty as easily thinkable, provided one doesn't begin with the assumption that further events must consist of existing units or places.[20] We conceptualized living process as eveving, meaning that all extant structur*eds* are taken into account and still the next event might be new. The structures do not function as themselves (so that what results is consistent with them), but just as they can function in the given eveving. Thus life events are inherently always new.

Therefore it is easy to see that humans would often find themselves in a quite new situation with a quite new implied next event. Such a next event has as yet no form. It is not yet structured (in the sense of explicit form and structure). But it is an extremely definite implying.

One can see this easily in that one always knows at such times without any trouble that what one thinks of to say and do is *not* what needs to come next. One can easily think of thousands of doings and sayings that will not carry forward one's bodily being in the situation. It is difficult, and a new creation to do and/or say what is implied, and will carry forward (or "meet") the situation. Thus it is easy to see how definite this implying is, even when we don't yet know what to say or do.

But the use of language does look like an arranging of preexisting units, and now each unit does seem to function as itself, and it is not restructured in how it now functions. Or so it seems. More exactly, the creation of fresh speech is still as above, with this difference: discursive units function as carrying forward *their own* context(s), and only thereby do they then also function in the fresh process. The way they are now freshly used does indeed add (and cross with) their own context(s), so that every use of a word or phrase adds to its meaning. Something like metaphor goes in every use, as fresh meaning is created by the crossing of the words' usual context(s) and this one. But each word-unit closes itself off, and cannot be sound-merged with the others. Each carries forward its own context (s), and only in doing so is it then (in regard to meaning, not sound) freshly modified somewhat.

(f-12) Deliberate

The capacity to stop and then sense, without doing anything, that one might do one of a number of possibilities, is deliberateness.

Every versioning is already the capacity to pause action, to keep the action context "the same" through a string of changes that don't change it as action would. But such a pause forms; it cannot be deliberately introduced.

Once there is language, a new eveving occurs with each unit. Each unit is a system of possible nexts, a system of its own. What it does in a given use, now, is to reconstitute (to version, to let me feel and have) this situation, *as* one of the word's context(s). I let the word version this situation now, for me, and it does that by reconstituting this context as one of its own. But so does the next word, and even if I am not talking, the word-system is implicit in what my situations are. Much that could be said is implied, and more: sayings are implied that I might find no way to actually say.

Speech is deliberate, and much action and interaction has also become deliberate. It can stop at any time, and is actually pausing at all times. Each bit of it is a pausing. What was behavior has been absorbed, and the pausings (after the FLIP) have become the main processes, the interactions, and lone gestures and makings.

Emotions provide an exception that we must consider later.

There is also a pathology of deliberateness, due to the "thinning" which makes each bit of interaction usually much less bodily potent than when the whole space was simpler. Only rarely do we change our situations radically enough that we really feel it. Most often this occurs emotionally.

There is also a way, to be understood in VIII, of making such bodily powerful and situationally radical changes. One would think that complex human living ought to be thicker, not thinner—so much is always implicitly involved in any action. But this can only happen in the way shown in VIII. While we continue with culturally patterned interaction, so much is now implicit which is not wholly carried forward, that the same actions that once were "thick" are now thin (using these adjectives to describe the quality of the bodily event). They still enable us to eat, or have intercourse, to work or create, but we are not full-bodiedly being carried forward, often.

(f-13) More than one context; human time and space

We have discussed human space (internal/external space, interaction-life-context), and can now add: the system of mutually implying interaction-contexts involves speech (gesture) sequences. These are mutually implicit in each other *both* via the relation of the contexts, *and* as word-units. The word-relations have additional aspects, those stemming from their origin in longer sequences, and these relations are how each word-unit is now a system of implicit sequences of many other units.

Each word is its own eveving, its own carrying forward of its own context(s). One is therefore always in two contexts, the word's own (the kind), and this interaction context now (the kind*ed* one).

Each word brings its context, that is to say, its relations to many other contexts. Each kinded interaction context, now, also consists of implicit interactions that would be other situations if they happened. Speaking now to this person, all I ever did or do and could do with this person is implicit, as well as all the situations that would thereby be altered, and all the people of those situations, and all I could do with them. While no person is totally unified, I call this whole system the interactive life context, knowing that it might actually have some disconnected places (empirical holism: it is an empirical question whether "all" or some are mutually implicit in all or some others).

This was true as the interaction-contexts formed, but there was then no way for a person to reconstitute and live in (feel, have) some of the other contexts now implicit. For instance, having made hunting tools, and used them, on the way home there was no way to feel and have the next hunt, so that one would still recognize the tools, as *such*. To do that would be to see the tools as universals, as that kind of thing, as belonging to that kind of context, and there was no way to have kinds. (No "thirds," we called it.)

But even though there are now word-units, these still form from the context one is in. How does their existence and use enable one to *be in a* situation one is not physically in? Once there is the FLIP, then the interaction, not the physical present, is the context one is in, we said. Thus "present" has a different meaning. It is "this situation," not "this physical behavior space." It includes all the interactions I might have with this person, and all the situations as they are mutually implicit, and all those physical times. These are now not only past experience implicit in the makeup of an event, but situations I can reconstitute and live in.

We all know humans can do that, but can we think exactly how? With words we can reconstitute other situations. But why would these words form? Through the mutual implying of interaction-contexts the next event might be in a context that was only implicit before, and in a different physical space and time. But why could one not move that way before? In behavior space such a movement was physical and would be a concrete change in physical space and time. But the interaction contexts implied each other before the FLIP. Yes, but then the whole system was only a pause within a given action in a given physical context. So the FLIP also makes it possible to live one's way from the present interaction-context to one that is made present, but isn't physically present. And to this must be added that kinded interaction (explicit use of words implicit in what every situation is) is deliberate. Each re-eveving is a new opening to implicit contexts, and the fact that then there is another re-eveving immediately after, enables many shifts from one physical context to another in a brief time. It looks as if we could move anywhere with our attention, and to any time. Actually we cannot. We still cannot move to something that is unconnected to whatever we are now living in, feeling and thinking. It must "come up." But the mutually implicit relations are now available at each word, and at each kinded act.

Humans live in many contexts, and this opens a complexity I must discuss in another time and place.

(g) When is the FLIP? Cessation of sound-formation in language use

In the notes to f-5 we last considered this question.

Short unit formation, we said, is probably the point at which use begins, since language use is of such units. Patterns collect before, and reconstitute not only the present context, but as long sequences they are not a repertoire to be used.

When and exactly why does language cease to take in new sounds? This is the same question as when no new "first dance" sequences can occur any more, or when art begins. Why would a new dance no longer version a context in a new way?

As soon as new interactions (or elaborations) form without new sound-gestures, obviously that is the point at which language continues to develop but without new sound formation. So we can ask our question this way: why would language develop further by combining existing sounds, rather than letting the sound-quality keep newly forming and versioning?

As interactions elaborate, further, that is *not* done by rearranging fixed units. Each interaction is a fresh event, not a use of fixed moves. Two points here: the development culturally is not in units, and also each new individual context is not an arrangement of units. Language of course develops along with interaction contexts, but its development is in terms of the same ancient stock of syllabic word-units.

When and exactly why did new sound-formation cease? Language continues to change, of course, but not by taking in new sounds. Old words are drafted into new uses, new words are fashioned from old words or syllables that are already meaningful. Even Linear A, the ancient language of Crete prior to its great civilization, when at last it was deciphered, turned out to be a kind of Greek. Sound-formation ceased very early. Once language has formed it is amazingly conservative. An infinite variety of sounds that are not language is possible, yet these are no longer drawn in to add to language. At some critical point the basic stock of linguistically used sounds is closed, and what is thereafter added must always consist of already meaningful sounds.

With every new crossing there is a *phantastic differentiation.* All the aspects that existing gesture-patterns version, and let one have, are now elaborated by the new pattern-dimension. Each multiplies with the whole cluster. A vast number of new facets becomes noticeable, experienceable, capable of being felt and had. Thus each crossing vastly increases the number of facets that are capable of being separately sequenced. The variety that is possible increases very greatly. The fineness of definition and structure—that is to say the number of facets that must be carried forward (eveved) by a next act—becomes quite great, and life becomes complex. What a situation is and implies (means) becomes subtle.

Even so, we said, there can be a new first dance, which again versions some elaborated situation by sheer sound-pattern (or visual, or movement pattern). Why would this become impossible at some point?

We also saw that soon given sound-patterns carry forward not as part of the way the whole body looks, but as sheer sound. We called these "patterns themselves," rather than a whole bodylook or sound. These are still patterns of sound-quality, however, and new "first" sequences are possible even when sound-patterns already carry forward as themselves. When can they no longer?

Today it is clear that sheer sound-expression is still powerful to carry the body forward. We have it in music and in tone of voice. Why can it not, today, add to language? Why can it not, as a first dance would, version the whole of a situation? Suppose I try it. I am in a complex interaction with someone, I am stopped and find no act or speech to carry me forward. Something is implied, quite focally and definitely, but I don't know in words or acts what that is. Now I grunt, and my companion certainly senses something. There is some communication here. Why is it not a "versioning" of our situation? Much of the situation *is* versioned by the grunt. But how much? "Versioned" means you get to live, feel, have and sequence the situation. To what extent, in hearing the grunt, is my companion having and feeling the situation? Relatively little of it is conveyed thereby.

Of course, the interaction was conducted with deeds and words till then, and *as an addition to that* the grunt can be very expressive and communicative indeed. But only *within* the interaction context, not at all as a versioning *of* all of it.

Talking can be used to conceal, too, and bodylooks and sounds can then especially be very informative—but again only *within* the complex interaction.

This is the "within" after the FLIP.

Ellen made a dance about the man who smashed the *Pieta* in the Vatican. But from the dance alone one could not have known what it was about. It was a dance of sadness. (The *Pieta*'s sadness and the sadness of the smashing.)

A new bodylook sequence is now *within* a *wider* interaction context, because it no longer versions the *whole* interaction context. How the bodylook patterns and sound-patterns are is now never as differentiated as the patterns-as-such already are.

The first time the body-sound quality no longer versions the context, it is within it. Versioning means reconstituting the whole context—each bit is a version of the context. If less than the context is reconstituted by the pattern, then it has remained within the context.

But let us go over this again. Something is odd. Just as the gesture sequence for the first time remains within the context, instead of versioning the whole of it, that is also the moment gesture contexts take over, and are no longer only pauses with behavior contexts. Isn't this contradictory? No—it is the *interaction* context that is now too wide to be wholly versionable by a new sound. The new sound remains within the interaction context. Thereby the interaction ceases to be a versioning of the behavior, and becomes the context instead.

There is really no interaction-context until the FLIP. It is still a behavior context with elaborations. When these elaborations become more complex than sound can version, then they are the context, that is to say wider, and the sound happens within it and becomes one sequence *among* the interaction sequences, and never again a pattern that versions the whole of the implicit interaction sequences at once.

The FLIP is the same moment as the cessation of new sounds entering the language. Since there are a variety of languages (but very few, if we consider the basic stems), the FLIP and sound-cessation happened somewhat later (but not much) than cultural and linguistic variety. Therefore variety probably goes very far back (there are and have always been various species of any type of living being). But the common structure of language is its type of structure, not its specific "rules." The search for universal linguistic properties, as currently conducted, is as silly as the search for universally applicable human or cultural traits. It is silly because one seeks these commonalities in the wrong place—in the contents, the developments that came later. The *type* of structure that language-and-culture are is quite the same all over. (I will say more about this in another place. See Gendlin 1967 and 1977.)

We have located the FLIP and cessation of new language sounds together. Now what about use? Does it begin at the same point? And is that also the same point at which short units fall out? Certainly we saw that short units must be re-eveved unit by unit, and that is use—because the reason for their falling out (and the re-eveving by unit) is exactly that they are each an eveving, a carrying forward of their own context(s). There are thus two evevs, two contexts: the word's own, that has to be re-eveved by the body. Yes, short units and use are together.

Now, are the FLIP and cessation the same point as short units and use? Shall we say that the short units formed, and that was why the behavior context could no longer be whole-versioned by sound? Or shall we say that the FLIP and cessation happened, and that is why the short units then began to fall out? Which of these helps us understand the other?

Before the FLIP a pattern collects (reconstitutes not only this context), but it is a pause in behavior. This means the pattern collects and is a kind, but the context is not kinded, it is only versioned and felt.

After the FLIP the pattern collects as before, but now the context is carried forward by the pattern—not versioned. The pattern-sequence is now like action (interaction) and carries forward the situation. Contexts are now carried forward (not versioned), and only so can there be two contexts, the word's own and this one. Why? Because the word carries forward *its context*. This isn't possible before there is a context that a word can carry forward! In other words it is not possible before there is an interaction-context.

My difficulty has been to forget that there are not interaction-*contexts* till after the FLIP; until then there are behavior-contexts elaborated by pauses. Such a pause cannot have been its own context carrying forward. Clearly, units that carry forward their own context could not have developed until after the FLIP.

· But more: as soon as there are interaction contexts, as soon as sounds carry forward contexts (rather than versioning), the short units would fall out because the first bit would have carried forward and changed the context. It would not have been paused, it would have been changed.

Another way to say it: before and after, sound-patterns reconstitute patterned contexts. But before the FLIP, "patterned" means the context has pattern-pauses in it. Afterwards "context" means interaction context, pattern-context. So the context has come to be of the same nature as the sound-patterns, and only so does the word have "its own." The collected context(s) are *its own* (it had these before the FLIP, but "context" was then behavior context) only because now there is the fresh present interaction-context.

We have clearly shown that the FLIP makes the doubled contexts, the word's own and this one.

Only then would the short unit fall out because it would have made its change, it would have functioned as a word, it would have been *used*.

Use, we see, is of course always *in*. One uses a word *in* a context which the word reconstitutes along with its own.

We see also that there is never again a reconstituting or versioning *of the whole*. There are no more "new first dances." There is now only always one sequence *among* many other possible ones *within* the context. (Even if "versioning" means "talking about" rather than carrying forward the interaction context, it never again means versioning the whole.) All sequences reconstitute the context, but never the whole.

Appendix to (f). Details do not drop out; universals are not empty commonalities.

The distinction of kind and instance (universal and particular) does not exist before VII. Animal situations can be called universal (the animal responds the same way to any tree) or one can say they are all particular (the animal responds to just this tree, always, not the category). Before a distinction exists, it is not really correct to say either, and one can make some case for either. The human observer brings the kind-structure, and the instances.

We do not assume the kind-structure to begin with. It is poor to say that reality is organized in "typicalities," as people like to say. Instead of helping us think about what universals and particulars are, they merely assert what we all know.

It is not the kind-structure that determines how kinds arise. Also, a great deal that is explained with the kind-structure really antecedes it, not only in time and development, but also in the priority of thinking.

Idealism assumes (so to speak) that an adult, developed philosopher meets Being (so to speak, on the street) and they introduce themselves to each other. It is the first time they have met. The philosopher contributes the kind-structure (reason, the forms of unity in judgments, and so on) and Being contributes sensation-bits (as in Kant), or perhaps it contributes an as yet indeterminate other. The human side of this meeting brings possibility, future, connections, order. In such a creation myth the human side is left un-understood. Idealism is an instance of the more general way of using the human observer to determine everything, whereupon, of course, that observer cannot be studied inside that system. Indeed, idealism is the philosophy that went with the science that depends on this idealized, generalized human observer. If now we wish to think also about the observer, namely we ourselves, it cannot be in concepts that assume an unclarified observer in their very structure.

We have seen that in living process itself there is a much greater and different order, and in and from this we want to see how kinds arise.

Even after they arise they are *not* determinative of more than a small portion of the order of living. The kinds, and the elaborated situations that are developed with the kinds, are not an independent system. Rather, they are new versions of the much larger order that existed before, and is now lived, felt, sequenced, and elaborated.

Past experience functions (see IV) in any present. But this is not determined by a kind-structure. It is not the case that there is a system of similarities, such that the past experience knows which present to function in, or such that the present experience knows what kind it is, and so also what past experiences (of the same kind) to pull out of its file. Even today, long after the kind-structure has developed, past experience still functions in vastly more ways than along the lines of the kind-structure.

One can say, in reverse, that the function of past experience *makes* similarity-relations. It is because past experience *can* function in just this way, that the present and the past have just these new similarity-relations, now. The functioning of the past, now, is the same event as the occurring now. What the present now is (how it forms, now), and what past is relevant now (is similar, now) are a single formation, the occurring now.

If we examine any present experience, we can find very many relations of similarity to very many past experiences. You are reading. All past experience of reading should function now, along with all discussions of philosophy, along with all discussions of language, that you have ever had, along with all instances of the same kind of excitement or annoyance which this argument now generates in you, along with all your relations to other people which were something like your relation to me, the author here, right now, along with all the times you argued similarly. But in what respect exactly shall we say you argued similarly? The same sort of conclusion, the same sort of reasoning, the same sort of overly righteous tone, the same way of giving examples, the same type of endless sentences—any number of facets could be lifted out to be the respects in which a similarity might exist. I have lifted out a few that recur in various of my writings. You will probably have thought of quite another similarity than my string of examples, above. Indeed, without *your* way of arguing (in some instance you think of), I could not possibly arrive at the right similarity, the right kind to use here. That shows that the similarities are determined by the two experiences we cross! Without the other experience, a given one cannot be defined as to kind.

Please notice also, that words don't exist to mark many of the kinds I have made in this example. I have had to make new phrases to lift them out. Every experience is capable of giving rise to endless numbers of kind-relations, similarities, depending on what we compare with it. (See Gendlin 1997a, chapter V.)

It is evident that any experience is vastly richer than the existing verbal kind-structure.

The function of past experience (of "everything," in the formation of a present event; see IV) is organic. If we falsely assume that it is the function of *separate* aspects, then we have to say that a vast multiplicity of respects exists, in which past experience functions in the formation of any present. But this is not a multiplicity of separates. It is a multiplicity of a different kind. (See IV.)

Animals "remember," people say, since animals recognize this instance as the same as last time. This obviously doesn't depend on language. (Animals can learn similarities between two things, two places, two kinds of events, which are made with language.) Human situations are recognized by animals, which were originally made by humans and could only have been made with language. Thus language is implicit, in an odd way, even in a house-pet's experience.

The cat knows the difference between the living room and the dining room, and the difference between a car and an airplane, between the clothes that go with going out, and those worn at home. It does not need the language implicit in these situations, in order to recognize them. But this is the function of past experience, not the kind structure. The similarities are not just those that the words collect.

We cannot assume a single set of kinds in nature, and certainly not as determinative of nature.

The organic crossings in how life process *goes on in* (see VI) determine the mesh of organic further structure forming now. Only metaphorically can we think of it as a vast mesh of not-yet-separated similarity-relations.

Our scheme is of course only one way of making new concepts (new kinds) from this organic process. Our scheme does what our scheme is about. The fact that the kinds we articulate are always only one set among many possible ones is inherent, and is nothing against it. Rather, it is one aspect that the scheme must let us think clearly about.

Carefully defined, internally clearly structured concepts are a further development, on a new level. Here we are still trying to understand how words form—and as we will see, each word is a gigantic system of implicit sequences and contexts—and not like a technical concept. But for us too, our new concepts first emerge as an unclarified family of uses. Only after we use it a while are we able to take the further step of structuring a concept internally. (See Gendlin 2004a for an articulation of how we have been doing this, and how it is possible.)

Certainly we will not confuse ourselves by asserting that some formal system of internally clarified technical concepts is the structure of nature or of experience. Rather, we want to see what the power of such concepts is, how they arise and remain related to experience, and what they do. Their "truth" lies not in a photographic relationship or equation.

The function of past experience does not involve kinds. When an animal runs, this does not bring along with it all the other instances when it has run. (As we saw earlier, one wouldn't know which of very many such similarities to invoke . . . it is running, it is breathing, it is running away from . . . , toward . . . , with . . . , in the sun, and so on.) The animal runs in behavior space, and not in a kind-structure. For the observer "running" may be a kind. The observing ethologist creates many new and odd kinds in observing each species of animal. Behavior does not collect, it is not made of similarity-units, not made of "a" running and "a" breathing. It is not kinded.

But human action is only kinded in just a very few respects, compared to the vast multiplicity of how past experience functions.

The kinded respects which first formed us as humans, which first constituted culture, are very powerful.

In the sections on pyramiding (in VI) and on meshing (VII-A) we saw that the original sequences are always still capable of occurring, if later developed ones cannot. The inherited body implies all these sequences.

These basic culture-forming kinds are *not* commonalities, as though everything else were "only" detail. I mean, for example, that "cat" is a common structure, and Siamese versus Abyssinian are additional details that do not, in any way, alter the shared catness. What a cat is can be known independently of these additional details.

Instead, every new formation is a crossing, so that the original culture-forming kinds are organically elaborated and altered, as well as continuing to function in their original meshed way.

The elaboration of interaction-contexts and the elaboration of gestures and sound-patterns are one development. There is no separated word-system even though, as we saw, language has its own contexts and its own interrelations among words.

Every human action and experience is kinded, it is "a" such. But this is so, not at all only along those kinds that we can verbalize in existing words and phrases. There are always vastly many kinds, that we can verbalize, of which a given experience can be made to be an instance. Then we say it "was" an instance of that kind, or that similarity. We can say it "was" after we explicate. This time relation is inherent in explication.

We cannot experience this rabbit without implicitly versioning "a" rabbit. This requires not just rabbits, as the cat might know. It requires the visual look of "a" rabbit, which would let us recognize a picture of a rabbit as the picture of "a" rabbit. It requires the patterns of movement of "a" rabbit, and the collection rabbit(s). We experience it not only as this but always also as "a." Experience is kinded: the kind-structure of collected context(s) is implicit in all experience.

Situations are kinds (they are "kinded") created by versioning, that is to say, as instances of a collected context. A human is *a* mother, *a* son, *a* ruler, *a* peasant, *a* man.

The first kinds are "archetypes," original kinds, types of interaction contexts. In these the people acquire role-identities, not as single individuals but in context with each other. And, of course, these are structures of interactions with each other, that is to say they are situational structures: the ways *a* husband acts in relation to *a* wife, *a* younger person toward *an* elder, *a* wife's brother to *a* husband, etc. We will return to this.

Here it is crucial to see the inherent connection in one cluster of the different dimensions we are deriving. Please do not settle for a merely factual recognition that humans have language, and also roles and interactional identities. Everyone has always known that. The point is to become able to think about the inherent way these are internally connected so we can think about what they are, to develop concepts for them.

If we see how human situations are always such situations (even when unique, because had uniqueness is a further development), we can also thereby derive the IOFI principle (Gendlin 1997a, chapter V). But if I derived it here there would be too much more to say, which belongs to VIII.

From the inherent connection between language and situational structure we can also understand how it is possible that we can articulate in language what we feel. What we feel is interactional has to do with our living—in situations—with others. (Even the hermit is in a situation away from others. Further developments alone are of course possible, but on the grounds of our interactional human nature.) We can "find" words to say what we feel because feelings, interactional situations, and language are one system. This is so even when we have to devise new phrasings and metaphors.

Because patterns reconstitute (let us feel, have) behavior contexts, therefore a relation of universal and particular is created. Both sides of the distinction are made distinct together. (As in the case of formation of the "external/internal" distinction, we have to guard against thinking of what was before the distinction as if it were either one or the other.) Before versioning sequences collect, everything is neither universals nor particulars. Now a sequence carries forward "this" context by versioning and reconstituting the collected context(s). Both *collected* contexts, and *this* context, arise first in such a sequence.

In one sense the *third* doesn't distinguish; it carries forward the present context *as* a merged member of the collected context(s). But of course, the people know they are here, now, and not in any of the other collected context(s). How? We see that in the very way this collecting happens, there is also *a new kind of space and time*, a new "here, now" *and* a new "other times and places"!

New marks develop to mark the distinctions between the collected context(s), "this" context, and "a." This is another VII-derived symbolic distinction. Even with these distinctions, the pattern always reconstitutes the collected context(s). One cannot say "this rabbit" without reconstituting rabbits. Similarly, "a rabbit" reconstitutes rabbits.

The patterns "this" and "a" are of course only results of this distinction. They don't make that distinction. It is the collecting which makes it, by reconstituting the context(s) in what thereby becomes the particular context.

A pattern is always both universal and particular, all the contexts in this context. The *collecting* is a crossing, but not the *lateral* crossing in which the *different* sequences that form a cluster cross with a new first-dance-versioned (pre-formed) cluster. Here there is a crossing of all the "same" contexts with each other. All of them are actually reconstituted and versioned in one versioning. These too are not side by side, like a card file of instances. They are meshed (see VII-A-o) in eveving.

We see now that a universal does know when to form! Aristotle and Kant were wrong to think that a separate "practical wisdom" must say which universal applies in which particular context. There is no need for *another* judgment to say when the given one applies. It seemed so, because universals have been considered empty of their instances, empty of their detail. What was common was supposedly abstracted away from what was different in each instance. We find it not so! The third reconstitutes all the particular contexts meshed, crossed; that is how it forms in this one.[21]

The present context is not merely an instance of what was collected already. Even when they are fully formed, as currently for us, they go right on forming. Every new application of a third adds to its collected context(s), and crosses with the earlier applications so that what the symbol "means" changes (or, one can say, a new way it can apply is found). The present context is crossed with the earlier ones, in the very formation, now. Conversely, the context in which the sequence now forms is carried forward *by* the third's own carrying forward of *its own* collected context(s) (among which the present one is now constituted). The present context isn't just discovered to be a member of the class. To think that way assumes everything we must try to understand. Rather, the present context is *made into* one of the collected context(s) *by* the formation of the sequence now.

We are still discussing fresh formation, not yet use. The fact that the sequence forms (i.e., it can form because it does) shows that *the present context can be reconstituted as this collection. Otherwise the sequence would fail to carry forward now.* But both collected context(s) and this one are mutually changed thereby.

Each formation changes how the sequence will again apply, that is to say, it changes the other contexts (the other instances).

This is nothing like dropping out the details!

Details are and have to be part of the eveving, each time the sequence forms. Only the present context with its details determines whether the sequence can form or not! If the details were not part of the formation, each time, how would one know what details to "drop out"? That was exactly why Aristotle and Kant saw a problem here which could not be solved. Universals, if they lacked the different details of their instances, would have no way of functioning in the "decision" of just which details to drop out. Such an empty universal could not tell you to what particular situation it applies. But in fact they form in particular situations.

The issue stems from the deeper error in Kant, of rendering nature as mere incoming bits which are then organized by rational universals. Many other errors stem from this. The animals have to be mere objects in such a view and our own animal nature gets utterly lost. To be sure, our "animal nature" is very much altered and elaborated by human development, but neither people nor nature make sense as bits + empty universals. Even our *thirds*, full of the crossed detail of their instances, are insufficient! We have seen how much organization there is in nature before thirds ever form. Without that organic order, they could not.

Universals (thirds) must be understood as forming in and of actual situations and their actual character. They also, in forming, carry situations forward, and in their original formation they further created what situations are.

Human situations are *kinded.* The particular is also *a* one of its kind. To grasp this relation, we must let go of the old notion that universals are abstract, or are mere fences that collect particular instances. As Whewell said long ago, of course it's easy to "abstract" horse nature, if someone has kindly selected a series of horses for you to see, one after another, with no other thing between. *Nor will it do to say that kinds are all arbitrary, you can cut any way you want.* There is indeed a vast variety of ways to classify, once classifying as such becomes a capacity for us. But still, it can only be done with the actual characteristics of things and situations. *Just as, coming into human pattern space, the object reveals its own look and sound-pattern, so also can they be collected only as in fact they are reconstituted together by one sequence. Cats never have puppies,* but any other way of classifying, too, will collect what is reconstituted together, and not any old heap. Therefore the actual things and situations, contexts, with their detail must function in the formation of universals.

For us "falls out" always means the whole context is implicit in what falls out. We say universals fall out from crossed contexts they reconstitute. Similarly, the bird cannot be an object without the scene—the bird falls out from a series of scenes which must be present too—so the universal cannot be had except as all its contexts that it reconstitutes. But the relation is not exactly the same, because the scene-changes which let the bird fall out are a string, whereas the collected context(s) are crossed and reconstituted together. But birds and universals are both often taken as if they were objects that exist without their contexts.

Thirds *make* those contexts "the same" in kind, which they cross, and from which they fall out. They make them "the same" *by* reconstituting them together.

All the situations in which we form the given sequence are reconstituted *in* the present context which is also reconstituted. All are versioned, not just this one. But they are all versioned in the versioning of this one.

That is why our thinking and talking is so very much richer than it seems when considered as empty universals. There are no empty universals.

This explains a good deal of what I say elsewhere more descriptively, about how a *given sentence or phrase means so many different experiential aspects. The having of an explicitly stated meaning is very much more than the explicit statement.*

So long as we play given routines we need not be too aware of this fact. But as soon as we try to think newly, or to understand something for ourselves, however old it may be, we must allow the functioning of this texture of crossed instances, as well as crossed clusters of interaction contexts, themselves bodily elaborations of behavior and life process.

Symbols are not at all merely "about." They change us, they engender a bodily process. They carry us forward. A universal is not separate and on another level—it is a way of having, living, and feeling the particular(s).

What is symbolized is what I call reconstituted, that is to say it occurs, it is carried forward and felt. When we speak of a situation, we live in it. It *is* present, even if it is physically non-present. It is our present interaction-context.

That is why we never use words except in some context, even if it is to give an example, in a philosophical discussion, of using a word without a context.

Einstein thought in a situation, of course. He was concerned with his (and everyone's) incapacity to perform certain operations and get certain predictions right. Since he knew a lot of physics and math, and since knowing is bodily, Einstein had (as he reports) a "feeling" all along of what the answer would be like (Wertheimer 1945, 183–84n7). This feeling was his bodily implying, and he could "have" it because he had symbols (versioning patterns) by which to reconstitute that situation. He could not yet carry the situation forward, which would mean "meeting the situation," doing what is required (in some way, not of course in a predefined way). But he could reconstitute the situation.

Similarly, even if one says only "Oh, well . . ." or "Whew," or some expletive, one thereby reconstitutes the situation. We say one "knows" or "feels" what situation one refers to. I say we live in that situation, it occurs, there is a string of versions of the body's implying it.

Are the universals poorer—can one say that the particular is always much richer than the kind structure? No, that would be to assume kinds in the old sense. Rather, we can say that only some aspects of the complexity have given rise to kinds. But every kind brings with it the whole complexity of the collected context(s).

That collection is surely richer than the present particular context which is made one of the collected context(s) and is crossed with them, as we carry this situation forward by using the words. The present context can be different, but in speaking we carry it forward *by means of* carrying forward the collected context(s), one of which it thereby becomes. This may fail to carry forward much of it, depending on the words. What we usually say in situations is quite poor, and carries forward the present situation only in a distant way. But this is not always so—we can also carry it forward very deeply. Never the whole of it, however (see VIII).

Thinking with the Implicit

(a) Introduction

> For hours I would stand quite still, my two hands folded
> between my breasts, covering the solar plexus. My mother often
> became alarmed to see me remain for such long intervals quite
> motionless as if in a trance—but I was seeking and I finally
> discovered the central spring of all movements, the crater of
> motor power, the unity from which all diversities of movements
> are born.
> —Isadora Duncan (1927, 75)

Isadora Duncan stands still, sometimes for a long period. She senses dance steps she could move into, but they don't feel right. What would feel right is not sure yet. She is "seeking," she says above, *looking for, waiting for* the right feel to come, *willing to let* it come.

This seeking, waiting for, looking, and letting is a kind of action. It is a way of relating to, *interacting with* . . . What? Where? It is interaction with a right feel, a new kind of feel which *will come* in a new place.

This feel, and this new space, are both made in this very interaction. (This is an instance of our principle "interaction first": only from the interaction do the participants come. A new kind of interaction makes new participants. See IV-A.)

Her new looking, waiting for, letting, ...—these change what comes, but it is still not right. She responds to its changed way of feeling by being differently toward it in some way. She *points to* a facet of the feel of what she would dance, *pursues it.* In response to the *pointing* and the *pursuing,* the feel itself becomes more distinct, like something there, a datum, an object, something in a space that wasn't there before.

As it forms, the "feel" understands itself, so to speak. It carries its own "yes, yes . . ." with it. She is "in touch with herself" in a new way, not just a self that was there before, waiting. Rather, a new, changed, more right "feel" is there, and is the "being in touch with." Then she dances what she could not have danced before.

The dance itself is the kind of sequence we took up in VII. What is new in kind is the *formation* of this new kind of "feel," the sequence she goes through while standing still.

How is this formation different from how a new dance might develop in VII? There too new sequences develop from the body, but without the long pause in Duncan's description. Novelty develops in VII directly, in a way I will now call "directly cross-contextual" (dir-c-c). What I so name is this: the body has, of course, the whole of the usual contexts implicit. When the body changes so that something new is implied and required, there is a crossing between this extant system of contexts and the new way the body is. The body directly bodies out a new sequence, without first the pause we are now discussing.

In this new pause there is a new kind of "feel." But in VII too there are feelings. Let me recall how we thought about these. Having a feeling is a sequence, a string of events that take time (make time). In VII one has a feeling only along with the VII-type of symbols; one uses words or one imagines actions, and only so does one have the feeling in a private sequence. Therefore, it was possible in VII to have a feeling first, and then dance from it. How is our new sequence different? The difference lies in the new kind of formation of a new kind of "feel."

Our section VII concerns traditional culture as it was for most people until fairly recently. "Culture" can be defined as the structure of situations, the patternings of human interaction. Culture is very many contexts implicit in each other. Contexts are situations. Situations always involve interaction (even being away from others, being alone, interacting with oneself, these are special cases of interaction).

Feelings of the usual kind are part of how our situations are culturally structured. We *have* the feelings, and by "have" I always mean a sequence, a stretch of time—we have them in certain "slots" in the interaction. The usual, culturally patterned interactions would not continue on their regular way if one of the participants failed to have the "slotted" feeling. If you do not feel respect for the saint, chagrin when called to order by the authorities, pleased when given a gift (and so on), the culturally structured interactions would then fail to work, to continue as usual. Your body would then imply something else, rather than what usually happens next. Either nothing further, or something else would happen. (Even pretense is something else, of course.)

Thus, the sequences of feeling, although often private, are part of the routines. If someone defeats you in some conflict, the cultural pattern may call for you to feel frustrated anger and also not show it. Despite this privacy, the other participants have your private sequence implicitly as part of the situation they are also in, with you. How you and the others interact later on will then make sense to all, on the basis of what you have lived together here. Thus our private inner life is largely an inherent part of our patterned situations with others. (See VII-B.)

Aside from such actual sequences during which we feel, there is of course also the simpler fact that any action (and, in animals, any behavior) involves feeling, but not as a *separate* sequence. Any action or interaction is a carrying forward of the body and so we feel our actions. I call such feelings the "in-behavior" or "in-action" type.

Since cultural situations are very complex, and each situation implicitly involves others too, which are also complex, a very great deal more is bodily lived and felt in this "in-action" way than is ever sequenced as such in those rather few "slotted" sequences we consider our feelings.

This whole complexity is carried forward by a VII-sequence, since it is implicit in every sequence. However, it is never felt *as such*. Neither slotted feelings nor in-action feelings are a feeling of the whole system of contexts as such. Implicitly, each carries that whole forward in a certain way, but another sequence would carry it forward in a different way. Each goes on in the implicit context that includes all the others, and therefore each is within the whole context of the others. In VII there cannot be a having of the whole, except as implicit in either this sequence or that.

Now, I am going to show that an VIII-sequence carries the whole forward, and is the having of that whole. The new "feel" is a feeling, having, sequencing, of the whole. Let me work up to showing this.

Take a VII example: See how the whole is *not* felt or had in the way I mean, although it is implicitly carried forward in some one way. For example, once I found myself grinding my cigarette out on the tabletop. It was what some people would call "very expressive." As I did it, I felt what I was doing, of course, and I felt the situation that led up to it (as we do in any ordinary action). But I did not do what Isadora is describing. I did not let a feel of the whole situation form for me, first, and then act from it. I had and felt the whole situation only inaction, in this spontaneous act. I had to go back afterwards to try to see what made me do it.

Of course, what I felt was anger, but that is too simple. Emotions "break back," as we saw in VII, that is to say they don't usually carry forward (meet) *the whole* situation. (That is why we often regret later what we did emotionally. Other facets of the situation, which were not carried forward, are then in evidence.) So even if I had first felt my anger (in a private, slotted sequence), I would not thereby have felt *the whole* situation. My spontaneous behavior also did not carry the whole situation forward. No sequence in VII-symbols ever does, whether the symbols are verbal, or pictured and imaged, or acted out as in this example. Something new did occur (I don't usually do this), but it was not what happens in Isadora's pause.

Duncan could have danced in this spontaneous way without waiting. Or she could have danced from any point during her waiting. Some dance would have arisen. Instead, she engaged in something else.

At each new moment after pausing she senses the whole context directly, as a "feel" (which isn't quite right). No previous kind of sequence we have considered could do that.

We noticed that the space in which Duncan seeks her source of a right movement has some features in common with an interpersonal interaction space. She *interacts* with some "feel" even before *it* is quite *there*. She seeks it, looks for it, waits for it, lets it come, pursues and points to what has come, senses its rightness or wrongness, even before it is clearly marked as an *it*. These are like activities one might do in relation to a person or an object in ordinary situational space (which we derived in VII). Interaction is usually (and as discussed so far) with a person or a thing. One pursues someone or points to something. Now something like such interactions are occurring in a new space made by these activities, and these interactions are between some new puzzling sense of *her*, and this new kind of "feel."

In our way of thinking about any sequence, a bit of body-change is made by some environmental change which in turn carries the body forward into a new bit of body-change. For example, when I look for something in a situation, the scene I experience is altered by my looking, and what I then see affects in turn how I further seek, that is to say, the next focally implicit move from my body is changed by how the environment responds to my last move.

Or, another example, how I move in space changes how all the objects can now be approached from my new spot. This, in turn, affects my next bit of motion. So it is with any sequence.

In our new kind of sequence, the move she makes toward the as yet vague feel has an effect on this feel which in turn affects the next move that arises from her body. Only now these moves are not dance steps, not words or images, but her interaction with this feel, her pointing or pursuing or waiting for. And the new environmental changes are changes in this "feel."

From each bit of this new sequence, Duncan could have danced. Instead she feels the whole from which such a dance would arise, and feels this whole as not quite right. She makes some move toward this feel, and it changes so as to carry her body forward into a further move (we must see later about this new kind of carrying forward, how it happens). In this way, the new sequence is a string of changes *in the whole context*, a kind of change in this whole which could not be made by dancing.

Each bit of this new sequence is a changed whole. Each bit would lead to a different dance than the last bit. Each bit would also lead to a different talking, if she were to try to say what "not quite right" now feels like, and to different images if she were to image. Each bit is a new whole.

But in the sense of VII the situation throughout remains the same. It is this relevance, this sense of being about to dance, which remains unchanged in the VII way, that is, she is still not dancing. She is still waiting. The same VII-situation waits, and is paused. The VIII-sequence changes in a new way what stays the same in a VII way.

Each new whole is thus a *version* of "the same" dance situation, in the sense of VII. As with other new kinds of sequence that we developed in earlier chapters, our new sequence here consists of a string of versions of the same, paused, earlier context.

From this sequence of versions, something quite new falls out. As always in our scheme, the *had* feeling or object falls out from the string of versions. That's what "a feeling" always is. *It* is the carrying forward continuity of the series of body-states, the changing which we sense as "a" feeling (and we can only sense over time).[1]

This new kind of "feel" isn't just there, waiting; it forms in this new sequence.

Both her moves toward the "feel," and that "feel" itself, are of course Isadora Duncan, her one body. As she changes her interactional relation to the "feel," the "feel" also changes, and as it changes, it leads to, implies, or enables a changed stance toward it.

Where does this happen? In a new space generated by this new kind of sequence. If you tell an ordinary person to stand "next to" some feeling or emotion, the phrase will not make sense in that use. "Where do you mean 'stand next to'?" the person will say. The new VIII-space is not familiar, has not been constituted by this person. In VII people feel things in their chest and stomach, that is one "where," and also in their situations, that is another "where." In VIII a new space opens.

Until now, every sequence we have discussed consisted of bits of bodily change and bits of environmental change, and this is the case here too. In every sequence some kind of environment carries the body forward into a bit of changed implying (which then makes for a further change in that environment, which again carries the body further). But in our new sequence there doesn't seem to be any environment. But it only seems that way.

We have already seen that environment is always partly homegrown. The environment that carries behavior forward isn't just sheer physical externals at all, as in the old notion of external stimuli. Rather, it is constituted by, and part of, the body. (See VI.) Similarly, inter-human inter-actions form a new environment (at first the bodylook; see VII). What is the new kind of environment which here does the new kind of carrying forward?

We cannot simply say that the new environment is the direct ref-erent, the "feel" I have been discussing. That would be like saying that the behavioral environment is the objects. We want to understand the formation of this "feel," just as in VI we could not begin with objects. We wanted to grasp how they form. We said here that the "feel" falls out from the changing versions of the whole. (This is analogous to how I presented the new sequence in VI. The sentience in-behavior was there seen to fall out from a string of body-changes.) The new environment is (a new kind of) bodily sentience—at least new in being interacted with, in this new way. What before was there only in-action is now interacted with, and now carries forward. We have yet to understand how it carries forward.

It is important to emphasize that the new sequence does not begin with the direct referent. It does not wait there, to be noticed or interacted with. Rather, the direct referent is a datum, a new kind of object, which forms, falls out from the sequence.

The sequence begins with looking for, letting come, waiting for, ... what is not yet "there." And where does one look and let? That space too is new, and is generated. As one looks, so to speak, in the usual body-sentience, this looking finds itself carried forward by a change in a somewhat different space. How this space is generated will become clear shortly. But it is not quite the usual way one feels, for example a pain, or hunger or tiredness in the body, and yet it is not totally different from these, either. Let me make the difference clearer.

While the changes in our new sequence may seem slight, they are actually each an enormous change. Duncan calls it a discovery of "the crater of motor power, the unity from which all diversity of movements are born," as quoted earlier (1927, 75). It is a new kind of source. There is no dance or speech or act of the VII-type, which could make that much change. After each bit of such change, *everything* is different. Each bit is a new whole, a changed whole. The whole dance and all speech or action which would arise would be different than would arise from the last bit.

I have already distinguished this new kind of "feel" from emotions or slotted feelings. These familiar feelings also make change, of course. What one would say or do after such a feeling comes is different than before. But they are within the whole context. Our new sequence consists of changes of the whole.

I must now distinguish this new kind of bodily "feel" from the more usual body sensing. Let me first let Duncan make the distinction, then I will do it. Duncan writes: "The (old) ballet school taught the pupil that this spring (of all movement) was found in the center of the back at the base of the spine. From this axis, says the ballet master, arms, legs and trunk must move freely, giving the result of an animated puppet. This method produces an artificial mechanical movement not worthy of the soul" (75).

Similarly, today there is a lot of work done with the body and bodily sensing. For example, one can move one's attention slowly up from the feet to the head, sensing for tension anywhere, and relaxing it. In doing this one is working with bodily sensings as just bodily, and not as a sensing of a whole situation.

Other methods involve the discovery (or rediscovery) that old childhood events and emotional sequences are, as it were, stored in the body. There is currently a lot of excited puzzling over how this can be. In certain kinds of stressing of muscles and other work, these old sequences come out, and are spontaneously acted or expressed. If the body is understood in the usual physiological way, this must be very puzzling. Our model can let us think clearly about it, as the body always focally implies a next step, and also implicitly includes all sequences that ever were, in a mesh so they are implicit in each other (and also pyramided over each other; see VI). But in these current methods, the old memories and actings, and emotions are, of course, not the person's current life implying. The old sequences and the mere emotions are also only partial, as all VII-type sequences are. It is something quite different to have (feel, sequence) a bodily sentience of any of one's *whole* situations.

Much follows from this difference, which I will discuss later. (The old patterns are not as such the constituents of our living. The "Eternal Return of the Same" and the "archetypes" will be understood very differently once we grasp the new kind of sequence developing here.)

In the new kind of sequence the bodily "feel" is the body's implying of the next focal move, now (which is a focaling of many, many implicit sequences), and the new sequence is a string of versions of this, a string of changes in it.

Duncan was one of the pioneers of this new level; Stanislavski was another. Even today he is misunderstood to have said that actors should feel the emotions they portray. He did not like emotional acting. What he favored was sensing the whole scene, the whole play, the whole situation, living oneself into that whole.

> Because of the lack of better means, the stage director will squeeze emotion out of the actor, urging him ahead as if he were a horse that cannot move a great load from its place. "More, more," the stage direc-

tor will cry. "Live more strongly, give me more of it! Live the thing over! Feel it!' (Stanislavski 1948, 475)

It would seem that there was nothing simpler than naked passion and nothing else. But the simpler a thing is, the harder a thing is to do. The simple must have a great deal of content. Bare of content it is as useless as a nutshell without meat. The simple, in order to become the most important and move itself forward, must contain in itself the entire gamut of complex life phenomena. (474–75)

Besides talent, an inner spiritual technique is necessary. (475)

Here we see that new concepts are needed, otherwise we will not be able to capture the difference, let alone understand it, between emotions (and feelings in the usual sense) on the one hand, and this new kind of "feel" which, as he puts it, contains "in itself the entire gamut of complex life phenomena."

I only had to think of the thoughts and cares of Stockman and the signs of short sight would come of themselves, together with the forward stoop of the body, the quick step, the eyes. . . . And these habits came of themselves, unconsciously, and quite apart from myself. From where did they come? From where? The creative ways of nature are beyond human ken. (Stanislavski 1948, 405)

Concepts fail him here, for the formation of that new kind of inward datum which contains "in itself the entire gamut of complex life phenomena." We are now making the concepts for how this forms.

Stanislavski (like Duncan—and they did talk with each other) asks his pupils first to be still and let a "feel" form, that has its own rightness. Only then should they stand up and act—so that the acting might be from this newly formed inward datum. The right postures and movements will come. He too thus insists on a *pause in VII-sequencing*, a time when one doesn't act, or speak, or engage in any of the type-VII sequences.

We can also see again that there is a change when this new datum forms. How one then acts from this datum is different than if one had acted earlier—and the difference is more and other than the kind of difference type-VII sequences can make. *Everything* one then does is different, as lived from out of this changed bodily sense. The whole gamut of implicit sequences is involved in this changed formation. Therefore ways of standing, speaking, and looking come, as if of their own accord, and are appropriate.

Stanislavski calls it being "able to create something new of an inner nature" (401). I am concerned with Duncan and Stanislavski not at all because what I care about is art or drama. What, in himself, Stanislavski uses here is his whole body's implicit richness of situations and inter-actions, all changed at once in this particular focal implying now. We need something like this in any life situation, and also in any new theo-retical thinking. He livingly processes such a bodily implicit whole, and from it spring changed and more right actions and thoughts.[2] What new kind of sequence and what new kind of "feel" is this?

How might I have *had and felt the whole of* my situation that made me (what we roughly call) angry? And what new kind of sensing is this, which pauses the usual VII-sequencing?

Einstein wrote, throughout his fifteen years of work toward the general theory of relativity, not only that he had a "feeling" of what the answer had to be, but that this feeling guided him. What is he saying? Not that he had a personal feeling. Rather, that his knowledge of phys-ics and mathematics was insufficient to enable him actually to solve the problems, to formulate equations that would predict correctly—but that his body, totaling and focaling all that, formed for him a direct referent which he could feel as such. He couldn't speak from it in terms of phys-ics, but for fifteen years it was living physics forward in a bodily way. He could not live it forward in equations and measurements but as "felt."

Original thinkers probably engage in direct reference quite often, although by direct context crossing too one can sometimes "come up with" an answer or a step on a problem without having had the felt sense of the whole problem *as such*. Making this method systematic is not only useful in thinking, but reveals a whole new field of rules, a new kind of logic, a new way of understanding what the powers of thinking always were, and strong additions to these powers.

(b) Direct referent and felt shift

In the next section we will see why, we will be able to think clearly about why; here I want to describe.

A direct referent does not always form. Certainly it does not form necessarily just when we wish. And when it forms, it is then whatever it is that formed, and perhaps not at all what we wished or expected. Another way to put this forming is to say that a direct referent *comes*. It can come only if we let it, and I will describe this "letting" more exactly.

When a direct referent forms and comes, something has jelled, something has happened, something—a great deal—has fallen into place. Direct referent formation is (a new kind of) carrying forward. We will understand this later.

At first, there is a period of unstable coming and losing hold of. One senses "the whole situation" or "the whole problem," and then that sense is gone again.

There are ways of helping people know how to let a direct referent form, which are much more exact than I describe here. (See Gendlin 1981.) Even so this will seem very specific, perhaps more specific than the reader is accustomed to enter into the details of experience.

It helps, at this unstable stage of direct referent formation, to find an initial descriptive term for the quality of this unstable sense of the whole problem. We call it a "handle." The whole problem feels . . . unresolved . . . a little icky . . . yes, "icky" names it just right. (This could be a personal problem or it could be how we have just formulated some theoretical problem, quite well so it seems, and yet . . .)

Let us say it is a theoretical problem.

Once the handle fits, one can keep using it over and over, and the felt sense of the whole problem, that uneasy sense now called "icky," will *come* again each time. "It" comes of its own (and one must wait for it, by attending in a bodily way.) "Ah . . . there it is again, yes, that's right, icky."

(Or it might need a more fitting word, phrase, image, or sometimes even a body-posture—any kind of VII-symbol.)

If the handle functions as it should, the direct referent will form more stably. There will be an internal "yes . . . yes . . ." quality, a bodily sense that this is just exactly right, even though one doesn't know what "icky" refers to. (One has all sorts of rapid ideas what it might refer to, but these are old information and must be put aside.)

If the direct referent comes, now, each time the word or words are repeated, each time the direct referent is waited for, there is each time a sense of relief, something shifting, releasing, stirring, in the body. This might be a very slight stirring or a big release. Yes, that's it all right, icky.

This release or relief or stirring will then occur much more strongly when, after some time, the felt sense opens and shifts in a major way. One then also finds out what is so icky about the seemingly good formulation of the problem—and usually it's rather different than one would have thought.

There may be many small "fallings into place," or one big shift. Now it is all open, and one can say, though it might still take time to find words or actions. One can say what the trouble "was" and is.

For example, "Oh . . . yes . . . yes . . . this formulation I just made covers over just that funny spot where I think something interesting might come, it's too simple the way it is even though it looks good. Somehow I've forgotten the problem I had so much trouble with yesterday, today here it looks all solved, but that's because the interesting difficulty has disappeared."

Or, it might be, "Oh . . . yes . . . yes . . . I never like it when it all comes down to *that* kind of explanation . . ." Then there will be another step, the person will tend to articulate further what it is that "I never like it" contains implicitly about "*that*" kind of explanation.

What at first seems a fuzzy unease, a seemingly merely personal reaction to a theoretical argument, implicitly contains complex and often new ways of seeing and understanding the theoretical issue.

As we already saw (in VII), thought is not at all only the moving around of fixed entities, concepts that are defined, "pieces" of knowledge. Thought is always very largely implicit and, as I tried to show (in Gendlin 1997a and 1992b), the implicit is not some fringe or periphery around what we centrally think. Rather, the sense we are making, the central point we are making, is had only as a carrying forward of an implicit complexity. What is implicitly functioning is the point itself, of what we are saying or thinking, just then.

Therefore, what is new here is the direct reference. In all thought the implicit functions, and in all novel thought there is some new aspect specifying, but it might occur in what I termed direct context-crossing, spontaneously in reaction to what is presented. (See VII-B.) I will later explain why the formation of a direct referent makes such a great difference.

Such a sense, like "icky," could be taken as a personal feeling as if it were only about personal matters. Not at all: it is an apprehension of the whole theoretical problem, an apprehending of more than can yet be formulated.

Similarly, with personal problems, the sense of the whole problem is very different from the more usual feelings and emotions. (Even the latter are, of course, ways of living and sequencing some situations.) A sense *of* the whole is always a way of carrying forward complex contexts of sequences possible in the world, often in a single focal way that is not yet possible in the world.

Both our theoretical thinking and our living are no longer as routine as they were in other times. In our time, the culturally patterned routines don't quite handle our situations. As we saw, each development brings with it many more implicit developments, (implicit type a) that have not yet actually occurred. Thus our complexity grows greater with each novelty, than is apparent from what happens. Situations develop which cannot be fully carried forward by any extant way of acting, nor is there always easily a direct novel creation which does. Our sensitivity, we might say, is greater than what we can devise to carry forward.

The circumstances under which our full bodily carrying forward comes, are more complex and less frequent, less easy to bring about. In more and more situations where a simpler, more traditional person would get angry, work, go forward, we may be blocked with no good way, no full-bodied way. How to be a father, or a wife, or a student, or whatever, in our situations is not so obvious, not routined in a way that works for us. We have to devise it anew each time.

Because emotions come in certain "slots" in interactions, and because our situations include new demands which one cannot carry forward, the emotion may not come, and because emotions are full-bodied, people think the whole problem lies in having one's emotions. But, as we saw (VII-B), emotions "break back," they carry forward less than the whole situation. The whole would be something else.

Even aside from the fact that our routines don't work anymore, the complexity of urban educated literate living consists so largely of symbolic actions rather than bodily doings, that they are "thinned" (VII-B). Of course, when signing something or pushing a button, such that a vast change is made, we normally do feel that quite distinctly in the body. The stomach sinks, the heart pounds, the hand shakes, or, if the action is fully carrying forward, there is a flood of relief and a new dawn in life. But how often are our actions that change-making? Usually the whole remains, only slightly altered.

To carry forward the whole of a situation, and to be in a full-bodied process, is rarely possible within the patterns of situations.

Just how would it be to live full-bodiedly, to carry forward *the whole of* routine situations? It would be a new stage.

Some new kind of "environment" could render the whole of our situation, and let us live it forward as a whole. Let me be clearer:

Suppose someone has insulted you. Now you are hurt, angry, chagrined, let us say, as you are supposed to be in our cultural routine. The routine defines both what "insulted" is, and what and when these emotions come. To a large extent we do, of course, still live and feel within these patterns, and so, let us say, you are angry, hurt, and chagrined. If you are asked why, you would point to the obvious. You have been publicly called such and such a name, and that certainly is the reason. Can't everyone understand that? Wouldn't anyone feel this way?

Let us say, roundly, that, yes, anyone would feel this way, at least in our culture.

And yet—if you had several people here each of whom had been insulted today in a similar way, each of whom felt angry, hurt, and chagrined, still there is another level on which one might ask each of them, further, why they feel this way. To answer this, each would have to attend to the fuzzy edges, the unclear part of *the whole* situation. Many people don't know how to do that, or even that it is possible. Some people do know that there always is this fuzzy edge, if one looks for it, waits for it to come in, lets it come. (See Gendlin 1981.)

Then very different specifics would emerge for the different people.

Like anyone else, this specific person would be having feelings of chagrin, anger, and hurt. One has a tendency to go over and over these emotions and the situational context that goes with it. To let a direct referent form, the person has to stop going through these VII-sequences, but the stopping isn't just a blank. It is a different activity, which makes a "pause" in the usual activity.

The different activity is sensing the whole thing, as a whole. Later I will say more about how this is done. Doing it, the person would find a holistic bodily quality of the whole thing, which is at first murky.

Finding a "handle" for it, the person might say, it all feels crummy. I feel crummy.

If the person now talked a lot, the sentences would be old. "All those people watching, what will they think, I'm mad, I'll get him back you wait, I don't like being made a fool of, etc. etc."

Reverting to these usually old VII-sequences, the sense of the whole would be quite lost again.

Instead, let us say the person uses the *handle* ("crummy") to let the sense of the whole thing come again. "I remember 'crummy' . . . is *that* still there? . . . [waits] . . . ah, yes, there it is again . . ."

Letting it come, and perhaps again come after it is lost again, there is an unstable period. When "it" is "there," it can so to speak be touched, tapped, asked, wondered at . . .

Then there is a *felt shift*. "Whew . . . yes, that's what it is . . . wait . . . I can say now."

The person might now say, or not. The direct referent has formed, or we can say if we like it has re-formed (direct referent formation includes all these steps.) It feels open, now, to speech and action, one knows it, it is self-understood, even without words.

"Oh, I don't care what they think, but I was at fault and I *hate* to see that, that's what the crummy feeling is. Funny, I knew that before and still I didn't, in a way. . . . Yup, that's what it is."

After a little while it is either all cleared up and the person is ready to go ahead, live, think, move, or (more often) the problem is not solved in one step. There's still a bad feeling, now the person circles around and around this being at "fault," hating to see that, excusing it, not excusing it, ethics, etc. All this is very different than before the shift, but it is again old thoughts that don't resolve anything.

Again, now, this changed whole needs to form as a direct referent. Again there will be a handle, say "unfree" is how it feels. That gets it all right! With that word, the new direct referent can keep coming back. When it shifts, there is a big relief. "Oh . . . it's not the fault part so much, it's like I have to be in this crummy way I was, and I have to go and be inside the ugly way I've been made to look. I keep climbing back into it," then there might be a lot of relief and then another round, perhaps ending in "Oh . . . yes, whew . . . I stop my good energy that way, when I climb back in there, sure . . . yes. I can stand that cruddy place all right, I'll even fix it I think, but I've been stopping myself ever since this happened, backing myself in like it isn't OK to surge forward anymore. Whew . . . what a relief. Now I can."

But it is very unlikely that these same specifics would emerge for one of the other people who had been insulted that day. They too would be similarly fuzzy at first, similarly poetic in their details, but different.[3]

A second person might find: "Well . . . ah . . . I'm angry. Hmm . . ." and after direct referent formation at this point, ". . . Yes, I see . . . uhm . . . (sigh, breath) I feel like killing the bastard. It's not too safe for me to feel the way I do. Yea, yup (breath). I'll do something stupid, not kill him really, but stupid. I don't like this part of me woken up. It's hard to control." And after another step of the same kind, "yeah, it's not controlling it that's the problem. It's the way I don't like being that way. That anger isn't so dangerous if I'm willing to have it for a minute, but it hasn't seemed like I could have it and hold it, even that long. Whew . . . If I can hold it I can think what I *want* to do."

Now the reader might say, well, what does all that prove, of course we are each different. But what has become of the cultural routine— didn't we say anyone would react this same way? Just how we are all the same and all different is no simple question.

The usual routined cultural pattern has none of the above statements, nor the actions which these people may now do. Only allowing the whole situation to be carried forward in a new kind of way, not by a sequence within the pattern already given, did these emerge. What is said here, and the possible specific actions have never happened as such before. They are new in the history of the world.

This is why the language is often odd, newly formed. ("I have to go and be inside the ugly way I've been made to look.")

But haven't we all felt that way at some time? Isn't this merely a poetic way of saying, perhaps for the first time, what is a recognizable facet of anyone's experience, or at least of many people? Even if we haven't experienced it, we do grasp it immediately. Someone paints an ugly picture of you, and if you feel it's partly right, you make yourself go and be inside of it, and that feels bad. Is that new in the history of the world? It's merely a poetic person who can differentiate and express that.

Later I will discuss why what one says and does from a direct referent is again understandable.

Direct referent formation enables such poetic novelty—but the novel phrasing is only a result. The prior important sequence is the formation of the direct referent, the having and feeling of the whole situation as a directly felt unclear whole. This having, this sequence, is a carrying forward—only so can we have and feel, over time, a way of pausing and sequencing the whole—a changing of it that isn't the kind of changing which taking an action would be, or speaking in a usual way without direct referent formation, using only what was clear. No one can find, think, or say such aspects.

We all have—and even in the most traditional culture everyone has—such complexity. It is and remains implicit, and unchanged, unresolved, bodily cramped whatever way it is. There are not direct referents there, in some "unconscious." The unconscious is the body. But direct referent formation is a new kind of sequence, not known in other times except to a few odd people. Direct referents are not there, implicitly, but the whole complexity is there, and is implicit in every sequence of action, feeling, and thought. When a person does engage in direct referent formation and then speaks, we can understand and "recognize"—not literally what *was* there before, but more exactly, what *now forms from* what was there. What was there was implicit complexity, implicit sequences, some never yet sequenced, but also all that ever were, situations mutually implicit in each other, the interactive life context (not totally unified, to be sure). *From* this complexity of ours the speaker to whom we listen, forms, in us, what we call "recognizing" that we always "were" like that, too. And yet when that "same" meaning forms, it is made of some different implicitly functioning experience. Ours.

I will say more in the Appendix to VIII about these quite new relations between novelty, uniqueness, universal understandability, generality, and particularity. This section has revealed, but not resolved, how these notions must now be rethought.

(c) The new kind of sequence

We understand our sequence, so far, only in that certain interactive moves toward a not-yet-here "feel" generate this "feel," and generate a new space in which it forms.

We have also seen that each bit of such a sequence is a changed whole, a changed *version* of "the same" whole situation, the same whole relevance. We saw that such a change in the whole cannot be made by a type-VII symboling sequence (although in another way each such sequence has the whole implicit in it in its own way). Each bit of our new sequence changes "everything," and from this string of changed versions, the new "feel," the direct referent, falls out and is had, felt. This *having* (or feeling as such) of the whole was not possible in VII. It is a new kind of bodily sense of the whole complexity itself. To have it one must pause the VII type of symboling.

Many people today still cannot be for even a little time without some VII-kind of symboling sequence. They must always have thoughts or images or be doing something. Then the new sequence cannot develop. Of course, such people have feelings, but these are always had only by means of thinking or imagining doing something in some imagined situation.

Body sensations are of course also familiar to everyone, including those that come as emotions. The heart pounds, the stomach sinks. These are located in the body. Emotions make a large shift also; once they come, everything is different in a way with them too. What one would say or do, once the emotion has come, differs from before. But the emotion does not sequence (does not let one have a feel of) the whole situation.

The location of the heart pounding, for example, is experienced in the usual situational space, that is to say between the table and the back of the chair I am sitting in.

On the other hand, the change in the situation (which the emotion that comes, has made) is experienced in the situation around me.

The relation between these two changes is also experienced, but not clearly. The situational space is not located "in" the body in the same way as the heart's pounding is. In VII *we said* that the body implies all our situations and focally implies our next move in each (even if we cannot find a doubled sequence.) But this is not usually felt in the body as such, as a sense for the whole situation, as a datum located in the body.

If the bodily sense of a situation is to be experienced as such, most people have only very vague, general VII-sequences available. One feels "tense" or "at ease," "expansive" or "constricted," "good" or "bad." (These descriptive quality words are only physical and general, yet they are the best entry to focusing.)

In direct referent formation one both keeps the situation the same, and one also lets it change. One keeps it the same *by holding* the relevance, the point, the sense of the whole thing, the same. It is *this* situation (and all that is involved in it), which I wish to sense as a whole. I hold on to this relevance. But also, I await the coming of a new kind of feel, the felt sense of the whole business. I can only *let* it come, I can't make it. In letting it come, I allow my body-feel to stir, to move, to do whatever it does independently of my deliberate control, while I do employ my deliberate control to keep the situation, the relevance.

Holding and letting is something like holding a frame, but allowing whatever comes to come within that frame. The image of a frame is an analogy. (One can actually visualize a frame and let an image pop into it, but this is the formation of an image, not of a felt sense. An image forms in image space, not in this new space we must still describe.)

Holding and letting sound contradictory, but are one and the same act, like a holding and waiting. As one does so, there are murky bodily changes, and only after some seconds of these is there then a distinct datum, a "this," the felt sense, the direct referent. It comes, something like the way an emotion comes, in the body, of its own accord, but in a somewhat different space than the literal space in the body. Indeed it is literally in the body, between the table and the back of the chair (if we are sitting there), but it also is in its own new space. I sense the felt sense "there" and I am next to it, pointing at it, in this new space. The space is not distinct until the direct referent comes.

Whether a direct referent actually forms, whether it comes or not, cannot be controlled. One can deliberately hold and wait, point and sense, but one cannot get a direct referent to form and come at will.

For example, if I am dissatisfied with my formulation of some theoretical problem, I can certainly *say* the words: "Oh . . . now I have a sense of what's wrong." But I cannot thereby make myself have such a sense of what's wrong. I can begin with what I do have, some diffuse, unfocused dissatisfaction, but this is not yet that "feel" which is a version of the whole. There is as yet no "it" that has *come*. And there may not be that day, whatever I do inwardly or outwardly.

I can call my diffuse dissatisfaction by some name, using some noun, but there is not yet *a* direct referent there for me. (That is why Duncan didn't yet want to dance for such a long time.)

We see from this that a direct referent formation really is a kind of carrying forward. Carrying forward is always something that might not happen. Much else can happen, one can (if one wishes) talk, image, act, make tea, but none of that gives one that coming of the sense of the whole.

When one is practiced at it, however, there is quite often little difficulty in letting such a referent come. Even so, there is a further distinction: I have called it a "felt shift," and described it earlier. (Iberg, 1990, calls the pre-shift stage "parturient" and the post-shift stage "nascent.")

Once it has shifted, one can speak or act not just in the countless unsatisfying ways always available, but in a focaled way that will carry forward what is implied. (Even that is inaccurate; one may have to do more, it might be only a step, one might still have to arrange the action situation in many ways.) But one can say or do *something* that is a just right next step. Then one might have to engage in further direct referent formation for further steps.

It isn't quite right to separate the coming, and the shifting, of the direct referent, as if they were always two distinct events. Sometimes they are. But the direct referent, the "feel" of the whole problem, itself is closed and still in formation until suddenly it opens, and "what it is" falls out. "It" has jelled. Now one "knows," though it may then still take some time to find words or actions.

What I have to say about the direct referent as an object from now on refers to it after it has formed as an *it*, and that means that some shift will have been experienced, though it may not yet be that shift which lets one go out and do or say all of what one needs.

So there is a distinction between the direct referent still during formation (as when Duncan waits, the whole thing doesn't feel quite right) and once it is formed. Of course, what I can then do may only be to state what the trouble was. Even so the trouble has just changed very greatly, even as I now say what it was and still is. I *can* now say.

(d) Relevance and perfect feedback object

In the new VIII-sequence one feels the relevance as such. Feeling is a sequence of changes, a string of versions. In being felt as such, the whole (or the relevance) goes through versions. In sensing or feeling it as such, it changes. (As we saw, it changes very greatly.)

When a direct referent falls out (it jells), we can then also say (or dance, or act from) what the whole problem "was," what the relevance "was." But of course this saying is from a changed relevance. In a VII sense it is still the same, the same situation or problem or concern we have been *holding*. While the same in that respect, it has now fallen out as a new "feel" from the new sequence, and from this "feel" we can speak in a new way, to say what it "was" all along.

We have often said that an explication is not the same as what was implicit. Implying is never to be equated with some structure. Loosely, if we have often seen cfing by the same thing, we can say it is what the previous moment implies. So hunger implies food. But something else too might carry forward in a new way (for example, intravenous feeding). Even if new, carrying forward will be recognizably different. What was implied will then no longer be. In contrast, there is always a vast variety of events which would not carry forward and thus leave the implying unchanged. You are hungry and you go out in the rain. Now you are still hungry. If you are on the way to a restaurant, this going out might be a version of your continuing same hunger which you are carrying forward in a special way—but which must still be carried forward by feeding somewhere some time.

Our new sequence is also again a versioning on a new level. At some time the direct referent formation will succeed and Duncan will dance again. (Perhaps not that day.) What now, exactly, is the new carrying forward of the VIII-sequence, this new versioning? When it *comes* (jells, falls out, becomes "nascent") then I have (feel, sequence) what the problem "was." That is to say an object, a datum, *has formed,* and is now no longer changing and forming. There is an *it.* This *it* is my sense of what the problem is or "was." I have or feel it now.

I am now going to explain that this object is itself a further living, a carrying forward, a kind of solving, of the problem. It *is* what is needed, but on this new plane, in this new environment (so that I will still have to do things in the old environments). It is a kind of solution, an object that carries forward, and yet it also is a sense of the problem.

Therefore, one's first description of a direct referent usually is "Oh, that's what the whole problem is." But really much more change has happened in this formation than one first notices. This ascription to the past is not quite right. *This* (the direct referent) is not literally how the trouble has been all along. Something new and different has formed.

Each slightly changed version of the relevance carries forward. This means it is in some way what was implied. The body lives on, lives forward, lives on by the erstwhile stoppage of the problem or not-right situation. "Not right" simply means that something was implied focally, and couldn't happen

In this new space, it seems, something can happen which was implied, whereas in the old VII-space of our actual situation it couldn't. The direct referent forms from a sequence of (in a way) fulfilling what was required.

There is therefore a great physical relief when a direct referent forms. Many processes in the body return to their more usual way, and no longer carry (see IV-A) the stoppage. The interaction in the situation is still implied, still awaiting being done, perhaps still quite unclear or impossible, but the body has lived on and the stoppage has been resumed by a new object, the referent.

When the direct referent comes (forms, falls out, jells), it is from a sequence of "perfect feedback," each bit being what the previous bit focally implied, required. It is therefore not only a sense of the difficulty, but a new object made by a solving of the difficulty (in a new sort of environment.)

One has lived past the stoppage which the problem literally was. Now, from this changed relevance, in this changed whole context, one formulates what the problem was in a new way. One formulates the problem in a world in which the problem is solved, in a context changed by that solving.

(Therefore, if any further steps in the VII-situation are needed before a way there can be found, it is important to hold on to the direct referent of the problem, until enough sequences from it can form, so that the interaction context is changed accordingly. Often that is the case; one cannot always instantly speak and act so as to resolve the situation. But any speech or action now instances the solution, and feels right. They will change the situation so as to instance the solution. Then an action becomes possible, which may not be there at first.)

The direct referent is a perfect feedback object.

How contradictory all this would be if we had only VII-concepts in which to say it. Just what we feel as the problem is the solution. (People do often say this! "If you can state the problem, you've got it half solved," and other paradoxical statements. A paradox is a new concept not yet formed.) Also, just as we can sense how it has been all along, it has really changed fundamentally. It was not, before, really as we now say it "was."

We must quickly distinguish: without an VIII-sequence too one can say what a problem is, and one can have many feelings and emotions, and do many actions. These are then usually what I call *negative instancing*.

Instead of being an instance of the solution (of how the whole context is, such that the problem is solved), they are instances of the problem (how the whole context is, such that one cannot proceed. There is a problem). One's statement of the problem is then itself an example of the problem, and lacks just what the problem is the lack of. One's effort to fix something is once again just another instance of what one was trying to fix.

From the direct referent, the statement of the problem and other actions are instances of the changed constellation, the carried forward whole, the solution.

The body has given itself an object that carries it forward in just that way in which the bodily whole focally implies.

Of course, something is still missing in the VII–interaction context, the situation, but this can now be fashioned.

The carried forward body (the stoppage no longer carried) now crosses directly with the situation, and the sayings and doings that form are instances of the new whole.

When a direct referent forms and comes (jells), and opens (becomes "nascent"), then the carrying forward has happened. It comes as it can and only that way. Its features are not what we might predict, usually, certainly not what we can control. Sometimes it is not an it, but two things, or three facets. Sometimes it is an odd juncture, two things neither of which is "it," but how they cross. A direct referent has its own character.

There is a great change in a direct referent formation, a carrying forward of the whole in accord with a focal implying that could not previously be carried forward. This lets us understand why direct referent formation takes time (how the direct referent isn't just there, waiting, but must form) and also why it has its own character. One cannot solve a problem any old way. There cannot be a feedback object, a carrying forward of a complexity any old way.

The change in the formation is not the same as the change inherent in feeling the direct referent once *it* is there. The formation is murky—then suddenly the further formation is what the direct referent falls out from as a stable object or datum. For some seconds or minutes, sometimes months, the falling out does not occur. It is nothing like turning and reflecting on what is there waiting. It is a very special formation. When it falls out, every bit of that sequence is exactly what the previous bit required, and the object made by that sequence is a perfect feedback object.

(e) Schematic of the new carrying forward and the new space

As with the other new kinds of carrying forward we formulated in earlier chapters, this new kind involves a kind of *doubling*, a way in which the *body finds* itself carried forward in a new way, and we must also again say exactly what in this *new cfing* can be understood in terms of the old, and what cannot. We also want to understand the *self-understanding* internal to a direct referent, the "Yes . . . yes . . . ," the sense that "it all fits." Each bit of the sequence locates into what the previous bit focally implied. What kind of *re-recognition* is here?

A new kind of sequence, for us, is *doubled*. In one sense (of course a special sense) it is the old kind of sequence, but in another sense a second, doubled, carrying forward is also occurring. For example, behavior is a new kind of body-process, and makes a (new kind of) bodily change. But also, the body's new environment (see VI) also carries each bit of body-change forward in a second, new way. Similarly, in VII, the gestures are (a special kind of) behaving, but they also involve a new doubled kind of carrying forward by the bodylook. While dancing, one would still avoid falling off a cliff. In that sense the movements are behavior and go on the ground as other behavior, and in behavior space and its objects. But the "simple movements" of gesturing are also a carrying forward of one body by the other's bodylook.

Here the special case of the old sequence is the *interacting*, the pointing, waiting, pursuing, etc. These are of course special, but they are of the old kind, a special case of them. (One has to interact with the incipient direct referent in a "friendly" way, for example. One has to "welcome" it, and so on.) But in this new kind of old sequence a second carrying forward happens: the whole body-sense finds itself carried forward. Changes in body-sense are a new environment, a new sort of registry. The interactional move one made, and the resulting datum's coming, are a new kind of old interaction. But the carrying forward of the whole body-sense of the problem is a new, second, carrying forward. Let me explain:

If there were only this new internal kind of interaction, it might be like relating to some datum—say, a pain—in some new way. The pain might then also become different, perhaps better. Or, say I have a worry, and I shelve it. When I can, I take it out and worry some more. Then I put it away. If this succeeds or not, there is here something like the interaction I am talking about, but there is not the new VIII–carrying forward.

Just as a gesture is not only a simple motion, but also a string of versions of the whole behavior context (see VII-A), so also the interaction with a direct referent is not only some inward dance, but each bit of sensing is a version of the whole life situation, or the whole theoretical problem. Again a new kind of en enables something seemingly simple in the new en to be versions of the whole complexity of the previous sort of en. What seems like simple change on the new plane is also enormous change on the old plane. All the VII-sequences (all the speeches, actions, and interactions implicitly in the situation) are versioned, altered, carried forward as a whole.

A direct referent is thus as different from the usual feeling as a bodylook-cfed gesture is from an ordinary behavior.

A direct referent is like a symbol with regard to the whole of the symbolic human interaction world, insofar as relevant in this situation or concern.

There is only one body, so that it isn't puzzling why a change in stance toward the "feel" that is awaited also changes that "feel." Similarly, the change in the "feel" is also a change in the body, and thus in the body's focal forming of the next stance. So also on the new level: the direct referent falls out when a bit of "feel"-change, carrying the whole complexity forward, is such that its bodily effect makes for another bit of feel-change which again carries forward. Until then there is a bit of change, but not yet the sequence.

To define the sequence, our old notion of "re-recognizing" will fit again. "Re-recognizing" was our way of thinking about what is usually called "expression." Something that is done is an expression, when the body responds to it by *finding itself carried forward further*, and in so finding, the environmental effect is recognized by the body as (a rendition of) what it just did. Expression is never just one unit. There is a response to it, once it occurs. The response to it, by the body that emitted it, is a recognition of what is outwardly perceived as being an environmental version of what the body just was. Expression is made; we don't want to assume it. The way a new environment can function to carry forward is first found.

The direct referent is a kind (a new kind) of expression. Each bit is a new kind of bodily sense of what one just was, and one finds oneself carried forward. Retroactively the changed body-feel is what the body just "was," and this relationship is the new carrying forward.

If this finding-itself-expressed is a body-change which again makes a "feel"-change that is re-recognized, if again it is (an explication of) what was just implied focally by the body, then there is a sequence.

These new body-feel changes are a new environment, a new registry made in a new kind of sequence.

As we usually do, let us ask how body-sense already had some carrying forward power. In VII we found that certain behaviors called "animal gestures" already made very large shifts (as when the fighting monkey turns and the fight is over, or never even begins, ceases to be implied). All through VII a body-sense implies the whole complexity of one's situation, only this is never felt (had, sequenced, cfed *as such*). When an emotion comes, it makes a big shift (but doesn't carry the whole situation forward). Slotted feeling sequences similarly make big shifts; they are also body changes, and hence changes in how the body implies the whole situation. That is all not new. Only the doubled way a new kind of environment carries the whole forward, that is new. Body-sense has not, before VIII, functioned as a kind of environment in its own right. (Analogously, in the higher animals there are many whole-body expressions that a human can perceive as expressive of the animal's whole situation, but the animals do not respond to this in each other. The whole bodylook and sound is not an environment of a separate kind for them, and only certain looks and sounds are reacted to—and even then only as behavior.)

Doubling can also be understood as two kinds of implying. Each bit of body-feel would focally imply some VII-actions, -speeches, -dances, and so on, and implicitly involves a vast number of these. But each bit of body-feel also implies the next bit of body-feel which will carry that whole complexity forward, carry that whole relevance forward. (This is similar to how each bit of gesturing implies a changed behavior-context, but also the next bit of gesturing.)

Therefore one has the sense that one could say, and does know, what is happening, and yet the change is more than thousands of words could ever say. It is a change in what would be said (and done), and could be symboled in some vast number of VII-sequences from the new bit, but how then the next bit carries this one forward is *more* than could ever be said. We must better understand this sense of knowing. It is not really that one "could say" or think it at all. Yet there is an internal understanding, I call it "self-understanding," but must later say much more about this. All these many VII-sequences that are now changed (type-a implicit; they have never yet been sequenced in their changed way) need of course not, and cannot ever be sequenced. Some of them are enough to change the VII-situation so that one can act in it.

The internal self-understanding in a direct referent sequence is how each bit occurs into the previous implying (as our model from IV would say it). Each bit of occurring locates itself into the previous implying, is an explication of that implying. The many VII-sequences which are each a kind of understanding (actions too, in VII, always involve understanding: we know what we're doing, the way we are being carried forward), all these sequences of understanding are now carried forward at once, as a whole, and all their understanding is implicit. That is one way to think about the "Yes . . . yes . . ." quality of a direct referent.

But until now we always *were* bodily, but never *had* the whole relevance, the whole situation. So there is also a new kind of understanding here, a sensing and having of the whole relevance, carried forward by another version of the whole relevance. All the implying is carried forward and we feel *that* relevance as such, from version to version.

Animals sense space, but it is full. Empty space, especially geometric space, is a late human derivative. Empty space is due (as we saw in VII) to the symbolic character of gestures—the way they version a whole complexity although in themselves simple. Gestures go on, not only in the actual physical space, but also in the complex context which they version. This context is "full," but the space in which the gesture physically moves is now different. It is no longer the behavior context itself, that the gesture occurs in. Rather, gesturing generates its own space, and that is empty space in which there are simple movements.

When an animal moves, it does so in behavior space, in the full context of all other behaviors, implicit in each other, forming a context, a space. Only the symbolically doubled space is empty, so that mere movements can occur in it independently of how all else is changed by each move. This is because the gesture (while still amidst the behavior objects, while it must still avoid hitting a tree or falling off a cliff) is not really in that space, but in its own doubled space. The complexity being versioned is not here, only the empty space is.

In this respect the doubling here in VIII is again twofold: the space in which the direct referent forms is in one sense empty (just this new kind of self and this new datum) and in another sense, of course, all of the bodily implied complexity which is being versioned. So the new space is empty in that the VII-complexity is not literally here, and yet that complexity is more fully carried forward than in any possible VII-sequence.

The vastness of that space is therefore understandable: it isn't the kind of space that situations are. We are in them. Here is a space *in which* THE WHOLE SITUATION MOVES. We are not in the situation anymore, but in the new space, and we are here, the situation is now a something, a new datum, there, over against us.

Once a direct referent has formed, what one can do in the new space is also different. Now one can "put it down," or "receive," one can let it wait for later, one can ask how one would feel without it (awaiting a new feel in the body, which again, must come, cannot be invented), one can stand next to it, tap it lightly to sense what more is involved in it, or, if one places each new problem to one side and lets each further problem be a direct referent again placed, one comes upon a vast plane. The big problems lie there like huge boulders, now small in comparison to the big open space.

Like VII-space, this space is symbolic in its new way (not like VII). It is a space generated by the moving in relation to the direct referent, and seemingly one stands outside the situations.

The space is made by the sequence. The sequence is a bodily carrying forward of this new kind (Whole-Whole-Whole). The body-sensing is the new rendering, the new registry, the new environmental versioning of what the body is, implies, just was.

The space is of course *not* the body-sensing, the space is empty. Space, for us, is always a result, an "in" that is generated by a sequence. Any sequence goes on in its own generated space. We first had space in VI when any given behavior altered how any other behavior is now possible. Let me recall this.

An animal does not move merely, it behaves. We might say it moved from left to right, but that kind of empty space and pure motion is a result of VII, of motions that are gestures and are doubled, as I just showed, and freed from the present behavior-context (except for bumping into things). The point of a gesture is not that, having to raise my arm to vote, for example, I must not hit the man next to me as I do it. I must look out for that, but the gesture goes on in the situation we are voting about— usually far away and not in this room where people sit around a table. My vote may change much that is not in the room, of course. Thus a new kind of space is created in the room, empty space, really symbolic space. The animal, on the other hand, behaves. As it moves (what we see as) to the left, going after a mouse for example, all the other behaviors which are implicit are not done, but if they were, they would have to be done differently. The behavior goes on in a full space, in the context of the other behaviors (like my raising my arm in respect of the people and objects near me, not in respect of its gesture-character which is independent of that, and goes on in empty space and versions an absent situation). A full space is one in which the other implicit sequences and this one are on the same plane, in the same context together. Considered symbolically, my VII-situation is a full space: whatever I do alters all the other sequences I might then do. Having voted, I cannot now do things in the same way as before—though I may have continued sitting where I was, or I may have moved, that doesn't matter.

We have seen that it is important not to think of space as mere position, and positional relations. These always require an observer who remains a puzzle because the observer is human. To an observer positions A and B are "related," but this doesn't mean there is any actual relation between A and B as events. To understand how an observer related spatially we have had to think all of VII. Already in VI we saw that an animal in behaving changes not just positions, but how other behaviors could now be done. Of course, moving there, the animal cannot approach a given spot in the same way as from here. But also, in chasing the mouse its adrenaline has flowed, its circulatory system has altered, the behaviors that are implied by the body (and are implicit each in the others) have been altered in how they would now occur. The animal behaves *in* a mesh of possible behavior sequences. Each behavior is a change also of the implicit others. The behavior occurs *into* this implicit complexity, and is always within it, and never carrying forward of it all. Only symboling does that.

Similarly now, we understand how the VIII-sequence can take one out of one's situations, just as the gesture takes one out of the behavior context, by doubling and carrying forward on a new plane, and as a whole.

That is why the VIII-space is empty, and yet is sensed as so full of the life meanings being carried forward as a whole complexity.

The vast space is not the space of VII only bigger, it is made by a carrying forward with a new kind of medium. The object that falls out (the direct referent) is a new kind of object.[4] That object and its space, form together. So the space is necessarily bigger than the object.

The self corresponds to the space, not the object merely (corresponds to the space and object). The body-feeling as direct referent is now the object, the "perception," the specific facet of the environment. But the body implies the whole new kind of environment, the whole space.

That is why the self seems so vast, and so clearly not merely the having-of-the-object. However large the direct referent formation change, the space is much larger.

But what is this space? Should it not (by our scheme) be all the direct referent formation sequences implicit in each other, like behavior space was? No, it is rather like the new consciousness of the first VII-sequence in VII-A.

We can think about this new kind of "empty space" along the lines of VII-A, where the symbolic simple movements had with them (from the first one) their "empty" space. They were still in full space as behaviors (not bumping into anything) but they were doubled and, as gestures were not in the same space as behaviors. Nor were they in an (as yet not formed) context of such new sequences. Empty space remains, of course, even after such an interaction-context forms, since it is the space that goes with the simple movement. *Its "emptiness" is its versioning of the previous context-type.* That is why it was symbolic space.

Of course these VII-concepts have to be used in an VIII way here to instance the direct referent of direct referent formation; we don't want to reduce VIII to VII-terms unless we use them in an VIII way. But the terms let us think about the character of this new "empty" space, and especially about the new self (self-locative carrying forward) which is now the body-side of this new carrying forward.

Just as the merely positional geometric space of location points must not be taken as basic, because then one forgets its derivation from symbolic movement, so also this new VIII-space must not be thought merely empty in a simple—and especially not in a positional—way. Positions are always in relation to someone, and space is that someone's mesh of implicit sequences, how each alters when one occurs. All this is lost sight of when a space of mere positions is constructed, unless we remember its derivative character. The capacity of a human observer to live a continuity between here and there, or there and over there, derives from movements that are versionings of (and thus physically independent of, and on a new plane from) behavior contexts. When (see VII-B) the new interactional symbolic space becomes encompassing of the old behavior-contexts, then people live in symbolic interaction contexts instead, and physical space comes to seem empty, but it is still doubled, always. It becomes a mesh of mere movements and position, because the life events are now in symbolic interaction space (see VII-B-1). In moving and relating moves in empty space we version our interaction contexts.

Of course, we would feel *more* ourselves since so much more is carried forward, which equals bodily changed, = felt, = had, = sequenced, = occurring. Locating into it is now not a consciousness of self (as in VII) but a new level of "of." To think about this we must first see in what new sense the direct referent formation is universal in its own new way.

(f) Rapid statements of points that instance direct referent formation

(f-1) How an VIII-sequence makes changes in the VII-context

Each bit of the new sequence is a changed version of the whole VII-context. Each bit carries forward (satisfies) the requirement-context that the previous bit was. A direct referent, a feeling of the whole, would not fall out as a datum, if this were not so.

The change made by this new kind of carrying forward is not a change possible within the context of VII-sequences, and could not be made by a VII-sequence. It is a change in all of them *of the sort we called "meshed"* (VII-A). They all change, but not in a way any of them could bring about in the others.

(f-2) Any VII-sequence from the direct referent is like a new "first" sequence in relation to the VII-context.

There can be a new "first" sequence only either by a renewed versioning (as when we developed VII, each "new expression" or new dance made for a new crossing of all the VII-sequences with the new expressive pattern; see VII-B); or this can happen from the next level only (as now in VIII), once no new expression in the bodylook environment can carry forward the whole (see VII-B).

With regard to VIII, all the VII-sequences from the direct referent are "second sequences" and direct referent formation is the "first" sequence. But within VII, each sequence after the direct referent is like a "first" sequence, that is to say, it changes the whole context, all the other sequences.

But let us recall the difference (clarified in VII-B), since new or changed second sequences too change all the others. The second sequences are the working out, the occurring, of what was already type-a implicit in the first sequence—that's just why it is a first sequence, because it implicitly involves a whole new cluster of crossed new second sequences. (When they actually occur, of course they make further change.)

Each statement from a direct referent acts like a new first sequence in VII. Each implicitly involves (type-a implicit) a whole cluster of "applications" *to everything* in VII, not at all only to the given situation or problem or theoretical topic.

This is why, as we see in *Thinking at the Edge* (Gendlin 2004a), such statements far exceed what at first is their only literal significance. Each can be a model affecting any consideration.

As a VII-statement it only applies to what is "under" its generality.

(f-3) "Monad"

"Monad" is the term I use for how a direct referent applies to everything, that is to say, to the working out of all its second sequences (each of which, we just said, is a "first" sequence within VII). For me, "to monad" is a verb. I want to say that a direct referent "monads out into everything."

(f-4) VII-statements from a direct referent instance that direct referent.

The reason such statements have powerful new properties is because they aren't only changed VII-statements; they come from the direct referent and carry the direct referent forward indirectly, implicitly. Each such statement actually monads-out the direct referent that it instances. Therein lies its power.

Of course, we must remember that a direct referent only forms (falls out) if the sequence carries forward, meets the implying of the whole. Therefore there is an implicit correctness, a validity in any VII-statement in regard to the whole VII-context that was carried forward.

Also, we must recall that "everything" is not a lot of things next to each other, but many sequences, each of which implicitly contains the others. That is why the whole cluster changes (in some carrying forward way). Every VII-sequence, if changed, implicitly (type a) involves changing its whole cluster—that's why I call it a "first" sequence within VII. But it also instances the direct referent which is a different sort of change of the whole. All the VII-sequences from a direct referent will be instances of the same direct referent the others instance. The whole that the direct referent formation carries forward (and that the fallen-out direct referent is) is not only the kind of whole that *any* VII-sequence implicitly involves. Rather, it is the having (feeling, sequencing) of a whole never capable of being sensed within VII, and not itself capable of being said or acted in VII-sequences.

(f-5) The new "universality" of the direct referent

The direct referent falls out from a new level of versioning. It is "of" (versioning defines "of") the VII-context(s) in a new way, a new kind of having, a new way of doing what in VII was properly called symbolization. For VIII I will put this new kind of kind into quotation marks. A direct referent is a new kind of "symbolization" (without symbols)! It is a new kind of rendering of something (the whole VII-context), now rendered in body-sense.

(f-6) The old universality of VII is implicit also.

It is important not to confound the new universality and the "symbolization" with the fact that in direct referent formation the VII-context(s) as a whole, in being carried forward, constitute a change in all of the VII-universals. Of course, the direct referent has VII-universal significance since it is a carrying forward of a VII-context consisting of mutually implicit VII-sequences. However, they are changed in this new carrying forward which results in VII-universals, that is, statements, or kinded interactions. But this is a VII-result from the new universality. Above we stated the new universality itself. It is different.

(f-7) The whole VII-complexity, not just the collected kinds, is carried forward and universalized in the new way; we can now derive the IOFI principle.

We saw (in VII-B) that words collect, they cross all the contexts to which they apply, each new context crossing with those already collected. This collected crossing differs from the lateral crossing of all the contexts implicit in each other situationally.

We saw there also that VII-universals are nothing like the empty generalities with the details dropped out, that they are usually considered to be. One uses a word with the collected sense of all the contexts in which it ever applied. (Even apart from individual experience, the contexts in which a word applies are implicit in the cultural system so that one has this implicit use already in other contexts and in other words, even if one has not individually used a word in enough contexts to have a personal experience of it.) All these contexts imply each other laterally, that is to say, our different interaction-contexts imply each other. In VII-B I showed all this exactly. The VII-complexity, the interaction contexts (mutually implicit), are fundamentally elaborated by the collect-crossing of language, but there is also much more complexity than language makes into kinds, and collects.

Direct referent formation carries forward much more than just the language-kind system. It carries forward not only the VII-universals—the "thirds," the words and possible sentences, the collected life interaction context, the collected interaction-context(s)—but also the whole complexity of all the mutually implicit contexts which, as we saw, are not dropped out when we speak. And it also carries forward aspects that are not collected in words at all. (See Appendix to VIII.)

For this reason a direct referent can be the source of countless new VII-universals, not only changed extant ones. This *derives the IOFI principle* (Gendlin 1997a), where we did not explain why it is that any statement, taken qua direct referent, is capable of leading to countless new universals—or, as I said it there: can be *an instance of itself* in countless ways. (Exactly: the having, the direct referent, of any statement can give rise to countless new general statements of which the given one will have been an instance.) Put mildly, the given statement—rather, our having of it, that is, the direct referent—can be an illustration or example of countless generalities, new categories. For example, this point I am here making can be an instance of (at least) new conclusions emerging from what we already said and thought we fully knew; how implicit complexity functions; how universals come to be; the way newly specific points are not really logically "under" what was more general; monading a direct referent, here about direct referent formation; how a new aspect is continuous with the previous but not logically derivable from it by deduction; and with a little intervening creativity almost anything we ever said here can also be made to have been instanced here. Such a list would not ever exhaust what could be "generalized" (as it is usually put) or "universalized" (as I call it).

Direct referent formation, by carrying forward the whole complexity, not just VII-"thirds," has made a type-a implicit universal of "every" facet of that complexity.

(f-8) The direct referent, and the new universalized complexity, was not there before direct referent formation; the direct referent is not a "reflecting upon" what was there before ("from 1/2 to 2").

The direct referent falls out from the string of carrying forwards. The direct referent is therefore not at all something that was there before, waiting for us to notice it. The "turning" which one thinks to do is there, but it is a new sequence, and creates a new datum, not what was literally there.

The complexity of VII which was always literally there is not the carried forward one. It is the not-able-to-be-carried-forward complexity. You can say they are "the same"; this one carried forward in VIII is the one that couldn't be carried forward in VII. True, but the datum, the direct referent, is new, and is from the carrying forward sequence.

This has been the case throughout. To feel something is to have it, to sequence it, to have it fall out from a sequence. What falls out (they used to call it the "commonality") is a product of the carrying forward of the sequence, not what was literally there before. (Thus I put "was" in quotations when I speak of explicating what something "was.") Even in VII the danced behavior-context is the one altered in this new versioning, not literally what it was. Even in VI the body-stoppage is the one versioned in behavior, itself a new kind of bodily change.

I call this the principle of "from 1/2 to 2." This rough way of naming it brings home that what is roughly called "reflection" is not a turning to see what was there before, unseen. It is not as if "1" was there, and reflecting, as in a mirror, we get two ones, making 2. Rather, both ones are created in the new "reflective" process. What was there before can be called "1/2." (Of course, I don't mean this to apply literally as quantities.)

This is why, without direct referent formation, one cannot state the problem or be aware of the lack that one is instancing. To be aware of the trouble is to have it, to sequence it, and thus to carry it forward in a new kind of sequence. That is why there is no way to have or feel what is not being carried forward. This goes a long way, as we will see, to explaining the character of the so-called unconscious.

(f-9) Direct context crossing makes novelty but still instances the lack.

Novelty in VII also alters implicitly all the mutually implicit sequences, but the novel action or speech will instance the lack negatively, not through a carrying forward of the whole in a way that satisfies its implying. We can use the above points to make this difference clear between novelty in VII and in VIII. That is why it is quite slow in VII, why cultural contexts last so long, and why an individual cannot change by deliberate planning and decision alone—it will all instance the problem rather than instancing a solution. Direct context crossing lacks phantastic differentiation (see VII-B-g) though on the VII level it makes some differentiations.

(f-10) Many words, like "direction," are used in an IOFI way in VIII.

Any word and any sentence can be used in a direct referent instancing way. Here I want to point to one characteristic (among many) which then arises.

Words like "direction," "good," "possible," "right," and many others, when used in an VIII way, seem to be empty of content—and are not at all empty. Rather, they instance direct referent formation. One knows in advance that they will be intended as used from a direct referent. Therefore one cannot (before direct referent formation) give their VII-content, yet they have such content. Let me explain:

If I wish to move in a certain direction, in VII this means I know and define this direction. In VIII it means that I know in advance that this direction will change in direct referent formation. From the VII point of view this means only that I don't know what the direction will be after direct referent formation. But in VIII I do know—I know *more* than the direction I defined; I know that plus the openness I leave for the "change" which a direct referent formation can make in carrying the whole context forward.

VIII–carrying forward fulfills the requirements, the implying, of the whole VII-context or, more exactly, the implying by the body (which *is* the whole VII-context as the body constitutes it. This specific way of saying it leaves open that some of my situation may escape me, since it involves other people. Most of that *will* be implicit in my body-sense which constitutes the situation as I live it, much more than I *know*, but I may not be sensitive to everything that can be relevant).

Yet VIII–carrying forward fulfills the implying in a new way, through a new medium. Therefore much is involved in the carrying forward which cannot happen in VII and of which it would not be meaningful even to ask if it could happen in terms of the actions, interactions, and symbolizations of VII. In that sense VIII–carrying forward transcends the requirements of VII, and arrives at a bodily solution which *takes account of* all the requirements of VII, but in a new way that must then still be sequenced creatively within VII. Such changes cannot, of course, be delineated in advance in VII.

Therefore it would be foolish for me to decide the "direction" in which a solution to a problem must lie, before I solve it. Such a decision would only instance the problem. Yet I sense a direction and could say what it is. Instead I want *this direction,* but not as definable in VII, but rather as about-to-be "changed" in an VIII–carrying forward. So far as VII can possibly define it, it is *this* direction into which I mean to head. But **in addition** an VIII use of that word would intend the "direction" not yet definable. (I italicize "in addition" because the VIII–carrying forward will not lose me anything of this VII-stated direction, despite there being as yet no words in VII to say, or deeds to indicate, in what way my VII-statement is not what I intend to mean.)

An old way of saying something like this is: to want the will of God. One wants the best, and in the long run the most desirable, what one *would* want if one knew everything. (At least, so it is with the notion of God I am implying here.) Thus one still wants the specifics as one now sees them, but in addition one wants the best change in them. And furthermore, if this way of thinking were not the best, then one would want whatever the best would be. Finally, if "best" is not a right way to think about or feel about this, and if perhaps "wanting" isn't either, then whatever changes that would make are also intended.

In IV-A-e, our concept there of "eveving" already employed this kind of "direction" when we formulated how an evev becomes stable. Only now can this be said clearly. The concept of "eveving" is from direct referent formation, from VIII.

This discussion is also an instance of how VIII relates to VII-content generally. An VIII-sequence *is* a carrying forward of VII-content, but it is much more than that. This still includes, however, a fulfilling of the VII-requirements, only in a way that moves as one couldn't within those requirements.

We want something "possible," and direct referent formation will enable us to get it, but "possible" needs to be defined as above, not by how it would be defined in VII-statements of VII-conditions. (We saw throughout, and discussed in IV, how the model is false, which makes any occurrence only one of *antecedently* defined possibilities.) Again, here is that relationship between VIII- and VII-content to which I wish to point. We will fulfill the condition that the later actions and statements must be possible in VII, but from a carrying forward that itself is not possible in VII. The eventuating change will be possible in VII. Retroactively we will restructure the VII-context in a possible way, and we can then say how what we say and do is possible ("was" possible all along).

For example, as we develop as persons, what we consider good and bad changes. This doesn't mean that we come to be more evil. Looking back to, say, when we were teenagers, it would be sad if our sense of good and evil had not developed, become more subtle and complex, deeper. But it is also sad if we thereby lost something that was good. This would be contradictory if we had to stay with a VII use of terms. Here both "develop" and "good" were used in an VIII way.

Spiritual people currently often say one should not have a purpose, a direction, and shouldn't be concerned with good and bad. They mean this in a VII way of using these words. But there is a seemingly contentless way of using them, not defined only in a VII way, but rather, defined by VIII–carrying forward. Then one still has the best VII definition and sense one can have, but more.

Of course, if I structure my efforts to "develop" by how I now sense everything, I will structure myself to stay fundamentally as I am. I will make efforts to improve capacities that how I now am leads me to value, and I will do it in the way I now do things.

What was said here is instanced by a whole discussion of axiomatic systems, and of how it becomes possible to examine and move beyond assumptions. *The whole new model, in a way, instances the question of how something can develop which is not capable of being reduced back to the explicit structure (and its units and relations) which was.*

Also instanced here is the whole relation between *implying and occurring*. What is implied is not some explicit structure (not even what usually happens and has many times carried forward), but something that will carry forward. Occurring, when it occurs *into* implying, changes that implying not as if the implying were for an explicit structure. "Explicit structure" itself, as usually conceived, is a VII-term! In VIII it becomes something that can instance a direct referent, and thus apply in ways that could not be inferred from its VII-character.

It is important here to see how nothing is lost. Implying is not less determinate than an explicit structure. Implying is always *more* ordered, but in a different way (I have said so often, and can now be clear)!

The "*more*" and different kind of order is that of VIII–carrying forward, of direct referent formation which is *at least* what I have said of it. "At least," because of course what I said was in VII-statements—new ones, to be sure, and odd, formed from direct referent formation, but still only VII-terms! This matters greatly. Nothing I say in this work is intended to foreclose someone's better sensing and better knowing. It is all said in a use of words I have just now defined.

VIII–carrying forward *is* a carrying forward of VII's implying. It is not indeterminate, it demands more. It has all the determination of VII. A VII-statement doesn't lose any of its determination by instancing a direct referent (before or after a direct referent formation). VIII–carrying forward (which really defines the term "carrying forward") is beyond explicit VII-type structure by carrying it forward, not by making everything indeterminate or vague. In regard to VIII–carrying forward something can be "open" without losing its VII-order.

(g) Additions to VIII-f

(1) That is why in VII people can actually make (see VII-A) things. What VII-versioning alters and creates *is* possible in the VI–behavior contexts, but not within the way they are explicitly structured. If versioning were not like that, what is symbolized would not then in fact work in the behavior context.

(2) A direct referent can monad only because of the jelledness, i.e., having fallen out from VIII–carrying forward. Just feeling or sensing something does not have this property. Direct referent formation takes time; there is amazing speed, but it does take some time. Something happens. Until it does, one cannot monad. Although one can make VII-statements, they don't have the properties described.

(3) IOFI space is not without this direct referent formation. Having gone round and round issues many times, having seen many views, does not automatically make IOFI space. Only when direct referent formation happened, and in regard to it, can one use VII-statements in a VIII way. Until then the most one can do is leave the terms open for a direct referent formation, as I said.

In order to make something clear, terms in VII will be cut so that much else equally important and true is denied or covered over. In VIII words are used as instancing the direct referent, and not only as the explicit structure which does this denying and covering. IOFI space use has its own rules.

(4) *Self is "separate" from the content being carried forward*, in the space of the VIII-sequence. Data are therefore constituted something like perceptual objects always are (see VI), so that they are the perception-perception-perception string, while there is also a feeling-feeling-feeling string, both as one sequence. The direct referent, the new datum, the new object, is there; I am here. The fallen-out direct referent is like the perception-perception-perception, and the interacting separate self is the feeling-feeling-feeling (see VI-A). Both make the continuity of the carrying forward, but now the doubled implying is new: how each bit of direct referent formation implies the next bit is new: it is a *self-*understanding much wider than the VII-content even as a whole, since as we showed, the carrying forward is new, new in kind, in a new medium

(the body-sense as environment). Just as in VII the carrying forward was by no means nothing but versions of the behavior-context, but a new doubling medium, so here too. The self in this sequence is not the self of VII (from 1/2 to 2) reflected upon; it newly finds itself as a new wider self with a new object, the direct referent, not of the old VII-objects. (Of course, the self is not the new "object" either; an object is always different than, constituted by, over against, though from the same sequence as, that in which the self finds itself. The carried forward fallen-out context or space is much wider; see later.)

Even in regard to VII situations, each feeling in the feeling-feeling-feeling sequence is the whole, hence in regard to these the evev-evev bits are each of the situation.

Just as VI-objects involve behavior space, and VII-objects involve interaction contexts, so a direct referent involves a new space (that vast space in which the direct referent can be "placed" down alongside one-self . . . or at some distance).

The self or consciousness, now self-understood, is parallel to the space, or the context–carrying forward, context-self-locating, not merely the object, of course.

(5) *This was always the character of consciousness* in our model, the self-locating (see VI) and also the making a new space. (In VI it was the first space. In VII it was internal space, or rather, internal/ external space; see VII-B-a.)

(6) All contexts (or, since total unity is an assumption, very many) always were implicit in any one. But this could not be had or sensed as such. To have or sense is to sequence, to carry forward into a sequence. One could say in general, as Plato did, that anything, if fully known and pursued, would lead to everything else, but one could do this only in small steps and never to the end. In direct referent formation it happens completely. But it happens differently in each new direct referent formation. Therefore there are *many wholes, not just one as Plato thought.* One can say that one always forms "the same" whole in a direct referent formation, but this sameness is in quotes. *The* order of experience, nature, or the universe is understandable only as (at least) an VIII "order" (using the word as "direction" was used earlier).

(7) From any direct referent formation very many new universals can form, but from any one of these in some use a new direct referent formation can occur too. (Can occur, I said, but might not occur. Direct referent formation is a special kind of carrying forward, it isn't just to be assumed.) *Thus the universals that instance a direct referent need not remain only in the "system" that a direct referent is.* Direct referent formation from one of its uses leads further. A direct referent is a kind of particular, as well as

being universal, as we have shown. From any universal (VII-statement) in use, or at any point in living, a new direct referent may form. In this sense of VIII, a new "particular" can always be formed leading to many new universals. New or old universals can lead to such a new particular (in direct referent formation). This is a way in which *particulars are not under universals in the most radical way.* Neither do universals (VII-terms used in an VIII way) include a fixed set of particulars.

(8) *Phantastic differentiation* was our term for what happens when, in versioning, the whole complexity of some stage is carried forward by (some new environmental version of) the whole complexity. Carrying forward is always context-crossing: as in VI, the way the body implies the environment is different than the way the environment all spread out is a version of this same implying. Versioning always vastly differentiates what is versioned. Thus VII, in relation to VI, vastly differentiates, increases complexity. This complexity remains and is the new kind of carrying forward, so that carrying forward is always cross-contextual (body implying is carried forward by an environmental version of that same implying).

In making sensible the complexity implicit as any VII-context, so that it can be had (as we saw, thus implicitly universalizing or versioning all of it), a vast number of now-sayable aspects are created (type-a implicit) and can be said, thought, or acted.

What was a cultural pattern or a basic human type (archetype) becomes a texture of possible differentiations. For example, what in VII thinking is either so or so (e.g., either continuous or different, either determined or indeterminate, either internal or external, either in accord with this system or that) becomes in VIII not indeterminate, but a new texture enabling many new differentiations and concepts. (And so it is also in personal living.)

Our concept evev (everything by everything, crossing) applies again on a new level. We made it characteristic of any carrying forward process. Of course, the concept came from VII and instances direct referent formation. A new environment enables a new crossing of bodily implying with an environmental rendition, a new carrying forward, thus a new eveving. Everything, each facet, crossed with every other (using "every" in an VIII way so that the crossing itself determines the new multiplicity) makes each facet as numerous as the whole complexity was. Of course, that is only a VII-metaphor for what occurs.

(9) Just as animals have many expressive bodylooks that do not function in animal behavior (and become a new environment that carries humans forward), so also is there in VII a carrying forward by body-sense. As with animal bodylooks, some specifics of it did function already in animal behavior, but only as behavior, and only some of it. Body-sense

carries forward in certain VII-sequences but only as symbolized, and only partly, never as whole. Now the whole of it is a new environment and carries forward the whole of the body's implying.

Why is it that from such a sequence new symbolic VII-sequences are actually possible in VII again?

We already asked this kind of question in VII. We were not content with just accepting the notion of symbolizing, we had to ask why versioning with patterns of bodylook (or, later, derived from it) actually result in something that can then actually be done, or actually made. Why does symbolizing work?

To answer it, we traced how the patterns are not arbitrary but are inherently related to the behavior contexts. First this was because that bodylook is how a body is in that context, and later even what are termed "conventional" symbols turned out to have intricate but non-arbitrary relations to behavior contexts. It is nothing like two separate things, the symbol and what it is about. That split makes two thing-like entities, basically separate, that someone must then "conventionally" tie up. We saw instead that what patterns would form were already type-a implicit before their occurrence (see VII-B), and we saw how they develop. We also saw exactly how they reconstitute the implicit behavior contexts they version, how these are bodily implicit.

Here in VIII also, we want it clear how body-sense is a non-arbitrary versioning of VII-contexts.

Symbolizing or versioning is always in a new medium that is non-arbitrarily related to the old. Neither is there a one-to-one denotative relation of symbol and what it is about—if there were, one would have to assume that everything symbolized was there before, already cut apart and interrelated as symbols render it. Similarly here, the VIII-sequence doesn't just find, it makes (but not out of nothing, not arbitrarily).

The body implies the whole VII-context in some focal way. When this goes through a new kind of change, it doesn't lose that implying. The new kind of change being made is a carrying forward *of this implying*. And yet it is also new in kind and not a sequence of the kind that was implied within that whole. The phantastic differentiation is a differentiation *of* those implied contexts and sequences, and yet it is also doubled, so that both: the VII-sequences are different (they are already universals) and also, the new doubled carrying forward is not just of them. Well, is it then a carrying forward of VII or is it something different? If we must choose among these alternatives, then it is something different. But instead, let us keep just this relationship we have found, how symbolizing is *of*, but by being a versioning (a string of carrying forward versions in a new kind of carrying forward in a new environment).

The VII-context is kept the "same," although (like "direction" above) it goes through change. It is not carried forward in a VII way until later when we come to say or do something.

Another feature of this relationship between VIII and VII is that the change is the solution to the VII problem "*only*" *in a VIII way*. The VII ways to solve it must still be devised. New VII-sequences are instantly focally implied, but these may not instantly solve the VII-problem. They may "only" state the problem, what has been wrong. They instance the solution, but it may still require much struggle to devise it. (Similarly, the change made in a behavior context by VII-symboling is not guaranteed by itself to resolve the problem in the behavior context. It will be pertinent, not arbitrary.)

The relationship is as we have seen, and cannot be split between how VIII is of VII, and how it is not, in a simple way.

One can have the direct referent only as itself; it cannot be rendered in VII ways. Any VII-sequence from it can instance it, that is to say, we mean more by the VII-sequence than it, itself, carries forward in a VII way. It reconstitutes the direct referent, and is a "second sequence" in relation to the direct referent.

In VII, cultural change is slow; the complexity grows with each direct context-crossing but doesn't result in a changed constellation of the whole. We become "more sensitive" and may get to the point of not being able to carry forward in the usual ways, yet no new ways develop. Each bit of novelty changes all (or many) of the other implicit sequences, they now have the changed context implicit in them. This much change is however nothing like VIII–carrying forward of the whole. At last some new way of VII–carrying forward is found, through direct context-crossing, that is to say without a direct referent, without having, feeling, or saying what was wrong, and more importantly, without that change of the whole.

It is important to understand what I call "*increased sensitivity*" here in this sense. I also use the term "*hard structure*" for the usual carrying forward which continues to be the only way extant, despite increasingly failing to carry forward all of what we sense, and sometimes failing to carry forward at all. Much of our culture is currently in this condition.

Culture forms and re-forms further in the crossing (laterally, and collectedly) I called "direct context-crossing" (dir-c-c). Direct referent formation in terms of VII is such crossing of all implicit sequences by all. It is therefore culture-formation par excellence.

Culture was defined (VII-B) as the structure of situations, the interaction contexts. Direct referent formation elaborates just this (phantastically, we said).

After direct referent formation, what is now implicit as interactions with others in the situation has become vastly differentiated: all kinds of alternatives exist which were only "unconscious" facets (not separately) of implicit complexity. These facets "exist," I just said—I mean they are *as such*, that is to say they can be had, sensed, spoken of; they are universals, new kinds (as anything in VII is a kind).

Not only are the extant VII-sequences changed, not only are there many more new ones, not only are these new ones universals, that is to say they can be sequenced in VII (they can be done or spoken), but all this is not just a quantitative change, vastly more alternatives. *What* a situation (a context) is, has changed. It retains what it was, it is "the same" context, just as "direction" retains the direction and also changes it. After direct referent formation "the same" situation is different in kind, is many quite new kinds.

Direct referent formation is culture-formation—we must examine this further since it sounds so odd. This individual and private process is *culture* formation?

It is the formulation of new interaction-contexts, new implicit sequences of interaction between oneself and others.

Until very recently this was a very private and odd individual process, and even now those who have not engaged in it don't understand it. Therefore one of the problems with it was its individuality—and the question was how it relates to culture, to society, to others.

VII-symboling came about *as* interaction. Only from interaction did the VII-self come to be. A person acquired an inner life through private sequences implicit in interactional contexts. Something seemed wrong with VIII insofar as it was not like that.

But over the years that I have been working on this, the change in our culture has become so marked, and is swelling so strongly, the way people imply their situations and interactions is changing so fast, that it has become quite clear how direct referent formation is culture-formation.

In early parts of this work I say (what is still widely true) that our roles don't work very well anymore, the usual ways of carrying forward have broken down, one must pick one's way through each situation. Father, mother, daughter, son, wife, husband, employer, and so on, the role patterns—the "hard structures"—so often fail to carry a situation forward. We must (direct context-crossing) pick our way through them. To do it better we need direct referent formation.

But already this is becoming incorporated into what many situations are, how they are implied by people. The whole complexity implicit before is becoming something that certain situations "appropriately" involve—and those who cannot let a direct referent form, and then speak from it, are having to learn how to do that.

This is much more than saying out loud the sequences one once kept to oneself. People are having to learn to find that inner source of such speaking, and are rapidly learning from those who already have it. Especially, intimate relationships have utterly changed in this regard while I have been living and working, and observing. And what could be a more important cultural change than a change in what these relationship-contexts are, how they are implied? If you cannot talk about finely differentiated sexual feelings and behaviors with your partner, you are "closed" and you must learn. No use saying "It's fine, let's just do it, I love you." Not too long ago (and in many circles still) it was the other person—the one with the complex feelings all differentiated—who was neurotic and too complicated, odd. And this goes even more for personal interaction between two intimate people. What a wealth of differentiations have suddenly come into common parlance, which would have been squinted at with puzzlement not long ago. All this has become not just additions to intimacy, it has become what an intimate relationship situation is.

I am not saying that all roles and all contexts will now become intimate. Intimacy is one kind of interaction context. But the others will also change, first because so much that used to be implicit and hidden is now perfectly visible, perceptible, sayable. Where not long ago (and in many places still) all one could say was "He's odd," or "That's the way she is," now there is differentiated perception of, for instance, the boss's way of acting manipulatively, deviously, playing one off against another, withdrawing responsibility for now obvious intentions, and so on and so on.

Secondly, there is an increasing perception that the routines need not be just only as they have been. Less and less are people "threatened" (as one used to say) by any change proposed in a routine way of structuring all situations. More and more people demand the leeway to restructure in various differentiated ways. This line of change has not yet gone very far, but it is very noticeable already.

The change is so strong—it is literally a new kind of humans that are emerging. A person who has not yet found the inward source of these differentiations seems "closed" just to that which we are coming to think of as the person.

It goes without saying that "finding oneself" is therefore not finding something that sits there, waiting to be found. (From 1/2 to 2 again.) What waits is the not-carried-forward implicit complexity (not carried forward in an VIII way, a differentiating way). What is found is something very different, the carried forward, utterly changed complexity, and the self that is fundamentally separate from all this complexity in the new sequence in the new space.

I call the VIII–carrying forward on the evev-evev-evev side "*self-*

understood" or *self-understanding*. This is the "yes . . . yes . . . yes" of direct referent formation, the new kind of carrying forward of the whole. This understanding is fundamentally without words (though implicitly it versions and alters the words implicit in the contexts, of course, so speech sequences are implicit). Again one might ask, is the self-understanding the implicit symbolic sequences being carried forward? We have already been exact about this relationship, above. No, the carrying forward is new in kind, and doubledly what can be spoken is being versioned in a new medium. It reconstitutes (each bit is a doubled version of) the interaction contexts and their implicit verbal sequences, and understandable kinded interaction sequences. In its changed way it has all those old and vastly many new VII-meanings, but also its own kind of "meaning."

Just as bodylook gave VII the new pattern-dimension as a new kind of environment, so here body-sense carrying forward gives a new dimension of versioning, rendering, meaning. A new kind of meaning dimension arises here for a new kind of thinking. Again, from 1/2 to 2: thinking always involved implicit body-sense. Along with the sound-symbols (or any symbols) there always had to be the bodily carrying forward, the feeling-feeling-feeling string interwoven with the perception-perception-perception string, each perception carrying forward each feeling.

Patterns, we saw, are powerful. Anything coming into pattern-implying space has then *its own* pattern, not some arbitrary human figment. (See VII.) But thinking was always more than patterns, it was also the bodily carrying forward. Now this bodily sensing has itself come to carry forward the body, so that body-sense is an object, a datum. In terms of body-sense as a rendering environment, that aspect of thinking which was implicitly part of a sequence comes into its own in a very new way. It is not a matter of becoming aware of something that doesn't change as a result. "Coming aware" must not be thought about with the flashlight model. To "be aware" is a sequence. To be aware without changing something away is to "pause" it, to have a string of versions of that "same" thing, rather than carrying forward it away. Thereby whatever it is acquires a new nature which is then after all its own, rendered in the new medium. Just as symbolizing discloses nature in a new way and builds a world, so the new carrying forward environment does also. I will go into this new way later, but for now just this: from any point in a VII discussion or line of thought one can move in two different ways: first, along the implications of the symbols; secondly, to direct referent formation (and from it to new symbolic sequences again). Of course, direct referent formation doesn't always succeed. It makes a vast difference, however, when it does. One is led to thinkings that are impossible to get to in the usual way . . . but these are thinkings about the topic's own nature.

As with patterns, it is again the body which has given the new medium. What must be grasped is that in terms of the new medium, everything acquires a new way of being disclosed, but one thinks the nature of what is disclosed, not just something made up. This is, of course, recognizable in the new VII-type sequences which then emerge and can satisfy the requirements of VII (although they instance more).

Appendix to VIII: Monads and Diafils

Monads

We have left the system of "universals" and thing-like particulars far behind. Already in VII-B we saw that words reconstitute the context(s) and don't drop out detail, are not "abstractions."

We also saw how past experience functions (in general, in IV, but that already instances VIII, as did VII-B).

A direct referent doesn't classify or organize extant particulars—rather, it creates a whole new range of universals (universals are such, they apply in many instances). Although they can function as VII-universals and carry a "particular" context forward by means of their own carrying forward, they are all a different kind of system, *a cluster.*

Each VII-sequence from a direct referent (we said) instances that direct referent, implicitly carries it forward. All VII-sequences from a direct referent instance each other (instance the direct referent each implicitly carries forward).

I call the system of such VII-universals from a direct referent a *"monad."*

The monad is the system of VII-sequences—but there are any number of such sequences. One might have one, or three, or a great many. They will each be instances of each other via the direct referent they each instance. The statements in this work are like that! (In *Thinking at the Edge* I show how to use all this exactly; Gendlin 2004a). There is not an exhaustive system like Kant's twelve categories.

The direct referent contains all these many VII-sequences implicitly, type-a implicit. We can now better see what exactly "type-a implicit" means, although we already saw this (in VII-A, B) about "first," "second," and "third" sequences. In regard to the direct referent the VII-sequences are "seconds." When they actually occur, they make much more change than actually happened in the great change of the direct referent. This is important. We do not literally assert these occurring sequences into the direct referent—they have not then occurred yet. When they occur, this is an eveing (see IV-A), a crossing (tantamount to a new expression in VII-A).

Consider a dialectical example: Polemarchus in the *Republic*, having had his first definition of justice defeated (led into contradiction, it implies injustice) now has only the feeling of what he meant. The question is, does Polemarchus, seeing this result, return to his original feel of what he intended to define, or does he have more now? Has he learned something, more than that the literal statement he made leads to contradiction? I want to elevate to a principle the fact that *Polemarchus learns*.[5] I see that this fact instances how second sequences do not merely state something already in a felt meaning. In so stating they structure further, they are a further occurring.

As always in this model, the change a new sequence brings becomes implicit in the ones already extant. They have more meaning (they carry forward more implicitly) when they recur. Thus each statement adds to the others that it instances.

When a statement from a direct referent is "applied" to any topic, experience, context, this is not a mere logical applying, not a mere imposition of certain patternings or conclusions upon the topic. In VIII "apply" is in quotation marks, because the statement applies not just literally, but through the direct referent it instances. This direct referent crosses with that topic.

Of course, the direct referent already crossed everything with everything, the whole of the VII-context or problem on which it turned—and thereby also the whole VII-world as it was implicit in that context.

But just as each VII-sequence, in VII, implicitly carries forward the whole interaction context in its own way, another sequence in another way, so that there are many ways the whole is implicit, so also the direct referent has not literally already done what happens when it is crossed with another topic.

There are many new wholes in VIII. Each direct referent carries forward the whole world already, and then can monad (cross and "apply") into the whole world of different topics and contexts. The monad is the cluster of new statements which results. But a different direct referent will monad differently. Again there are many wholes. In contrast, dialectic assumes the same formal whole is reached by any avenue. This has a new meaning in VIII. All these wholes are not just different, nor the same. The "one whole" in VIII is in quotation marks.[6]

A direct referent is a type-a implicit monad. The above defines "type-a implicit," though its meaning will grow as we proceed.

A direct referent stays "the same" in all this monading, and this is a new sense of "same." Already, as it fell out from the string of versions of direct referent formation, it was (as usual) a sense, a datum, an object, as "the same" across the versions. (By their change the carrying forward versions enable one to feel, sense, be conscious of, ... an it, a datum, an object. See VI.) But now there is another way the direct referent stays "the same" through monading. It changes—as a "first" always does through "second" sequences. (See VII.) It is the "same" instanced, implicitly carried forward whole, but all the sequences each get elaborated as they come to imply the new sequences from the actually monading. The direct referent remains "the same" whole (as behavior space is always "the same" space, each new sequence elaborating the mesh that every sequence implicitly alters if it occurs).

Shall we ask why all this is possible? How again was it that the *unique* peculiarities of a given person's having of the VII-complexity during direct referent formation came to be universally valid, so that VII-universals can be new, and yet valid for anyone?

Of course, in ordinary science already, any unique instance has to exemplify a general law. Let us be old-fashioned for a moment, and look back to see within what assumptions this is asserted. If something happens at all, however odd, it instances some laws that account for it (so scientists would say). One instance is quite sufficient to pose the question of its lawfulness. One exception is enough to disprove a law.

So it is careless to accept the idea of human "uniqueness" just like that. If a certain human experience of some individual can happen at all (and if it did, it could), then the universe is *such* that it was possible. By "such," a universal patterning is meant.

But now let us turn and examine the assumption that the universe or nature consists of laws or generalizations or universals. Let us not uncritically accept that as if it were a fact that we can't get behind. Laws, generalizations, VII-universals are *patterns*; we saw in VII how they work. *If* something comes into a pattern-implying space, *then* it has *its own* patterning

Direct referent formation (we saw in VIII) takes all facets (no separated number) and crosses them (with a new environmental rendering of them) so that every aspect comes into pattern-space (pattern-space as implied by the body).

And this is true again as the instanced direct referent crosses with each new topic to which it (or any VII-statement from it) is "applied."

We saw in VII-A how a "first" sequence, there, is a "first universal." *It is only an incipient universal and becomes actually so only as it functions implicitly in the formation of second sequences.*

We saw in VII-A-o that what *would* function implicitly in a sequence if it occurred does not necessarily function implicitly when the sequence itself only functions implicitly. (If it doesn't, we called that "held.") We necd this point here, we are instancing it and clarifying it: if this odd principle were not so, all the VII-sequences of the monad would actually be in the direct referent, and all the change each second sequence makes would already be made by the very first second sequence. Or else we would have to say, no, these sequences are simply not implicit in the direct referent, and in any second sequence. Instead we have the term "type-a implicit" which lets more change happen when a type-a implicit sequence itself actually occurs. As they develop, so also do they continue to imply each other.[7]

As we saw in VI, there is another reason why crossing with a new environmental plane brings novelty. In VI, I called it "the open cycle can surprise the evev." Even though it is the body evev that projects, implies, makes the environmental version, it is done with the actual body-environment. Here the same point is instanced as the body-sense, though made by the evev's implying and being carried forward, nevertheless comes in its own (again bodily) way.

This is even more obvious when we speak of second sequences— they can "surprise the evev" in each bit, because they occur in the VII-environment (in the interaction context) and of course in the actional and bodily (b-en) environments which interaction contexts involve.

Looking back from this, the body-sense involves all these in a way— the body goes on in all these environments and body-sense is an aspect of physical life process, of course. These environments are not separate, of course; we have seen how each is doubled with a new way of carrying forward the previous.

All these environments are implicit in the body's evev, and differently occurring as the body-sense. The body-sense might physically encounter something differently than evev implies it. *In its concrete bodily way, it can "surprise," therefore.* And then, of course, the VII-sequences can do that again, in their environment.

In all these ways what is later specified (in VII-sequences) "was" already implicit (type a). Thus one can specify how some experience "arose from," or "is an aspect of" some other, via both instancing a direct referent and the further creativity of aspects which sequencing from the direct referent entails. In *Experiencing and the Creation of Meaning* (Gendlin 1997a) I only showed that this is so; here we can think about it. Of course, ours here is only one model of VII-concepts from the direct referent formation; there may be other ways to think about it. This poses a problem.

In "Experiencing and the Creation of Meaning," by merely pointing to all this (for instance, how something can be retroactively specified as having come from what it literally didn't come from), *I was perfectly certain of what I was saying.* Here, by rendering it in VII-concepts, I *cannot, it seems,* have that certainty. But I can, if I use my terms here in a direct referent-instancing way! The pointing in that book was after all also done with VII-concepts, in words and a scheme. The scheme was rudimentary, so it was more obvious that not the scheme but the pointing was intended. We don't need to lose that here! We can have the advantages it gives us, to be able to think sharply and clearly about direct referent formation, and still also let what we say instance the direct referent. (Of course, instancing a direct referent involves "pointing," that is, "direct reference," that is what a direct referent is.)

In this way we retain the inherent validity of the concepts made from the direct referent without overplaying this validity and falling into a VII view of conceptual schemes! From VIII we see the power of concepts not as a literal representational truth, but as a monading from a much bigger truth. *The bigger truth can give rise to many clusters of VII-sequences*; any direct referent is still only one of endlessly many possible ones that are equally universally valid in the old VII way, and hint at "one whole" in some way we cannot think about clearly yet. *Equal validity here is nothing like a relativism which takes away from the degree of truth that each relative version has. On the contrary, the monaded cluster of concepts from any direct referent is fully true in the VII sense*, and certain to apply in true and significant ways for any person and in any context. *The old VII notion that there is one truth only of a VII type is false in being too poor; nothing of it is lost.* Experience, nature, or reality is much richer than that old view wanted.

What then can we do right now, if we wish to have not only the clarity our concepts give about direct referent formation, but also *Experiencing and the Creation of Meaning*'s certainty? If we ask again why speaking from a direct referent is valid, and we answer again: a direct referent isn't just any fuzzy feeling, it must jell, and doesn't always form at all. When it forms, the whole VII-context of some problem or situation (with all its implicitly functioning other contexts) has actually been carried forward, that is, all these implied requirements have in some way been fulfilled. But now we say that all this is couched in some model—are we certain about all this business with sequences and contexts and requirements and versioning? Let us now engage in a *creative regress* to the felt sense of what all this instances. (I will now use different words, to point to it, but again these different words are intended to instance, not as literal. As literal they are simply in another model, one less well worked out.) We recall that, yes, experiences are in each other in some way. Yes, one can specify a texture that is always there. Something profound happens in the formation of a direct referent or whatever we might call it. We could just stick with describing what we can always do, letting our description be so poor that none would take it literally as a scheme.

Now, in having this regress we seem to have less than our model. Not at all, we still remember our model! We could just as well say we are bringing home to ourselves what our sharp conceptual statements are really about. We add to our model-sharp sentences the wider direct referent grasp which they instance. *And, our directly referred-to implicit sense of what we are talking about now has the sharp statements implicit in it! Polemarchus has learned!* We don't return, after conceptualizing, to the literally same direct referent, but to the "same" one. (Later I will say more about this IOFI space, as I call it, which instancing builds, and which is being built here.)

But if every conceptualization will alter the direct reference and always be implicit forever, what about a wrong chain of thought? Suppose we don't find out its consequences and learn from them? Suppose we think it right when it is not? Does it then remain implicit from then on in our supposedly valid direct referent?

So we can now think much more clearly about our own model: it's not merely that there can be many models but it's good to have at least one good one. It's not merely that our model is on a new and as yet unused level, but soon there will be more and better ones of this kind. That is so, but in our model we can now say why this is. We can bite into, think into, form sharp concepts into the underpinnings of why this is so. We can think about a new kind of truth that is much bigger.

Of course our concepts, and any concepts, are instancing the direct referent which as a whole can be had only by the direct reference in this instancing. But the concepts and statements can be used in a literal way too, that is not lost.

This is far beyond the usual vague statements (which remain true, of course) that we have from Plato, for example, or from Heidegger. "Any truth always also hides the truth," Heidegger writes (in *Wesen der Wahrheit*). Plato showed in every dialogue how any statement can be driven into contradicting itself if its implications are drawn out by logical procession until something results that is the opposite of what was intended. This was long ago recognized to lie in the very nature of conceptual structures. But now we can think about the nature of conceptual structures more sharply and we can directly use, rather than be baffled by, its limitations. These limitations are not negative, they only need to be understood. Then there is at least the knowledge of these limitations, and, when we wish, also direct referent formation and the instancing use of statements, which is beginning to become clear here. (More is written on this elsewhere.)

Just the opposite: *by having regress to this direct referent after a given attempt at a statement, just those aspects of what the statement does will be implicit, which are valid.* What magic! But of course . . . the statement insofar as it instances the direct referent and carries it forward indirectly does so only as valid. Much in the effects of the statement will fail to carry the direct referent forward, i.e., will fail to let it function to shape the statement. And insofar as that is so, the direct referent will not have functioned implicitly, will not have shaped what we said, and will not have been changed.

Therefore it is very powerful and corrective to refer directly to the direct referent between sentences as often as possible. If what forms doesn't implicitly take our formulation-attempt in, if nothing like that forms, if there is only a fuzzy confusion and no direct referent (with the *yes . . . yes . . . yes effect of self-understanding*), then it is important swiftly to return to the direct referent as it had formed before our latest formulation-attempt, and to discard that formulation-attempt.[8]

Has this not always been done in good thinking? In a way yes, in another not. Dialectic, for example, and other methods, indirectly of course employed the implicit functioning of everything one knows, as one thinks. Without that there was never thinking. Thinking *is* the carrying forward of the complexity that is being versioned. But very often there was only the logical guidance, arriving at systems and formulations that are only logically "spun." Empirical testing corrects that. In dialectic, a return to what one intended is added, and the powerful insight is also added, that new concepts can be fashioned, new differently cut boxes altogether, when a contradiction is run into. But both the merely logical + empirical testing, and the dialectic return and reformulating, proceed slowly, in that way I called "direct context-crossing." The steps are implicitly informed by all one knows, of course. But one must play out at length all that one can spin with logic, and then test it, then reformulate. There was no way also to constitute all one knows, that is relevant, as itself a datum, a new kind of object, which can be consulted between every two steps of thought, in a new kind of "empirical testing," if you will. (And we already saw what powerful and vast change the formation of such an object makes in the content itself. It is like a vast number of theories and testings, a vast number of dialectical reformulations, all at once.)

But what did it mean, how can we bring it home to ourselves, to say that monading from all direct referents is "true," or "valid"? I *mean that it can be lived in the world, that the world really can be changed and lived in this way; I mean at least that.* We have a way of thinking why direct referent formation enables such new statements and doings which can actually be lived in a world, a situation, a problem which they thereby change, but let us not substitute the good explanation for the direct reality. The validity is not our explanation of the validity.

Said the fellow in Catholic religion class after the teacher-priest had presented Saint Thomas's proofs for the existence of God, "Father, all my life I heard about God, and you mean *that's* what it is based on?"

When new VII-sequences are type-a implicit, this means they can be lived, done, sequenced, had, felt, in a sequence that makes time. As we saw, an occurring sequence like that is a new and further eveving; it isn't literally "in" the direct referent as it will be lived. In what way, then, has direct referent formation ensured that it can be lived? Only as far as the whole-whole carrying forward in the direct referent formation has changed how the body implies all these contexts. Is that *necessarily* enough change to enable the further change the actual sequence will make? No, we said that there. There might have to be many steps of speech and doing, and again direct referent formation. A guarantee would be an assumption that we cannot make, and in fact, often we need many steps, and we do not solve all problems. But direct referent formation moves powerfully in that "direction."

But again, why not? Can we think clearly why direct referent formation does not *necessarily* enable livable VII-sequences in just one step? We already saw how the VII-sequences can "surprise." They engage the actual en in a spread-out way, which was only functioning implicitly in the direct referent (in the body-sense and in the evev). We also saw already in VI that versioning is not guaranteed to change a context so a stoppage can be resumed. It is only pertinent.[9]

Diafils

A monad as I defined it is one kind of VIII-object. Now I want to consider another kind: I call it a "diafil."

A monad is like comprehension in Gendlin 1997a, and a diafil is like metaphor in Gendlin 1997a. I mean: as the direct referent monads out, it stays "the same." The whole cluster of statements from it, instancing it, and all the "applications" of those statements, is like one large *comprehension* of the direct referent. All are comprehensions of the direct referent in all fields.

Instead, we might let each topic and context cross with the direct referent *not only* in that way in which the direct referent "applies" and monads out, but *also* in the reverse direction, letting the other topic be a direct referent monading into our first one. If we do that we lose the relevance of our direct referent, and it is no longer "the same" as monading (IV-A-h-4).

For example, when early on I crossed explication with action, I let each of them alter in crossing with the other. (I did this because both were already facets of the direct referent I was working from. Therefore they already instanced that direct referent and the example is only technically one of diafilling. If we get clarity about this, then it is helpful and right to consider what I did there, and this kind of theory construction move, as diafilling.)

If we were to cross each new topic in both directions, we would eventually *arrive at wisdom*—though no single relevance would stay.

We have seen (IV-A-h-4) that the kind of crossing we called "sbs" (schematized by schematizing) is not the same in the two directions: between any two experiences different results occur depending on which one is used to obtain new aspects of the other.

Another way to put this is that there is not one fixed relation (or set of relations) between any two experiences. If there were, obviously it wouldn't matter which one you began by relating to the other; you would get the same thing both times. What we said about sbs (schematizing by schematizing) was thus an instance of the fact that new aspects are created, they are not all already given. Or, the same point is instanced when we say that implying is not identical with any explicit structure; if it were, again the relations would be already fully fixed, and a finite implicit set, with a "not yet" added.

Therefore the distinction between monad and diafil is not really possible; we cannot split between them. To do so would mean that we could split between keeping a relevance (a whole evev) "the same" in monading, as against letting it change in diafilling. But when two cross, each relevance is carried forward in some way, that is to say "kept the same" in some way.

There are many ways, not just one or even two, that two experiences can be crossed. In Gendlin 1997a I attributed this to the many "other" experiences which always function as the context. Depending on what we want, what the juncture of the discussion or line of thought just now is, what else is required to make a solution acceptable, the crossing of any two will be different. (Of course, we might be crossing as our "two" the whole sense of a problem at this juncture with the "whole sense of" another. Then the "other" experiences that function are already part of the direct referent. Throughout, I have not discussed the relationship between the set of functional relations in Gendlin 1997a and our discussion here. Of course both are schemes, and what follows here about schemes applies to them.) Another instancing of the fact that many rather than one way of unitizing and schematizing are possible, is the following:

We cannot say that a given new aspect, formed from a crossing between two experiences, was or was not already implicit (type-a) in the direct referent. This is because we can retroactively specify the direct referent as it "was," so that the aspect will be seen to "have been" implicit in it.

All this is another instance of the fact that we cannot split between what functions implicitly and what is *held*. Held/functioning implicitly is not a split between parts. (See VII-A-o.) It is a new distinction in how anything can function to shape something else. To function implicitly is to help shape something else. *A likeness is created when something functions in shaping something else.* (We are instancing the reversal of the order.) The given sequence or content now functions not fully as itself, and not with some preexisting part, *but in a way that was not in any way part of it before.* As we saw in thrashing (V), its function may be much more, and more noticeable, than it itself was. (Our metaphor for this was that when walking isn't possible because one is in the water, the movements of walking do not "partly" occur; much more movement occurs without the ground being there. Thrashing was not "part" of walking, before one fell in the water.)

Nor can we split between those sequences which do in some way function implicitly, and those which can't. The sequences are all implicit in each other (or, if we don't assume perfect unity, many are). Therefore we found that we cannot assume that all the sequences implicit in any one, when it occurs, also function implicitly when it functions implicitly. This is because of what we just said. A sequence does not function implicitly as all of itself, does not function implicitly always in the same way, nor in always an old way.

To version is to keep same *and* also change (carry forward). Versioning is always doubled. We have seen that monading is like that: one keeps the direct referent "the same" by carrying it forward in some other topic. I also call that other topic a *field*. That term is defined by this function in relation to a direct referent. *To monad is therefore an instance of "comprehension"* (defined in Gendlin 1997a).

Contexts are all implicit in each other, so that *one is always at some spot in all the contexts.* If it were all one logical system, then this would add up to one set of relations between each. Since it is more than that, *everything isn't settled* (and more than one VII-sequence is implied) *by how the contexts are implicit* in each other. Rather than simply stating what was already, the contexts are further enriched, though we then can say that (and specify how) they "were" already so.

We have understood direct referent formation itself in the terms we are using here, especially the crossing of many contexts. But it is direct referent formation which is instanced by these terms, so that we must not put the order backwards. It was always reversed and we set it right. (Instance of reversal of the order.) So we do not expect to reduce direct referent formation to these terms, nor do we intend to reduce monading of a direct referent to what we say here about monading. We are saying that monading is "at least" what we say here. Direct referent formation can be thought of as "at least" the crossing of all the contexts.

If direct referent formation is in this way diafilling ("at least"), we must keep in mind that *there are very many ways any two can be crossed*. This then lets us think how still more happens when the direct referent is monaded, and how there can be many direct referents of all contexts (and many "all contexts").

Direct referent formation we called "jelling," to describe the way it feels. But again, *there are many ways and also there might be many jellings, many "steps," and "shifts." Again, we cannot split between no shift, one shift, and two.* If we wish to know about such differences, monading out into VII will show us whether the problem is solved, can be lived or thought from.

If it does not jell, however, then there was not direct referent formation, and then one cannot do what we have been describing. That distinction stands between direct referent formation and direct context-crossing.

In Gendlin 2004a I discuss building a new field of terms. It will be neither an "application" we can ensure being only the monading of our model, nor something totally different. The model (our direct referent) will function implicitly in forming that new field of terms. Just as monading generally, our direct referent has functioning in it implicitly all the sequences we have made until now. How they will function in relation to a new field is not going to be exactly as we conceptualized monading, nor diafilling. Let us call it "monading-diafilling" and let it stand for what will be a whole continuum of different ways: for example, one may require further "applications" to be within one model, always going back over everything to make it one theoretical system. Or one may require the kind of consistency we have had in our model, permitting new terms to be more complex and not univocally resolvable in relation to earlier simpler terms, but without any contradictions. Or one may tolerate some contradictions, while working out others (wherever that is needed to be able to deal with what one needs to deal with).[10] *And this array is only one way of bringing home that there is not a simple split between staying in one monad, as against allowing development.* All these cited above are still a use of one model. Later we will see that many models can be used (see *Experiencing and the Creation of Meaning*, chap. 6, and the concluding section below).

Another type of differences along which we might have such a continuum is: if above I bring in everything we ever talked about in this work, crossing each with each, I would be making the terms more and more consistent with each other. One might say: all these topics already were instancings of the direct referent we have been monading; *of course* they easily lead to one system of monading sentences and terms.

But I could also consider a narrower subset of my model, and "apply" it to all the other topics, rather than letting my model be rebuilt by them all. Or I could widen my scope further, bringing in new topics and considering my model still being built.

There is a difference also, whether we let a new topic raise its own facets first, so that there is a set of aspects we require ourselves to deal with. If so, we let these import the structure of *their* relations. Or we might let our model or direct referent specify the aspects of the next topic and deal only with these.

We see, usually with a startle, how vastly differentiated anything is that we care about, and if we care to deal with it we must allow that. It lets us see how vastly different anything is from the simplistic schemes that we usually use to think about anything. With our model and method we can differentiate one or many steps into the actual complexity, rather than merely deploring the supposed poverty of thinking in relation to anything. That we can do this is very powerful, and that we can do it in many ways rather than only one is *more* powerful. There is not just one system of differentiation levels implicit.

I call this different "densities" of consistency.

We see that there are always many considerations along which one can make a scheme of such a point as this. Similarly I spoke of comprehension and metaphor in *Experiencing and the Creation of Meaning*, showing that any other consideration brought in can specify a scheme about their relation. And this is so at *any* point, *if one wishes to consider that point as instancing the most basic relation between experiencing and symbols* (as the schemes relate to experiencing).

This way of using "monad" and "diafil" is like the use of "metaphor" and "comprehension" in Gendlin 1997a. The terms retain their VII-sharpness and help us think and instance rather than to reduce the direct referent relation to themselves.

One way this manifests is that a given aspect can be formulated in both ways. We can use "monading" to explain diafilling and direct referent formation and much else, but we can also, with different results, use "diafilling" and also could formulate some still different terms.

Here I want to make clear only that we are not allowing VII terms to get fuzzy or lose their power. We are retaining their usual power and adding immeasurably to it. We will not just shrug if there are different results from two formulations of "the same" thing. We know in what sense (we can think clearly about in what sense) it is "the same" and in what sense not. We will look at the different aspects, themselves able to be direct referents, which are specified by the different formulations. We will see at any juncture whether the different aspects affect that juncture.

That effect itself can be pursued, direct referent-formed, and specified further. Or, if at the given juncture it makes no difference, we can know that later on it might. For now we can leave the difference, knowing that it cannot be ultimately removed, since that would be to impoverish experience down to one system. Why want that? We see that more than one have powerful effects. Why not allow ourselves to think sharply about something that is richer, I repeat, not poorer, not less determined, not less structured, not less meaningful, not up for grabs or arbitrary statements or actions.

There has been no way to think clearly about something more ordered than clear thinking sequences. Therefore people have misunderstood all this.

When terms instance a direct referent, they mean more, that is to say they carry forward more. Their effect on the juncture at which they are used is more. They make more difference in the context they carry forward. If this "more," or some of it, is to be specified, that too can be done, not exhaustively reducing it to VII terms, but in such a way that *we know better* what that effect was than the words say, and still also know in VII-sharpness what the words say.

Conclusion and Beginning

So far as the model itself is concerned, I stop here. I say this in spite of a whole development of terms that is to "come," which will immensely clarify certain important points left open in our model. (It is inherent in our kind of concept-formation that there are points left open. To fill them in would develop a new tier with its own new points left open.)

Our model, as I say, will continue to function implicitly as it has for each new stage up to now, but with more openness which we will define later.

From now on each new topic will be permitted to raise its own facets, not just those our model would lead to in "applying" it to the topic, and we will also be in IOFI space, not in our model.

I would want to use many models although there are not, as yet, many on this new level.

We will still develop clusters of mutually implying concepts and statements, but for each area. The power of the model will best be seen in this way, since often enough we will remain "within" it. But we want also to gain the other advantages.

Could I have stopped sooner? I set out from VIII (in the form of

Gendlin 1997a) and wished to arrive again at VIII after forming concepts by crossing with the other relevances (body, behavior, symbolization, etc.). Once arrived in VIII, I know I could continue on and on. I want to be able to think into how VIII "function*ed*" from the start. If I find that I need more concept-formation to do so, I will let that happen in doing so.

It is vitally important that this little discussion we just had be clear. So many people today believe they must choose between thinking sharply systematically *or* having and honoring the much richer living Whole. I hope I have shown that both can continually enrich clear thinking by using the implicit functioning of the directly referred-to Whole. It is by no means only for the power of the systematic statements themselves as such, that we want to think clearly, but also for how it enriches what we then directly refer to again.

As I will show more exactly elsewhere (with due carefulness for certain other concerns I have with them), Plato and Aristotle together instance what we have just discussed. Plato devised a method for concept-formation (dialectic) in which each step checked itself against the whole, and also informed the whole. Plato cared much more about this method than about any specific concepts, however powerful and superior they certainly were to what had gone before. Aristotle modified this method to fix concepts. He developed *one* consistent cluster. He knew very well that in each new context new concepts must be allowed to form. Whenever he "applied" his model, he did it so as to allow that model itself to become newly differentiated in each new context. ("It must be something like . . . ," he would say, and cite an earlier instance. Then he would let the new context develop new terms, not within, but not contradicting, what he already had.)

In spite of Aristotle's conscious fresh concept-formation with each new topic and in spite of his delineation of how to do this (*Posterior Analytics*), the result was the loss of the method of concept-formation Plato had originated and Aristotle had developed. People found it much easier to learn Aristotle's concepts than his method of concept-formation. Indeed, often enough they didn't even see the method at all. The "sciences" Aristotle carved out have largely remained, while the intricate overlapping way he did it is largely misunderstood. The *basic* concepts in many sciences, if not still those he fashioned, are often simplifications of his. (Current discussions of time and space, and motion, life process, self and other, individual and society, history and art, are examples.)

Should we blame Aristotle (if that makes any sense) for developing such a beautiful model? Ought he not to have done so? Do we wish he had followed more closely Plato's way of beginning anew and arriving at a different scheme in each dialogue? That cannot be the right answer.

There is a way, at least today if not then, to have the power of one or more good models, and still also have the power of concept-formation.

I wish to be my own Plato *and* Aristotle. I wish to offer not only a method as Plato did (*and Gendlin 1997a does*), but also a body of consistent concepts that do better in science than what we have had, and are better philosophy than what we have had. *But I want more still!* I don't want our model to have the kind of negative side that Aristotle's turned out to have in history. I do not wish the power of the new concepts to prevent people from knowing how they were formed, from using concept-*formation*. The method of concept-formation is much more important than the concepts. Also, what the method shows about the relation of concepts and experience is much more important than the ways in which I have formulated that relation.

How can one be Plato, *and* Aristotle and more? But they have already written and we stand on their shoulders—and Kant's too, Wittgenstein's and Heidegger's, and many more. If you really understand, you always move beyond, as I tried to show a little while ago.

But if this is so, are we doing away with consistent arrays of findings and theory in each science? One can't shift models all the time, or if one does, then no consistent bodies of knowledge will develop. We do need those. One or more new models might be of great value, say in medicine, or aerodynamics, but we would want them used in interaction with the existing science, not to disorganize it. Are we not glad that consistently formed data and propositions in these sciences have remained intact long enough to be thoroughly tested and expanded? Would we like to board an airplane built along the lines of some new model of thought? And did I not promise (and perhaps even illustrate in a few cases) that our new model can help science in the sense of resolving anomalies and enabling the further development of *consistent* bodies of data and propositions in these very sciences, not only in newly begun approaches?

How are consistent bodies of knowledge to be reconciled with concept-*formation*?

It has always been philosophy's task to examine the *kind* of concepts used in science (and the *kind* of method, assumptions, strategies). When scientists examine the basic *kinds* of concepts and methods, they are doing philosophy (although they may, as persons, be quite unprepared, and unfamiliar with how to conduct such an examination). Scientists may do this because of controversies involving different assumptions, or because of anomalies arising in the current model, or because they wish to develop as much thinking power as possible.

The distinction between science and philosophy need not be embodied in separate groups of people. It does require different sections of the library, different bodies of connected statements and findings. But the same persons at different times need to do both. I am against continuing the split between scientists and philosophers. It seems wrong to prevent the first group systematically by education from ever becoming familiar with philosophy. Then they cannot examine their own tools and assumptions. And I agree with Merleau-Ponty and Keith Hoeller that philosophers would do well to engage in science *continuously*, to examine directly the differences the philosophical assertions make. (Too often the official view was that philosophy does the science-examining task once. Let the scientist read it. The philosopher must know science— that has never been seriously questioned. But it has seemed needless to continue in constant interaction with science, on each page or in each paragraph. I find, as must have been noticed, that I must often discuss the philosophical point about kinds of concepts and methods together with a scientific issue that leads to, and is affected by, what I say philosophically.) Even so, the difference in task, function—an essential difference, between philosophy and science—stands, of course.

Does this mean, now, that "science" is always one connected consistent body of knowledge, but philosophy can change models and examine kinds of concepts, itself using many kinds? This has not been the case in history so far. Philosophers, even more than scientists, have usually developed just one model, one consistent system. (Plato is the exception.) True, philosophy, much against its will, has always contained many models. But most philosophers deplored this fact, as though philosophy done rightly would be in only one cast. With the basic system created, the philosopher applied it from then on, and looked to scientists to read it and apply it for themselves. Once in a while this also happened to some extent.

Heidegger, having completed his consistent model (*Being and Time*), refused to use it, and proceeded instead to the generation of new concepts, vague but vital insights. Rather than inviting everyone to apply his new basic model, he very nearly asked them not to. In moving on as he did, he knew something of what I am saying here. But it was a grave error not to work toward developing his "model" so that it could acquire the specifics it would need to replace the usual model. He ought to have done or invited the job I have done here. But he wanted to proclaim the "end of metaphysics," that is to say systems, consistent schematic philosophy. In wanting an end to systematics, he had a sense for going beyond systematics, but he did not know how. So he went backwards to vaguer, more naturalistic, more homey ways of speaking, and he went sideways to poetry. He did not solve the problem of how to have, if you like this way of saying it, *continuous philosophy*, that is to say, a continuous undercutting and reexamining, a continuous concept-formation, fresh emergence of form—and also still have consistent connected bodies of knowledge.

Just as the same person can at different times engage in both philosophy and science even though they are different activities, so also can the same person deal both with consistent model(s) and also with concept-formation, and this is so both in philosophy and in science. Nor need the different times be very far apart; they might be moments apart.

Having pursued some line of thought along the lines of a consistent and powerful model, having noted what this power just now gives one, why would one be unable to employ, moments later, a different model to see what that would lead to? To do this doesn't contradict the consistency of models; on the contrary, it is possible only because consistent models do have powerful results and different models have different results. Having been led to something relevant by use of the second model, there is no reason (if one wishes) why one cannot then formulate "that" in one's preferred and consistent model (including an examination of what difference it makes to do so). And if this is so for different extant models, it is also the case with innovative thinking.

The problem how to have both is as old as Plato, and rightly so, since he sought to emphasize concept-formation rather than concepts. He chides the mathematicians for never asking why, without changing "one" in one hand, and "one" in the other, they become "two" merely by moving one's hands together. This (among many other examples) meant one should inquire into one's assumed concepts, not just deduce with them. The "divided line" metaphor in the *Republic* distinguishes in its upper half between deductive science and dialectic (really, philosophy). But in chiding the mathematicians Plato did not at all wish to eliminate mathematics!

But Plato did not solve the problem, how to have both, and did not think merely to examine or reflect upon basic scientific concepts—he meant to change them, and did change them in every dialogue. But if that is what happens, how then have both? Of course, some innocent "philosophy of mathematics"—which would only reflect upon, but leave unchanged, the concepts and axioms mathematicians use—would pose no problem. Plato did not mean it that way. If the navigator asks not only how to get to Egypt, but also, as Plato wanted, why go there, and what purposes are worthwhile, naturally that would seem to disorganize the science of navigation. (Or would it get us out of the bind of technological splits between how and why, facts and values, physical and human, and so on? Would it lead to new concepts that could apply across?)

I am discussing two distinctions: philosophy/science, and systematics/continual formation. About both I have so far said that the same person can do both at different times, perhaps moments or sentences apart; that they remain distant; and that there is much more power in both than in discarding one.

Let me now say more about philosophy and science, from the viewpoint of VIII.

Just as the many universals that emerge newly from direct referent formation are *not under* other more general ones in one logical system (see VIII-g-7), so also is there no simple division among more or less general topics. Not only is this so in terms of scope of generality, it is also so in regard to context. Something in sociology, something very specific, let us say in just one subspeciality, noticed by only a few observers, may instance (through direct referent formation) very many sequences of great import to many other sciences. There are philosophical aspects in any statement or action. Conversely, no topic is strange to philosophy. It might sound like sociology and talk about society, it might sound like psychology and talk about the psyche, it might sound like physics and talk about matter and change, but it is never discussing just these things, always also how it is possible to discuss those, so that whatever is said exemplifies philosophical issues.

With direct referent formation this becomes true in a whole new way, since a direct referent is a cluster in which everything is changed, and all these changes are instanced by any one statement which might otherwise appear to be in just one field.

None of this means that the divisions between fields must be lost. We still need public bodies of knowledge collected and organized topically. It is in addition to these that one can also know how to instance more than just what belongs in one topic.

Similarly, the difference between philosophy and any science stands. Philosophy will always undercut, examine, reposition basic terms, concern *the kind of* concept one uses, rather than only the topic directly. But all levels of discourse are involved in a direct referent formation.

So we see that, indeed, it is not breakdown or limit, that our terms (all VIII terms qua instancing in IOFI space) do not resolve schematically. Instead we go forward into what is continuous philosophy.

Notes

Foreword

1. Gendlin adds this cautionary note: "But before we deprecate the current model even for a moment, let us be clear why science needs this perceptual split and these space-filling things. We make stable things and parts. I call them 'units.' (I call it the 'unit model.') Everything from the wheel to computers consists of stable parts that we make and combine. Seven billion of us could not live on the earth without technology, so let us not pretend we can denigrate science and its perceptual split and its units. We need them even to study and cure living things. The first sense of the word 'environment' I define is the environment that science presents. I call it 'environment #1.' Of course we will keep it, and keep developing it" (Gendlin 2012).

2. "From where does this philosophy stem? It moves on from Dilthey, Husserl, Sartre, Merleau-Ponty (and indirectly Heidegger), and also McKeon, Peirce, and Dewey, as well as Plato, Aristotle, Leibniz, Kant, and Hegel. My recognition of certain difficulties is very European, but my emphasis on situations, practice, action, feedback, transitions, and progressions is very North American" (Gendlin 1997a, xvi).

3. For a more complete account of Gendlin's philosophical origins, see the detailed essay by Donata Schoeller and Neil Dunaetz, "Introduction to Gendlin's *A Process Model*," available at http://www.focusing.org/gendlin_antecedents.

Chapter II

1. The order of implying differs from en, but this does not mean that the en is structured or patterned. We who are building a model employ patterns, and see environmental occurrences in patterns, but patterns are a later development. We derive them in VII. So we have to think of the environmental sort of order as happenings, like walking or feeding, which are not patterns although they might be seen as patterned in various ways. Never are they only patterns with mere concreteness or existence added to them. In logical inference we use patterns, but the process of generating them and inferring from them involves much more than the patterns. Thinking with patterns always involves a process that is more than they would be if they could exist alone.

Of course, the concepts we are making here involve patterns, but not only patterns. Thinking is also a bodily process (as we will see in VII-B). Concepts carry the body forward. Each brings its many situational applications along with it; we can tap into those at any point. The implicit experiential intricacy still comes with each term, even when one uses a theory as if it were closed, without attending to the implicit intricacy (and without attending to the implicit effort involved in putting it aside). The logical power—the logical inferences—require this. But we can reopen a theory at any point and in any application. We can use any theory both as closed and as reopened. (See Gendlin 1997a, VI.)

Our term "implying" employs the old conceptual pattern, but the sentences in which it occurs here enable it to imply more, which also changes the conceptual pattern. Occurring occurs into implying and changes it. The terms "occurring" and "implying" have to be thought together.

Chapter IV

1. In VIII we will discuss the kind of thinking that goes beyond the usual categories. (Gendlin 1997a shows a number of such "characteristics" of how experiencing functions in cognition. One I already mentioned is: the more determinants, the more novelty. Determinants delimit but they also enable. See also Gendlin 1991a and 1992b.)

2. The new thing happens and keeps the old thing from occurring. In building a model we seem to build from the bottom up, but as I will keep pointing out, we can in fact begin only from our human process. I am really beginning with VIII—with explication and focusing and fashioning concepts with and from those processes, terms which will eventually be able to carry those forward.

As Wittgenstein showed, language is capable of new uses that make immediate sense—they are not first a breakdown of the old meanings. I have tried to show that when we lack words, it is because our more intricate situation is already reworking the language implicit in our bodies and implicit in the "....." which only seems "preverbal." The "....." is not preverbal, but it is "pre-" the new phrasing which may come.

The implying of a pet's body has language implicit in it (because its experience has), but a wild animal's body does not. But the implying in any life process is capable of developing as we have developed. In ourselves we can trace back through civilized history our own culture, but also primitive culture, and the animal and the vegetative in us. The implying of life precedes all those levels and must be put first, at the very bottom, even at inanimate levels as the wider model. What was there before was of such a nature that what has developed from it was possible.

We must not model nature on mathematics and logic—as was done for so long. Math and logic are exclusively human processes. If we model nature on mathematics or anything that is only human, we exclude all forms of life but ours. In the case of mathematics we drop ourselves out too. Implying and occurring are human but not exclusively human. Implying and occurring lead to a wider model, within which we can derive the logical patterns too. But the former cannot be derived within the latter.

The order of implying is neither determined nor indeterminate, but more intricately ordered. This order is not understood in most philosophies, although it is just what makes philosophies possible. A philosophy changes how the basic terms are positioned, and thereby shows that the order we live in is more orderly and capable of more than can fit one system. It is why many models can be fruitful. Ours has special characteristics, but there will soon be other models with those.

3. I call it "functional accruing" when the environment-implying of the other processes (their en#2) is also implied by this given process. I say that the implying of en#2 of each of the processes "accrues" to the other processes. For example, not only certain digestive process events imply food. Circulatory and many other processes also imply food. Some seemingly tiny sub-sub-process in some remote tissue implies much of the many environments of many processes in the body.

4. Zeno's paradox showed that a thing cannot move if it must traverse an infinite number of actual distances. If an interval were infinitely divisible, and if each of these divisions were an actual span, then an infinite number of them would have to be traversed before the moving object could get to the other side.

The solution was to realize that infinite divisi*bility* of an interval does not imply an infinite number of actual spans.

Since a line is divisible at an infinite number of points (since points have no dimensions), the solution of the paradox also says that even an infinite number of slicings still would not imply an infinite number of fixed intervals between the slicings.

We could reformulate the solution by saying: *the multiplicity achieved by any one way of dividing need not stay fixed, while the motion is occurring.* The motion defines its own interval (it is a motion from here to there) in starting and stopping, and aside from that, interval units need not stay fixed, and do not define the motion.

If we formulate the solution of Zeno's paradox in this way, we retain the idea that an infinite variety of slicings does not provide an actually existing infinity of intervals that take time to traverse, and we can let the actual motion determine the slicings.

Our formulation can extend to events, not only to space and time intervals. The multiplicity that crosses need not be thought of as units that actually happen separately, in their own right.

We could apply the paradox, so formulated, to the old unit model: if all the interaffectings have to be separate actual occurrences, then interaffecting would take an infinite amount of time to get from one constellation to another.

But the multiplicity of space points, and also the multiplicity of aspects of a given whole event, are not separate occurrences. (Even as simultaneous they are not separate occurrences, but different aspects.) The further occurring is not defined by them as a fixed and literal multiplicity of separate existents. *Only the next event occurs. We can retroactively relate the further event to a previous one in any number of respects of comparison.* Thus we can retroactively construct an earlier multiplicity which supposedly lasted through to the later event, and ascribe just this multiplicity to the earlier one as well. In this way we can derive the old model's way of conceptualizing a transition. However, such a formulation will be much poorer than ours, because it will involve separate strings of comparison. For us the retroactively determined multiplicity will have been one in which all aspects affected all others and were in turn affected in how they affect others. But all these interaffectings did not happen as separate events. Analogous to the infinite number of points on a line, they are constructable, but not independent events with their own time-spans.

The traversing, or the occurring, is not fixed by static units. If the units are not lasting, then there can be any number of them, even as an infinite number.

For why space and time intervals, and independent units, are not actual events, see note 6 below, as well as Gendlin 1997e and Gendlin and Lemke 1983.

5. I am indebted to Hannah Frish for this example. She used the term "aura" for the way all that is felt at once. See also Goldfarb 1993, 180–91. Einstein said that he was guided by "a feeling" on the relativity problem. "Direction" in space is derivative from living, as I tried to show in Gendlin 1992b and 1997c.

6. In Gendlin 1997e I showed that the consistency of Newton's and Einstein's space is less basic than interactions. The assumption of individuated referents is not necessary. This assumption has seemed even more basic than consistent localization, but both are systems of mere comparison. Comparison does not need to supervene quantum mechanical interactions. Individuated referents alter depending on the respects in which one compares them, which in turn depends upon the grouping of other things with which one compares them. I do not deny individuated referents. We need (and in an odd way are .....) those. My point is that the individuation of referents changes without interaction, simply by deciding on a different comparison group.

7. To let our scheme of sbs itself be sbsed instances how all concepts apply (see VIII). What a scheme reveals when applied is not necessarily only what fits *within* or *under* it. Rather, facets which emerge from applying the scheme can change that very scheme. The scheme is further schematized by its own role in schematizing.

A simple way to say this: one need not apply a scheme blindly to something so as to notice only what can be said in terms of the scheme. It is more powerful to notice that what arises from applying the scheme can turn out to have further aspects that do not fit the scheme. The scheme itself can be further specified if one pursues those.

This is a way of thinking both about the use and *the formation* of conceptual schemes. A scheme first forms when something is used to schematize something else. I discuss more of this in VIII and in Gendlin 2004a. Of course we can use this model in that way.

8. We will derive "making" in VII-A. See also my derivation of the machine in Gendlin 1997e. Our science renders everything as if it were something made out of antecedent pieces. Chairs are not made by the wood or the metal, nor do they develop from a straight chair into a sofa. Patterns and positional time arise

together (as we will see in VII). The chair pattern is separate, and externally imposed. The wood can splinter and the nails rust, but this is not always positional time. Physics needs a more intricate time. See Gendlin and Lemke 1983.

Inanimate things are not just in positional time either. (See Rosen 1994 for a reflexive treatment of time and space.) ·

For a model that is less different from the usual than ours but does have some of its major advantages, see Bickhard 1995; Bickhard and Christopher 1994.

For physiological evidence that organismic process is not primarily something that happens to a body, and that perception is not prior, see Ellis 1995, 51–55.

9. In this sense we can say that the implying always "wants" life to work out, to go on, to succeed. Much that we find in focusing will become clearly sayable with this concept of the dual "was." The pathology may be implied next, but a healing way is also and more truly implied next, since what is implied is not this or that content, but a carrying forward. The more intricacy, complications, problems, in a sense the greater the pathology, the more novelty is implicit in the healing or carrying forward which is always also what is implied. And carrying forward is always still more than the implying. A sequence of actual further steps is even more, as one can see from focusing steps. (See Gendlin 1964 and VII-A-o on how carrying forward is not only more, but also brings more implying.)

The case of simply not carrying forward is quite distinct (e.g., doing a lot of other things does not carry hunger forward), but there are many kinds of carrying forward, as we will see later on. This is also why carrying forward an organism's *own* inwardly arising process connects it to its original implying, and is therefore so much more valuable than even the best imposed way.

10. On not dividing between "was implicit" and explication, see Gendlin 1997d and the section VII-A-o here.

For example, in walking, when the foot presses on the ground, the ground has to "already" have returned the foot's pressure so as to cause it to "have been" foot pressure. Kant solved this problem in the old model by making "simultaneity" a kind of time-"order" that could be consistent with the succession of cause and effect.

Similarly, the moving body's momentum seems describable as being-about-to-be-there, in a further location, but the momentum is an attribute of it here now. The implying *is* a real aspect of an occurring.

Kant saw that a pure positional time-order cannot exist alone. As Kant put it, time is not written on the events so that one could perceive time as such. Whether something must come before or after was determined for Kant by *explanatory* relationships between events—you must put up the walls of a house before the roof, but you can look at either one first, if they are already up. Kant took this to mean that time is a scheme of relations between events. He used the Newtonian model and was content to impose both positional and explanatory relations on time-positions.

Instead, we would say: *time is in the events, not between them.* That the roof comes after the walls is inherent in what a roof is, and what building a house is. Therefore time is not an empty ordering system that is independent of events.

In terms of quantum mechanics, what the actual interactions are (re)generates the systems of space-time localization. (See Gendlin 1997e and Gendlin and Lemke 1983.) Experiencing is time-inclusive and multischematic, as I say in Gendlin 1997a, 155). This means that many models of time can be devised from actual experiencing.

We need to retrieve and revise the way our American Pragmatists employed three terms. Currently in Europe it seems there can only be two terms, signifier and signified. It is assumed that a "third term" would be the Hegelian synthesis. So it seems that other than logical continuity there is only rupture.

This model also builds on Dilthey, Whitehead, McKeon, Heidegger, Merleau-Ponty, and Wittgenstein, as well as Plato, Aristotle, Leibniz, and others. Elsewhere I have discussed my debt to them, and my way of going on from them.

Chapter V

1. My use of "derived" is intended to mark that we are not simply asserting a commonplace (that much of nature has rhythms). We have built concepts or internal structure in terms of which to think this. These concepts and this structure are precise all the way back into our earlier concepts, and will be continuous with our later ones. Yet the new concepts are not reducible to the earlier ones; it is not an axiomatic system. If it were, we would forever be stuck in whatever concepts we first developed or began with, some arbitrary choice. If one can begin, ever, there is nothing against beginning often; I mean developing new and further conceptual patterns that are not logically derivative from the earlier concepts *alone*. But neither is it necessary to have sheer gaps which don't enable one to think, except with either these or those concepts. The continuity between concepts is such, rather, that the new developments further inform and precision the earlier ones. Terms are definable and *derivable* in terms of each other. Our process concept can now *derive* rhythm, something both ongoing and stable. (Of course, "stable" means what it says here.)

Of course, we did not get leafing only from our earlier concepts; we knew about leaves and heartbeats and intention movements in animals. In the latter we saw an example of how a new process and a new move can develop from a stoppage. Using that as a model instance, we were able to precision it here in relation to our already developed concepts. We are also interested in other instances where something new and very different occurs when an earlier process does not go through. See (V-b-2), which comes next.

In using such model instances, we do more than just assert them. We are not merely saying one thing after another. If someone says only that organisms have rhythms, that living things come in pulses, etc. etc., it would be fair to object that this tells no more than we already knew.

But how is the method used here different, if it too adds new instances and makes new concepts at each step? How can I claim to have "derived" *rhythm* from our concepts when I am visibly developing the concepts right here, to do so?

I do not just add that there are, for example, intention movements in nature. I take them as model instances to let them form new concepts for us, but more than that: I let them form new concepts *from* the concepts we have up to now. Or, to put it in the right order: when we roll the concepts we have up to a new instance, we do more than just slice up the new instance along the lines of the old concepts. To do only that is quite foolish and locks one into a given set. But it is just as foolish to fail to make use of one's concepts up to the given point. A third way exists: we let the concepts schematize the new instance, but we also notice how the new instance resists, does not fit, crosses, gives something new, in response! Taking what is thus found and permitting the concepts themselves to be elaborated by it lets the concepts be further schematized by how they schematize.

Such a new "response" from a new instance is not just any modification. Rather, it is just *the* modification which *these* concepts need in order to schematize *this* instance. There is therefore a continuity in this explicatory development of the concepts.

The concepts develop until they can derive the instance they are sbsed by. When it can be derived, the newly elaborated concepts are successful that far. (Sometimes this does not happen at once—a whole new context may have to be built over many such steps, before something used earlier becomes derivable. I usually point this out when it happens.)

2. The ordinary English word "relevant" could fit here, but we already used it in IV-A-d-2 for how the past functions in the present. Relevance is inherently the case; the past wouldn't be functioning in this present if it were not relevant; that it "functions in" the present means that it is able to participate in shaping the present, and to be regenerated now by functioning in this present. (See IV-A-d-2 and VII.) I want to let the word "pertinent" say a less inherent relation. Anything in the en during stoppage is pertinent, just as when one is trying to solve a problem all the information about it is pertinent. But only some of this information actually leads to a solution.

Chapter VI

1. This is not to deny that we can trace visual perception in the animal body and brain separately from other perception. But we must not read what we differentiate back into our understanding of a process that has not yet made that differentiation. (See part B of Gendlin 1992b.) If we do, we cannot come to understand how we form it in a later development. We will not have a grasp of the process in and from which we form it.

2. Here we are giving the word "context" an internal conceptual structure. For humans, the behavior context is called the "situation."

There are many occasions when one wants to say that something "occurs in a context." The phrase is as vague as it is important. Better concepts can be devised for (from) it, but ours give at least some more conceptual structure so that we can think further from saying that something "occurs only in context." See whether it doesn't show you something important, or enable you to conceptualize what you are trying to get at, if you think that the thing *in* context is falling out from *a string of changed contexts*. Rather than assuming empty space, so that the phrase "*in* context" means that the thing is *spatially* surrounded by everything else, but separated from it by its *position*, think of the "in" so that the thing is not separable. It *is* the string of contexts.

For example, the relation between action and situation is like that. It is in fact my model instance for this schema. An action goes on *in* a situation, but that isn't well grasped, if the "*in*" is considered in empty space like an object in a room. The action changes *the* situation it goes on in. The situation is thus "the same" one before, during, and after the action—if it were not, the action wouldn't meet the situation.

3. Implying is always for *some* carrying forward, not for a fixed form. When the environment occurs into an implying so as to form something new, we can say that the new sequence "was" implied. Therefore "implied" can mean either "implied" (a) has never occurred before, or "implied" (b) seems the same to an observer as a previous occurrence.

4. This is an example of the kind of model that Howard Pattee is looking for (see IV, where we discussed him). He needs a way to make sense of *seemingly* the same unit having very different characteristics in different contexts. Pattee makes at least two errors: he assumes a limit to order (see VIII) and thinks of a given molecule as "fully determined," no degrees of freedom, nothing indeterminate, which to him means the same thing as no openness for novelty. For us anything implicitly functioning is never determined to an explicit form. Secondly, the kind of determination he looks at is only explicit. He has no way to think about what functions implicitly—and that can make greater differences despite looking no different. Really this is two points again: the molecule can do more than he knows about, because it has an implicitly functioning side, and also, what he considers an exactly similar molecule in *another context*, isn't. The context is not only positional *around* something in the observer's space. The context may be implicit.

5. For example, every word comes with a "family" of uses. These are not side by side, but crossed, so that they form one sense of "knowing how to use the word." But in actual use this crossed family also crosses with the situation, so that the word comes to say just precisely what it says here, in this situation. (See Gendlin 1991a.)

In the situation the words **come** to us **already crossed**—the body produces them as part of implying the change we need in the situation. What makes just these words come to us is how their use-family crosses with our situation. Language will be discussed in VII, but we build our model here so that we will be able to use it there.

6. As has often been noted in philosophy, even human perceptions (taken up in VII) are not experienced as bits of sound and vision. We hear voices or trucks and we see people. But we need a theory of perception to think about this, as well as how bits of just color and sound arise (as we will see in VII).

7. If an insect attacks the leaves on one side of a tree, those on the other side quickly mobilize certain antidotes. How plants imply their body-process is

much more intricate than has been recognized till very recently. But I don't think they have the doubling we are deriving here.

8. Traditionally an object was thought of as a unity of "traits." The object is the underlying substrate (sometimes said to be supplied by the observer as *sub*ject) which supposedly holds the traits together. Sugar is white, sweet, and crystalline, dissolves in water, etc., but each such "trait" is shared by other things. What makes it sugar is supposed to be a unity of these traits.

From our viewpoint such thinking comes too late. Traits are abstracted entities.

Above we see the unity of an object in terms of mutually implying behavior sequences.

Objects implicitly involve the other sequences and their fall-out objects. They are internally related. An object implicitly involves how it (for we can now call it "it") falls out from other implicit sequences and their objects.

We derive how there are objects across many sequences. We don't just assume a world cut into objects, bundles of traits abstracted from behavior.

What objects are depends upon the organism's living, its behavior. A tree is an object for humans; we cut it down or sit under it or climb it or eat its fruit, and we move around it when it is in our way to something else. For some animals, the tree may be an object like that. For others certain leaves and branches might be home, and fallen out from many sequences, while the trunk may be an entirely different object together with the remaining branches. Nor need the different division be spatial, as in the above example. The moist trees after rain might be an object, and the rest might blend into everything else.

9. The above rendering of space, and objects in space, makes it possible to differentiate between what moves and what does not.

In Newtonian space, absolute empty space, only cat and bird are moving at all, the scene is unchanged. We have just derived some of the experience of steadiness and sameness which Newtonian space requires observers to have. But only in VII can we really talk about that.

From our schema we can see how simple the old model is, of mere comparisons of already assumed clunk-objects in empty space. We will derive this empty space in VII, but behavior space will remain its underpinning.

10. The short syllables of language (and their intricate syntax) may have arisen from compressions of longer sequences in a protolanguage. We will discuss this in VII. Another example: a new train of thought must be sequenced through. Once we have often done that, just its becoming implied may be enough to move us on. A short phrase may do it, for example "Oh, yes, that." We no longer need to sequence it fully as we did at first. The brief phrase changes the evev enough so that something further becomes implied. (I call this kind of compression "boxing.")

11. Merleau-Ponty should be cited and credited in this discussion. He did not provide a model, nor did he study our own explicative process which he used. But he was a pioneer in regard to the role of the body in perception, behavior, and language.

Chapter VII

1. Philosophy has recently overcome its long fascination with "sense data" and the error of beginning with them. But there hasn't yet been a derivation of them. Husserl wrote that we don't begin by hearing sounds, we hear birds and voices and doors slamming. Sounds as pure sensa are products of a theory, he thought. But this isn't quite right. Humans can and do hear sounds. We can hear a sound. We can hear a moan-sound and know it to be the wind, or someone's imitation. We can hear a shot and wonder if it was something else that made a sound like that. Pure sensa are derivatives not from theory but from expression, from symbolic sequences of the looks of, and sounds of ...... Only thereby are there separated senses. Then there can be just a sound. Only thereby can we theoretically think of ourselves hearing sounds and seeing visual stimuli the nature of which we don't know. The animal hears *something* and perhaps doesn't know what it is. We can hear *a sound*, and we may not know what it is the sound of, but we can always hear what it sounds like (even if it is strange and "sounds like nothing we know"). We can have, feel, attend to, the sound *as sound*. (Only then can the theory that Husserl rightly criticizes begin.)

2. The two laws of explication are placed here because we can derive them here. But here we only speak of a sequence that first functions implicitly, and then actually occurs in its own right. The parts are different in the two cases, and what is implicit is different. Later on these two laws have more meaning, when we can talk about language and (in the usual sense) about explicating.

3. For example, a frequent argument is that one can use only what is publicly observable as a basis for thinking. This usually misses the fact that our inner experience occurs in publicly observable contexts (in action contexts) exactly like language does. We have our inner experiences in contexts (situations) with others, and they have their public significance just as much as words do. Internal events are neither private (in the sense of not public) nor inconvenient for theory. To remain unable to think about them means being unable to think about most of human life. But how could such an absurd error be committed, as to try to drop inner experience from consideration in theory and even philosophy? It was because an outer/inner distinction was uncritically accepted. Thereby "inner" was taken as if it were spatially located out of sight, as if it thereby left no gap in the public world if it were not considered. And this was thought to be convenient.

One must grasp, however, that all human events (VII-sequences) are inherently external/internal, that is to say inherently symbolic, inherently one thing concretely while being *of* another thing. There might be other ways of conceptualizing this, but no omitting it can then hope to grasp anything human, including how we grasp nature.

To remain unable to think about the inherent character of external/internal means leaving the human observer unexamined, and thus also the very basis of the current model used in natural science. Thus natural science cannot be deeply examined, human science becomes utterly impossible, and certainly the relation between them has to remain a gap.

4. Was there something like this FLIP also in VI? It could not be exactly like the FLIP here from one space to another, because there was no space before VI. But there was a new consideration at the point when the open cycle became behavior-space.

5. That is why the space is empty. Of course, as to the movements of gestures themselves, again one cannot raise one's arm and at the same time reach for something with it. But this is now only a concern for movements, for locations in space, and not for the meaning of behaviors (which these gesture movements only version). When the gestures form the new system of space, the situations are interactionally related, and the empty space comes to subtend everything. Objects can then be positioned in that empty space, anywhere, just as if they could appear anywhere there is room for them, just as gestures can. This is then irrespective of what the object is, and in what context it could actually arise or be found, as in behavior space. They are then loose and arrangeable as to location. That is the "space" *we* usually mean by that word.

6. Even we today cannot bring up just any old thing; something must make us think of it, must "bring it up," for us, must relevant it (see VI).

7. It makes no difference if this second stage originally developed with a lone individual, or if others were present and looking on. Either way an individual is turned to an object, not to the others. The others are *carried-forward also* by what that individual does in relation to the object.

From the start it is implicit that the others are carried-forward also by the same formation. The dance which functions implicitly in seen-formation is an interaction with the others. They are implicit from the start. Since these gestures and object-seens form for this individual with the dance interactions implicit, they form also for the others. It doesn't matter if they first form for them alone, or if they are carried forward by first watching this individual.

The "also carrying forward" of others is implicit (at first it is type-a preformed implicitly, then after it occurs it further changes the context).

8. We have had three cases where it seemed a sequence forms in the wrong context. Each time we found that it isn't the same sequence. It forms a new context, comprising both earlier contexts in a new way. The three cases were the wind moaning like a person, the garden-versioning at home at night, and the "*third*" which reconstitutes its own collected context(s), thereby making the present context an instance. These three cases are different, of course.

Before the wind can carry forward a sound *like* a person, the wind's own wind-sound must acquire carrying-forward power. In that formation the person-sound functions only implicitly. When the wind sounds *like* a person, this likeness itself is sequenced, had, felt, carried forward. The people don't run out to comfort the wind, or to comfort some lost person out there, they know it is the wind. What is sequenced is the moaning-likeness-in-the-wind-context. At home, versioning the garden, one does not spade up the floor. Like the moaning-likeness-in-wind-context, the garden-at-home-context is a new one.

The likeness doesn't give the wind a personal identity, it does not elaborate the wind context in a basic way. The garden versionings do turn the garden context into an interaction context. What makes the difference?

The *carrying forward by likenesses* as such or patterns as such occurs in all three cases. But the garden-at-home develops into language, while the moaning wind doesn't. Why not?

To be able to carry forward likenesses as such is also the capacity to see pictures as pictures, as well as the capacity to show someone how one spaded the garden by standing up and making motions (but without cutting into the floor literally). Thus the capacity to form new likenesses is very basic and occurs widely. It is not language; there is no crossing, no formation of many similar but different symbols from crossing.

We can say that there is a likeness between whatever sound forms and the human sound that functions implicitly, but we had not explained how we can do that. We can say that the animals recognize a likeness if they respond to one thing as if it were another like it, but the animal responds to this present object. If the animal hears the wind sounding like another animal it will go out and search for that animal, not sequence the likeness.

We have often used our developed human capacities to describe what develops, long before the capacity to describe it so, develops. There are therefore three: what develops, what the developed itself can have or sequence about itself, and what *we* can say or observe or have about it, or else we cannot understand that observer who must then remain outside the system. Then we cannot understand our own scientific system either.

It is something very different, to live or do something, than to be able to say it (have, sequence, pause, feel, symbolize, version, take time to sense without changing), describe it, understand it. Much development and living goes between. Roughly, the living is like a first sequence, the between development like seconds, and saying, *thirds.*

9. Another way to put this is in terms of the schematic principle that a reflexive turn upon some context turns, not on the context as before, but on the context newly regenerated. It turns on a turned-upon context, not on a not-turned context. The carrying forward patterns-as-such regenerate the context so that it is the interaction context, i.e., has patterns-as-such in it (not the behavior context with patterns about a behavior context added on). The patterns are about a patterned context, a "situation."

10. The implicit must not be thought of as nothing but the explicit not yet. Rather, *there is a lot of difference between an a-type cluster and the later actual occurring*. (See "Polemarchus learns" and my discussion of *Meno* in VIII.) As one altered seen sequence actually occurs, it also changes all the ways the others are implicit. Actual working out or occurring is by no means nothing but what was implicit. We saw that the implicit isn't to be viewed as the same kind of structured something that occurring is. Later, after occurring, "was implicit" will be attributed to the structured, but this isn't the literal "was." We cannot split *between* what occurs and what doesn't but functions only implicitly, as we saw in VII-A.

11. Why did language develop in sound? (Once patterns themselves developed, they were just sound, or just visual, or just motions. As shown in VII-A, the different senses became differentiated. But why was it sound that developed language?)

Many reasons can be thought of. A main one has to be that sound carries in all directions so that one need not have been looking at someone to be addressed by that person. The infant's crying will carry to the mother even if she is just then looking somewhere else.

That sound-patterns affect us bodily by their quality is of course plain in music. The Ohm sound is still used for its specific bodily effect.

Both reasons are involved in why "conventional" symbols developed in sound.

12. Each new dance forms as a new whole bodylook carrying forward. As we said in VII-A, the whole development of patterns in the action contexts enriches the capacity for whole bodylook carrying forward, so that the next new dance versions such an elaborated action context (in which the other action contexts are implicit). The pattern space is "expressionized" and "actionized" reciprocally.

The object has always its looks and sounds, but this becomes more elaborate as more pattern-aspects come to carry forward. What *it* looks like and sounds like becomes more and more developed, although that is always its character (seen and heard in pattern space).

Similarly, the patterns of action and making grow, as do the patterns of objects, those used in action and making. They are all not arbitrary, even though the pattern *dimensions* are *derivatives* of expressive versioning of just certain human contexts.

13. The different behaviors or actions were physically interrelated, but not only for the external observer. There were many other physical interrelations than just that one cannot climb a chopped-down tree or that while running, an animal cannot drink from a stationary brook. The observer would see that. But the body is more complex, and much that the observer would think possible cannot happen together, either. Also, quite a lot can be one body event, that the observer would think of as different events.

14. As we saw (in V), this need not literally have been part of the dance. It can look quite new to an observer. It will be what can form, when the dance sequence itself is implicit and cannot. As we saw (with thrashing) what forms can be more, it need not be less.

15. Edward as a baby said "bye bye" with a wave whenever someone left the house and got into a car. Then we going out ourselves came to be called "going byebye." Then cars came to be called "byebyes," and our car was called "gooliga byebye" (the first part of that was his version of his name). Other people's cars were named by their name + "byebye." This is called "semantic drift."

16. It is not yet clear if we should think about this as *use,* or if it is still only the development of the units that are used only later. (It seems probable that we will later see clearly: yes, this short unit formation is also an original use.) Once short units have formed, there is use. Until short units, even though patterns themselves do collect, it is only past experience functioning.

17. Just exactly why, and at what point does language cease to take in new sounds? We now have several questions like this, about the exact point a development comes: we want to know that about the cessation of new sounds in

language, about the beginning of use, and about the FLIP when interaction-context space (inside/outside space) takes over.

Against these questions we can place the schematic developments we have clearly seen: the change from whole bodylook carrying forward to only just certain visual or sound-patterns themselves; the formation of interactive contexts and gesture sequences together; the collective reconstituting of patterns; the development of short units.

18. Appendix to f at the end of VII-B is a discussion of how details do *not* drop out, and universals are *not* commonalities with the differences dropped out. It has been moved to the rear to permit the present discussion to arrive at its conclusions more directly.

19. The above offers a way of understanding Chomsky's view.

20. The more development there is, the more novelty further happens. It speeds up geometrically. Humans are par excellence processes that can give themselves trouble, and lead to stoppage. All the way through it need not have been en-change, that made for stoppage; it could have been from the side of the body. See also the section on increased sensitivity. Any sequence is a string of contexts of many implicit sequences. Thus what seems the same action can recur, each time with different, more elaborated implicit sequences. A point is reached where the given sequence, too, can no longer occur, the given carrying forward can no longer carry forward. In modern culture this is easy to observe. We become "too sensitive," as it is called, to be able to eat, profit, defend ourselves, have sexual intercourse, and much else, under conditions that served perfectly well to carry our ancestors forward. We can still *do* a behavior, but are no longer carried forward bodily and fully, so then we cannot do what our bodies would need next to imply. Instead, there is a stoppage, a new situation with a new implying.

We cannot expect always to find ways to carry such new situations forward, although we must try. No simple return to less implicit complexity is possible. Call it neurosis or creativity, call the old times brutish or spontaneous, it doesn't matter. It is an error to think that we can want to return to the eternal return as Nietzsche saw it. Certainly he is right to the extent that we must find ways to carry forward our bodies, our work and procreation. No amount of behavior can substitute for body-process, one cannot be nourished from behavior alone. Similarly, the most complex human space must still enable us to eat, sleep, and have sexual intercourse. But these must not be viewed as empty commonalities, as though the detail didn't matter.

We are in the midst of a whole new stage of the development of the individual. Some huge proportion of people in the world are developing an inwardly sensed self that transcends cultural role-identity. The rest will soon find it too, since it is a cultural development. We need not be surprised therefore, nor is it to be deplored, when many of the traditional patterns are no longer possible for us. New patterns slowly develop, but we cannot expect to create a whole regenerated culture on our own as individuals. We cannot expect ourselves to discover all the new patterns we need to carry life forward in every situation. Certainly, some degree of this culture-creating is now the norm for an individual. Just as, at some stage, culture became various from place to place, so now also the individual variations are growing into a major factor. But humans are inherently interactional, and even with the greatest creativity an individual could be imagined to have, there is no guarantee that a way will always be found to carry forward an interaction.

I will consider this much more closely in VIII, as it cannot be resolved in VII, which is really devoted to traditional culture, as it was before this current began.

Novelty has always been in human living. Someone who could only interact in well-known routines would not be human. Here I was concerned to remind us that body-process events are never made up of extant units. Implying is always for some carrying forward, not for an already formed next. Stoppage is something that a developing process can make of itself, and not only due to a change that comes from outside.

21. Of course, a particular situation is inexhaustible in regard to the universals that can be formed in it (see Gendlin 1997a, chapter 5), and in that sense Aristotle and Kant were right—practical situations are like our details. But they misunderstood the system of universals in several ways: first, it's not right to ask: "which universal applies today?" They all do, and they all know to form today. But of course, secondly, this cannot be done from external observation of one's own situation, only from direct reference, which VII doesn't have. The VII person is cut off from this. Hence universals are *brought to* rather than forming from the richness of a particular. Bring-to and form-from are two different procedures. The world cannot be considered one system such that the two correspond to two systems of units, things, or considerations, aspects. Even of those that form from it, one might in a practical situation want to pick the one that focally carries forward. In developed VII but before VIII, full-bodied carrying forward is difficult. Too many form, not because they're empty fencings, but because it's hard to carry forward the whole focaled situation, none of them can, usually. *The individual situation is in principle beyond the kinds and inclusive of them.*

Chapter VIII

1. See VI and VII. If each bit were literally the same, there would be no body change and nothing would be felt.

2. This "rightness" is the "yes . . . yes" which comes in direct referent formation which I will discuss later.

3. Also note: the third step is clearly not simply some specific way of being insulted. The details are not "under" a general class definition, as we will see later.

4. Direct referent formation is analogous to the first VI-sequence. Recall that a bird only forms later, in a more developed context (behavior space). The space of the first sequences is the empty space (which also remains as the symbolic counterpart of the simple movements). (Later, after the FLIP, all behavior seems to be going on in symbolic empty space.)

Therefore the direct referent is not an object like the bird in a mesh of mutually implicit sequences of the new type—that is not a stage we have yet.

Rather, the direct referent is a doubled carrying-forward object like the monkey's gesture that is versioned. Rather than one big-shift emotion, the body-feeling here goes through a versioning on a new level.

The line that can't quite be drawn between the formation of the direct referent and the shift *in it* is analogous to a change coming for the monkeys as a result of the whole dance (their conflict behavior-context is changed so something new can happen). But we experience this as a shift in the direct referent, or *of* the direct referent. It is itself the perfect feedback-object (always, each bit of each new sequence is). It is the solution to the requirement context in each bit, but its fallen-out datum is already all that change. To go another step of change that is clearly different from this one (this formation one) would *require another direct referent formation,* not the role of a direct referent as an object carrying forward an implying of it. All carrying forward carries forward an implying of it in a way, but it isn't a carrying forward object on a new level, since that hasn't formed yet.

5. As we saw in VIII, Socrates's respondents do not quite form direct referents. When I say that in dialectic one is thrown back to what one intended and meant (since the statement has contradicted what one meant), this "what one meant" is not instantly a direct referent. The respondents usually complain about being confused, paralyzed, they don't know what to say. Or they give another quick answer. But even when the next answer is exactly a definition that follows dialectically from the contradiction, and incorporates what has been learned, even then it may be only a direct context-crossing: from the knowledge of before plus what has been seen, the new definition follows so as to take care of what made the contradiction. If justice is paying back what is owed, and a weapon deposited with you for safekeeping is returned when the depositor is crazy, you will hurt someone who did you no harm. So in this case returning what is owed is precisely *unjust.* Then the next definition of justice is to return a favor for a favor, and a bad deed for a bad one. One has learned that what one owes is a favor, something good, not the weapon or the money, or the thing borrowed.

Dialectic is therefore formal, both in driving statements to contradict exactly (unfairness or injustice follows logically from the definition of justice), but also in how the next definition is attained, exactly from what was learned in the contradiction. We don't need the formality of driving each statement separately into it.

Direct referent formation, on the other hand, changes the whole scene, the way all the sequences are now implied and what they are.

But each new definition in dialectic too changes all the boxes, the way the concepts cut before, and makes new cuts. It does this as a direct context-crossing does it, from a changed bodily implying but without first carrying forward that as such, as a new datum.

But the effect of sequencing implications out, and thereby altering the whole complexity as it is in the bodily implying—this is as true after direct referent formation, as without it. Therefore I came to name the principle this way.

Also, in its slower way on the VII level, the dialectic features the problem we are answering: How is it that one—in a way—*knows already*, so that one can recognize that this consequence is *not* what one intended, and nevertheless one has *also learned* something? Is it that what one now learns explicitly is what one already knows implicitly? Not quite! One's implicit sense of the question has developed too.

6. The different monads will all be valid.

7. More exactly: we might be talking of development, recurrence, or pathology. Once developed, all extants imply it—but when they happen in their changed way, again it is new eveving.

Once happened, are they not with all their new eveving implicit in all extant sequences? Yes, but not along the lines of only one logical explicit system. New entitizing and universalizing (new particulars or aspects, and new universals) can be made from any point, which were not literally implicit.

But all this is still development. Why is this the same point as "held"? Or, more exactly, there will be *some relation between type-a implicit and held*, since they both instance the direct referent here (of direct referent formation). What is their relation if they aren't the same point?

Isn't the point that an actual happening is something, is a change really, and not just a filling-in of extant "possibilities"? It changes the implying when there is an occurring, so how can it necessarily be one ossified system as if the implyings were occurrings-not-yet?

But is this same point quite the same in development and in recurrence? As recurrence, yes, it is again a formation (with exceptions [VI, VII] that don't matter here, about thinning and boxing). But that's not the question. Rather, it is whether what the occurred "first" functions in (the formation of) should be said to be implicit in a way that leaves further functioning-in (the formation of) open in the same sense as some implicits-in-implicits are held. *But "held" is that each functions only insofar as it shapes.*

Since not all sequences are literally *functioning* implicitly (many are held) in any given VII-sequence, therefore *what was held has not been crossed, as it would have been if it did function implicitly. We are therefore accounting with the "held" principle for why each new second sequence also changes the world, why this didn't already happen— indeed would have had to happen, in direct referent formation* and if not there, again in any one second sequence from a direct referent.

But "held" seems a small, quantitative way to say it unless we enrich "held" from here! It isn't that some sequences are left out, to be crossed with later, *but that how anything functions implicitly IS how it functions in this shaping*, in this sequence, in this eveving. All these points instance how there is not a fixed set of clunks that move around, how there is a different eveving in each sequence. How there are many wholes is instanced and clarified too.

8. This is not to say we won't keep the statement until later, for other reasons. It might be the only statement we can make now, of some finding or some observation or some notion that we wish to reformulate. But we will keep it at arm's length until we can formulate it differently. We might also specify exactly certain aspects of how it *doesn't* fit. This can only be done with the use of direct

reference, and by keeping the direct referent, so that the statements of what's wrong are statements that do instance the direct referent.

9. Later we will examine the relation between a direct referent monading out and the contexts, language systems, and other organized fields into which it is monaded. We can see that since these can differ, the VII-sequences from a direct referent can be various. But all that has been said, not only this, shows that direct referent formation is not yet actually the creation of the VII-sequences themselves. A further creation happens when these occur. They would be logically deductively determined in advance only if we wrongly thought of the bodily implied complexity of VII as equivalent to a system of statements, thirds, only. But within the creation of VII-sequences (from a direct referent) the same relations hold as in VII, between the interaction contexts and how language elaborates and alters them and reconstitutes them.

The cluster is type-a implicit in advance, and thus very finely determined, but as usual, the implying (of this cluster) could be carried forward in various ways—though getting even one is difficult, since it must carry forward so many fine newly implicit differentiations.

10. To work out a contradiction will always show something, specify aspects.

References

Bickhard, M. H. 1995. "World Mirroring versus World Making: There's Gotta Be a Better Way." In *Constructivism in Education*, edited by L. Steffe and J. Gale, 229–67. Hillsdale, N.J.: Erlbaum.

Bickhard, M. H., and J. C. Christopher. 1994. "The Influence of Early Experience on Personality Development." *New Ideas in Psychology* 12, no. 3: 229–52.

Brandom, R. B. 1994. *Making It Explicit*. Cambridge, Mass.: Harvard University Press.

Derrida, Jacques. 1982. "White Mythology: Metaphor in the Text of Philosophy." In *Margins of Philosophy*, translated by Alan Bass. Chicago: University of Chicago Press.

Dilthey, Wilhelm. 1927. *Der Aufbau der geschichtlichen Welt in den Geisteswissenschaften*. Volume 7 of *Gesammelte Schriften*. Göttingen: Vandenhoeck und Ruprecht.

Dreyfus, H., and C. Taylor. 2014. *Retrieving Realism*. Cambridge, Mass.: Harvard University Press.

Duncan, Isadora. 1927. *My Life*. New York: Boni and Liveright.

Ellis, R. D. 1995. *Questioning Consciousness*. Amsterdam: John Benjamins.

Gazzaniga, Michael S. "Forty-Five Years of Split-Brain Research and Still Going Strong." *Nature Reviews Neuroscience* 6, no. 8 (2005): 653–59.

Gendlin, Eugene T. 1964. "A Theory of Personality Change." In *Personality Change*, edited by P. Worchel and D. Byrne. New York: John Wiley and Sons. Also available at http://www.focusing.org/personality_change.html.

———. 1981. *Focusing*. New York: Bantam.

———. 1984. "Time's Dependence on Space: Kant's Statements and Their Misconstrual by Heidegger." In *Kant and Phenomenology*, edited by T. M. Seebohm and J. J. Kockelmans, 147–60. Washington, D.C.: Center for Advanced Research in Phenomenology; Pennsylvania State University. https://www.focusing.org/gendlin/docs/gol_2150.html

———. 1987. "A Philosophical Critique of the Concept of Narcissism: The Significance of the Awareness Movement." In *Pathologies of the Modern Self: Postmodern Studies on Narcissism, Schizophrenia, and Depression*, edited by David M. Levin, 251–304. New York: New York University Press. http://www.focusing.org/gendlin/docs/gol_2158.html.

———. 1991a. "Crossing and Dipping: Some Terms for Approaching the Interface between Natural Understanding and Logical Formation." In *Subjectivity and the Debate Over Computational Cognitive Science*, edited by

M. Galbraith and W. J. Rapaport, 37–59. New York: Center for Cognitive Science. Also in *Minds and Machines* 4 (1995). https://www.focusing.org /gendlin/docs/gol_2166.html.

———. 1991b. "On Emotion in Therapy." In *Emotion, Psychotherapy, and Change*, edited by J. D. Safran and L. S. Greenberg, 255–79. New York and London: Guilford. http://www.focusing.org/gendlin/docs/gol_2068.html.

———. 1992a. "The Primacy of the Body, Not the Primacy of Perception." *Man and World* 25: 341–53. https://www.focusing.org/gendlin/docs/gol _2162.html (excerpt).

———. 1992b. "Thinking beyond Patterns: Body, Language and Situations." In *The Presence of Feeling in Thought*, edited by B. den Ouden and M. Moen, 25–151. New York: Peter Lang. https://www.focusing.org/gendlin/docs /gol_2159.html.

———. 1996. *Focusing-Oriented Psychotherapy*. New York: Guilford.

———. 1997a (1962). *Experiencing and the Creation of Meaning: A Philosophical and Psychological Approach to the Subjective*. Evanston, Ill.: Northwestern University Press. http://www.focusing.org/ecmpreface.html.

———. 1997b. "How Philosophy Cannot Appeal to Experience, and How It Can." In *Language beyond Postmodernism: Thinking and Speaking in Gendlin's Philosophy*, edited by David M. Levin, 3–41. Evanston, Ill.: Northwestern University Press.

———. 1997c. "Reply to Johnson." In *Language beyond Postmodernism: Thinking and Speaking in Gendlin's Philosophy*, edited by David M. Levin, 168–75. Evanston, Ill.: Northwestern University Press.

———. 1997d. "Reply to Mohanty." In *Language beyond Postmodernism: Thinking and Speaking in Gendlin's Philosophy*, edited by David M. Levin, 184–89. Evanston, Ill.: Northwestern University Press.

———. 1997e. "The Responsive Order: A New Empiricism." *Man and World* 30: 383–411. https://www.focusing.org/gendlin/docs/gol_2157.html.

———. 1997f. "What Happens When Wittgenstein Asks: 'What Happens When . . . ?'" *The Philosophical Forum* 28, no. 3: 268–81. http://www .focusing.org/gendlin/docs/gol_2170.html.

———. 2004a. "Introduction to 'Thinking at the Edge.'" *The Folio* 19, no. 1: 1–8. http://www.focusing.org/gendlin/docs/gol_2160.html.

———. 2004b. *Let Your Body Interpret Your Dreams*. Asheville, N.C.: Chiron.

———. 2012. "Implicit Precision." In *Knowing without Thinking: The Theory of the Background in Philosophy of Mind*, edited by Z. Radman. Basingstoke, Eng.: Palgrave Macmillan.

Gendlin, Eugene T., and J. Lemke. 1983. "A Critique of Relativity and Localization." *Mathematical Modeling* 4: 61–72. https://www.focusing.org/gendlin /docs/gol_2153.html.

Goldfarb, Mica. 1993. "Making the Unknown Known: Art as the Speech of the Body." In *Giving the Body Its Due*, edited by M. Sheets-Johnstone, 180–91. Albany: State University of New York Press.

Goodall, Jane. 2000. *In the Shadow of Man*. Boston: Houghton Mifflin Harcourt.

Iberg, J. R. 1990. "Ms. C's Focusing and Cognitive Functions." In *Client-Centered and Experiential Psychotherapy in the Nineties*, edited by G. Lietaer, J. Rombauts, and R. Van Balen. Leuven, Belgium: Leuven University Press.

James, W. 1890. *The Principles of Psychology*, vol. 1. New York: Henry Holt. Retrieved from https://archive.org/stream/theprinciplesofp01jameuoft #page/n5/mode/2up.

Lorenz, Konrad. 1981. *The Foundations of Ethology*. New York: Simon & Schuster.

Mead, George Herbert. 1922. "A Behavioristic Account of the Significant Symbol." *Journal of Philosophy* 19: 157–63.

———. *The Philosophy of the Act*. 1938. Edited by Charles W. Morris, John M. Brewster, Albert M. Dunham, and David L. Miller. Chicago: University of Chicago Press.

Merleau-Ponty, Maurice. 1963. *The Structure of Behavior*. Translated by Alden L. Fisher. Boston: Beacon.

———. 2012. *Phenomenology of Perception*. Translated by Donald A. Landes. New York: Routledge.

Pattee, Howard H. 1973. "The Physical Basis and Origin of Hierarchical Control." In *Hierarchy Theory*, 71–108. New York: Braziller.

Rosen, Steven M. 1994. *Science, Paradox, and the Moebius Principle*. Albany: State University of New York Press.

Schoeller, Donata, and Neil Dunaetz. "Introduction to Gendlin's *A Process Model*." Available at http://www.focusing.org/gendlin_antecedents.

Skinner, B. F. 1938. *The Behavior of Organisms*. New York: Appleton.

———. 1953. *Science and Human Behavior*. New York: Macmillan.

Stanislavski, C. 1948 (1921). *My Life in Art*. New York: Theatre Arts Books.

Wertheimer, Max. 1945. *Productive Thinking*. New York: Harper.

Williams, Meredith. 1997. "The Intricacy of Mind and the Situation." In *Language beyond Postmodernism: Thinking and Speaking in Gendlin's Philosophy*, edited by David M. Levin, 120–47. Evanston, Ill.: Northwestern University Press.

Wittgenstein, Ludwig. 1953. *Logical Investigations*. Translated by G. E. M. Anscombe. Oxford: Blackwell.

———. *Philosophical Investigations*. 1958. 3rd ed. Translated by G. E. M. Anscombe. New York: Macmillan.

Index